A PHOTO-LOCATION GUIDEBOOK

PHOTOGRAPHING
WILDLIFE IN THE UK

ANDREW MARSHALL

*f*otoVUE
outdoor photography

PHOTOGRAPHING **WILDLIFE IN THE UK**

BY ANDREW MARSHALL

First published in the United Kingdom in 2016 by fotoVUE.
First reprinted February 2019. This reprint April 2022.
www.fotovue.com

Edited by Stuart Holmes, fotoVUE Ltd.
Book designed by Mountain Creative and fotoVUE – *www.mountaincreative.co.uk*
Book layout by Stuart Holmes.
Additional editing by Kate Cooper and Mick Ryan
Cover design by Nathan Ryder – Vertebrate Publishing – *www.v-publishing.co.uk*

All maps within this publication were produced by Don Williams of Bute Cartographics
Maps contain Ordnance Survey data © Crown copyright and database right 2016.
Map Location overlay and graphics by Mick Rayn.

A CIP catalogue record for this book is available from the British Library.

ISBN 978-0-9929051-2-5
10 9 8 7 6 5 4 3

The author, publisher and others involved in the design and publication of this guide book accept no responsibility for any loss or damage users may suffer as a result of using this book. Users of this book are responsible for their own safety and use the information herein at their own risk. Users should always be aware of weather forecasts, conditions, time of day and their own ability before venturing out.

Front cover: *Adult little owl sitting pretty.*
Nikon D4, 500mm + 1.4 x converter at 700mm, ISO 1600, 1/800 sec at f/5.6
Inside rear flap photo: *Andrew Marshall by Anna Riddle.*
Rear cover left: *Jumping red squirrel taken from a hide in the Scottish Highlands.*
Rear cover right: *Kingfisher at Otmoor RSPB reserve, Oxfordshire.*
Photo opposite: *Mother and cub otter crossing the stream, Isle of Mull.*

Printed and bound in Europe by Latitude Press Ltd.

Only a carrion crow saw them hastening across
the meadow to the leat, and its croaks followed them into
the woods where bees were burring round purple spires of foxgloves
and chiffchaffs flitted through honeysuckle bines,
Otter and cubs passed low and swift among the green seedheads of
the bluebells and uphill over blackening leaves, until they saw
the river again below them, where the sun points glittered
and a young kingfisher, one of the sons of Halcyon,
drew a blue line in the shade of the oak tree.

Henry Williamson, Tarka the Otter

CONTENTS

Short-eared owl out of the mist. Nikon D4, 500mm + 1.4 x converter at 700mm, ISO 5000, 1/800 sec at f/5.6

Acknowledgements

Thank you to my wonderful family, Charlie, Jake and Sam for allowing me the time and space to go on my crazy adventures to these far flung places chasing my dreams.

Thank you to Stuart Holmes for suggesting I write this book and for his life long friendship and companionship on other wild adventures. Thanks also for help and advice in the art of photography.

Thanks to Anna for African adventures and some of the wild trips in this book where we taught ourselves to take better pictures.

Thank you to all the photography and bird experts I have met in hides and wild places around the country, especially Del and all the Otmoor birders. Their knowledge and advice has helped me point my lens in the right direction, at the right time.

Thank you to Mum who always told me to do what makes me happy and my Dad who bought me my first camera, showed me how to use it and inspired me with his own photography, humour and art.

Andrew Marshall
February 2016

Foreword by Iolo Williams

I'll be perfectly honest with you, I am no great shakes as a photographer. I cannot begin to count the number of times I have looked back at the images on my camera with a mixture of dismay and despondency. Dismay because the photo looks nothing like what I saw, despondency because a once-in-a-lifetime opportunity has gone a-begging because I simply do not possess the ability to get the best out of my camera.

How I wish this book had come out 30 years ago.

Andrew Marshall has packed so many stunning images, so many tips and so much knowledge between two covers that I genuinely didn't know where to start. This is a man at the peak of his profession, a brilliant photographer who has learned his craft by spending untold hours out in the field. To be a great photographer, you must get to know your subject intimately; study its behaviour, its habits and its preferences, look for its favoured perches or resting sites, and get out at all hours in all weather. Andrew has done all of these things and more, and the fruits of his labour are here for all to see.

This book is a wildlife photographer's bible. It tells you some of the best places to go to see particular species, gives tips on field craft, techniques and equipment. It travels the whole country from the northernmost tip of Shetland down to Brownsea Island and from Skomer in West Wales across to East Anglia. Although it concentrates on the spectacular and the photogenic, it does not neglect the commoner species and it will prove invaluable to beginners and experienced wildlife photographers alike.

You cannot help but be impressed by Andrew's knowledge and ability. His images are beautiful, his writing concise and succinct. I have been enthralled by this book, so much so that it has inspired me to pick up my camera once more and venture out into that enthralling playground that is the British countryside. What I admire most about the man and his book however, is his continual emphasis on the fact that the wellbeing of the wildlife comes first. As Andrew himself says, a true wildlife photographer takes pictures of wild creatures looking at home in their environment. Bravo!

Iolo Williams
Welsh naturalist and TV presenter
February 2016

A surprised looking mountain hare in the Cairngorm mountains
Nikon D4, 500mm +1.4x at 700mm, ISO 500, 1/1000 sec at f/9

Introduction

The first question many people ask about a wildlife photograph is:

Where did you take that?

This guidebook describes some of the best locations for photographing the most interesting wild animals in the UK. Included is advice on what to expect, what kit to take and how best to get the image you are hoping for. It takes time and research to locate the best spots and without a full knowledge of a species' habit and preferences a trip to a distant location can often result in disappointment.

In making this book I have travelled far and wide and had some fantastic experiences. Some of the better known locations have proved unremarkable whilst some unexpected locations have excelled. Many of these places are not a secret but some are not well known. Some locations are free and open to the public, some are available for a small entrance fee and some are costly private hides. In the long term once you have honed your skills and learned about the wild creatures you wish to see you will find that the images that become most important to you are created during encounters of your own making and frequently on your own patch.

These locations are beautiful places to visit in themselves and you should go with an open mind as to what you might see. Every visit to these special places will result in different experiences, both of species encountered, individual behaviour seen and the light that portrays them.

Last but most importantly a good wildlife photographer takes pictures of wild creatures looking at home in their environment. The best advice in this book is to respect wild creatures and their habitats, and help to give wildlife the space to remain truly wild.

Andrew Marshall
Leafield, Oxfordshire, January 2016

Kingfisher (Alcedo atthis) Upton Warren August 2014.
Nikon D4, 300mm + 2 x converter at 600mm, ISO 1600, 1/1600 sec at f/5.6

The eagle and the moon. Isle of Mull
Nikon D4, 300mm + 2 x converter at 600mm, ISO 800, 1/1250 sec at f/13

Aims and scope of this book

There is a huge variety of wildlife in the UK. This guidebook deliberately targets the most spectacular and exciting species.

Getting Started

Whether you are just beginning to take wildlife photographs or have been for a while it takes time and effort to find answers to the common questions. What kit do I need? Where should I go to find wildlife, and when?

The aim of this book is to save you time, energy and money by pointing you towards some of the best wildlife locations in the country.

Of course there are no guarantees. Wildlife activity is influenced by the weather, the seasons and the time of day. Some species migrate, availability of food will determine sightings, and ultimately individual animals die. Nature does however persist and as long as we preserve environments suitable for the wildlife it is likely to prosper and endure.

To that end I would encourage the reader to support the trusts and charities that maintain these wild places so that the species will still be here for future generations to enjoy and photograph.

Honey potting

Wildlife photography requires peace and quiet to achieve good results. In planning a visit to any of the locations in this book or elsewhere it is wise to have a plan B in mind. It's always good if possible to avoid weekends and school holidays when most sites become busy.

On arrival at a location check the car park and if this is full or even looks busy consider changing your plans. Busy noisy hides are not ideal for photographing wildlife.

Some of the locations in this guide are small and suitable only for limited numbers of visitors. If a hide is already occupied consider using an alternative hide at the same location or try a different spot altogether. Where relevant we have mentioned other locations in the area which offer alternative subjects.

This advice also applies to individual animals. At Richmond Park for example it can become very busy at key times and individual stags occasionally are targeted by a number of photographers at the same time. This can cause stress to the individual. Also, having figures in the background of your shot is not desirable. There are plenty of stags here so walk away from popular areas and go in search of something different.

Short-eared owl (Asio flammeus) on a misty day.
Nikon D3X, 300mm + 2x at 600mm, ISO 3200, 1/500 sec at f/5.6

Getting used to the kit

Practice makes perfect; the more time you spend in the field the more you will learn, the more encounters you have the more successful images you will achieve.

You may already have some photographic equipment and are wondering if you are getting the most from it or if you need to upgrade to a faster frames per second model, a full frame body or a bigger, longer and heavier lens. The answer to this is that there will nearly always be a better piece of kit to buy, choose something within your budget and learn to use it well. There are better pictures taken with basic equipment by people who know how to use it than are taken with top of the range kit by people who don't.

Aims of the book

There are many types of photographer and even more kinds of photograph to take. Everyone aspires to taking great wildlife images be it to simply capture the moment to show friends and family or publish the photos and enter competitions. Subject-wise, some prefer a landscape type shot showing wildlife in its habitat and others may prefer a close up image showing only the animal or bird in sharp detail.

This book aims to benefit all photographers from beginners to experienced pros. Within you will find lots of different locations to inspire you and some tips and techniques for all levels of experience.

Species

Of all the mammals, birds, reptiles, amphibians and insects in the UK it was an easy choice of what to include in the book. When I first started photographing wildlife there were key species I wanted to photograph the most. These were usually the most spectacular and rare species; either colourful like the kingfisher, rare like the otter, elusive like the bittern or magical like the barn owl.

The most photogenic species are what we have concentrated on for this book: the beautiful, rare, enigmatic or dramatic. For the most part these are bird and mammal species. Also included are a few reptiles and amphibians to add some diversity and occasionally insects though these are so diverse and specialist that they require a book of their own to do them justice.

The limitations of this are that there are many species left out, some due to the space available and some, such as the phalaropes on Unst in Shetland, have simply eluded this photographer. I therefore apologise for filling the pages with birds of prey, kingfishers, puffins and otters but these are the species that get me really excited and hopefully you too. The techniques and skills described in this book are relevant to most wildlife so you can use them to photograph your own favourites.

Locations

My own experience told me that there are locations you can turn up at and expect a good show from the species you are expecting to find. For example Richmond Park in October will have red deer and they will be rutting. Donna Nook likewise will have grey seals in the winter. Otmoor RSPB reserve however can be a bleak and windswept spot with not a lot going on at certain times of the year. We therefore have a big mix of locations, some are more or less guaranteed wildlife hotspots whilst others require patience, numerous visits and good old-fashioned luck.

Locations were chosen on merit as the best places I know to have a decent encounter with the wildlife portrayed.

With wildlife nothing is guaranteed. Individuals well known to photographers can die (capercaillies killed by dogs and Thetford otters run over by cars are sad examples). Seasonal changes can mean short-eared owls or waxwings just don't turn up in the UK one winter.

These things said, this book hopes to give you the best chance to find some amazing wildlife in some fantastic and beautiful wild places.

Below: Cairngorm mountains , Scottish Highlands.
Nikon D800E, 17-35mm at 35mm, ISO 320, 1/320 sec at f/14

Absolute Beginners

A lot of photographers think that if they buy a better camera they'll be able to take better photographs. A better camera won't do a thing for you if you don't have anything in your head or in your heart." – **Arnold Newman**

Starting out

It can be very discouraging starting out in wildlife photography when we are constantly bombarded in the media by incredible images of wildlife. The standard of images seems unachievable.

This book is full of amazing images of wildlife. How many years must have gone into producing this book? Well, three actually. The majority of the images were taken over a three year period whilst working full time and with a family too.

But it's all about having the best equipment right?

Whilst I now use professional quality kit I started out with very modest equipment. Amazing images can be achieved with a basic compact camera or even a mobile phone. A few basic techniques will help you advance from snaps to amazing images.

Preparation

Getting good wildlife images is mostly about knowing the subject; the more you know the more photographic opportunities you will create. Learn about the creature's habits. Where does it live? What does it eat? When is the breeding season and is there any special behaviour associated? When is the best time of year or day to look? A great idea is to find Your Local Patch, see p340.

Learn about your camera by reading the manual, you may be surprised what your phone or compact camera is capable of.

Basic camera techniques help in all types of photography. See the Composition section on p.358.

Spend lots of time in the field observing and learn about field craft, p.352. One simple field technique is to wait in the right place and allow the wildlife to approach you rather than trying to creep up on it.

A good pair of binoculars are an essential tool for anyone looking for wildlife.

Equipment

Work within your limits and those of your equipment. You cannot hope to take good quality photographs of a sparrowhawk in flight with a mobile phone camera. You can however get fantastic images of herons, badgers, puffins and animals that are used to humans by being in the right place at the right time.

Practice using the equipment you have, it may not be the ultimate in quality but you can still learn composition p.358 and work on field skills to learn how to get closer to the wildlife.

Upgrade your equipment slowly using second-hand equipment if necessary as your budget allows. See Equipment p.348.

My youngest son Sam shot the puffin below at age 12 using an old Canon Rebel DSLR and a Canon 75 to 300mm lens. Similar cameras and lenses are currently available used from the internet for less than £250 (including standard lens) and £100 for the zoom lens.

Incoming puffin by Sam Marshall, age 12. Canon Rebel DSLR with 75-300mm at 85mm, ISO 400, 1/1250 sec at f/7.1

You can photograph the family pet with any camera, it's great practice for getting to know your camera.

Basic Camera Features

Zooms are great for getting you closer to the wildlife or, if you are already close, it can be very effective to fill the frame with the face of the animal or bird.

Compact cameras and phone cameras often have good macro capability, look for the flower symbol on the mode dial: ✿ This is perfect for close-ups of insects, butterflies and anything you need to get really close up to.

Using landscape mode, usually a mountain symbol: ▲▲ will give you the maximum depth of field, meaning most or all of your image will be in focus. This is useful for capturing a stationary animal within its environment.

Use the sport mode: 🏃 on more basic cameras for capturing anything that moves. You will need to ensure you keep the subject within the central focus point and track the bird or animal with your camera as it moves.

Subject matter

Most people drift into wildlife photography having started out taking the usual snaps of people, landscapes, pets and holidays. If you decide wildlife is really your thing then it makes sense to start learning basic skills with animals which are already close and approachable. Pets are perfect for this and many lessons can be learned from trying to capture the twinkle in the eye of a pet dog or cat and these skills easily transpose to your first meeting with a wild fox.

Captive wildlife

The next stage could be photographing animals and birds in zoos or wildlife parks. The fact these animals are captive means they will be easier to approach and unafraid of human presence. These are great places to practice watching out for behaviour and concentrating on focusing and composition.

Go Wild

The next stage from captive animals is wild (but used to human activity) so city parks such as Richmond Park p.218 and Regent's Park p.230. Here you still do not need to worry too much about fieldcraft but can potentially get fantastic results. The chances are you will get some images you are really pleased with and you can now consider yourself a wildlife photographer.

Forums and social media

Don't be shy about posting pictures on forums and social media such as Flickr and Facebook. These can be a good way to receive affirmation that your images are good. Most people are supportive and positive, be prepared to accept constructive criticism but remember your opinion counts too. To a degree photography is individualistic so do not be put off by stupid comments. The important thing is to enjoy what you are doing so if you like the picture you have taken then regard that as a success.

Photography courses

Take a look online or in the back of any photography magazine to find a whole host of courses designed to get you close to wildlife and help teach you some of the necessary photographic skills.

On the computer

Some basic tweaking can transform an otherwise dull or boring image, or one where the subject is far away. The most effective procedure is cropping; cutting away part of the photo that adds nothing to the image. Also cropping to place the subject using the rule of thirds to create a more pleasing and balanced composition, see Composition p.358.

Minor tweaks to brightness, colour, contrast and sharpening can add punch to a dull image, just don't go overboard with your adjustments, try to keep it real.

Don't beat yourself up

Getting good photographs takes time and you will not always come home with a great shot, but part of the enjoyment is just being outside in a wild place.

Wildlife Seasonal Highlights

SPRING: March, April, May

As temperatures rise in spring the breeding season gets underway. Check out the woodlands for signs of activity around fox and badger dens.

With the bluebells emerging the backdrop turns from brown earth and dead leaves to the green of the first shoots and then to that fabulous blue. Timing is everything and each year is different, the warmer the spring the sooner the bluebells flower. The time frame is short and within two weeks the bracken may be too high to see the fox cubs at their den. Your Local Patch p.340.

Birds are breeding and courtship displays such as great crested grebes and mute swans are beautiful behaviours to watch and photograph. Otmoor p.176 and Ham Wall and Shapwick Heath p.272.

Mountain hares start changing their coats from white to grey but you can still catch them contrasted against the moss and grasses in the Peak District p.140 or camouflaged with the lingering snow patches in the Cairngorm Mountains p.52. Ptarmigan also still dressed in white are easier to spot as the snows melt.

In March you might start looking for the mad March hares. Some brown hares may still be boxing now but in my experience most of this activity happens earlier in the year from January to February. See Otmoor p.176.

Short-eared owls begin to move north again to the Isle of Mull p.28 and Shetlands p.66. Badgers emerge in the

warmer weather, see Sibford Gower p.168. Red squirrels and avocets are active on Brownsea Island p.206.

The first really warm days see grass snakes emerge from their winter hibernation, basking in the sun to warm their cold blood and gathering in groups to mate. Likewise frogs and toads can be seen en masse in March as they congregate in ponds to spawn. Look in the wetland reserves such as Lakenheath Fen p.242 and Strumpshaw Fen p.256.

April sees black grouse lekking at Ruabon Moor p.298, and in the North Pennines p.116 and on the Glenlivet Estate p.42. Pied flycatchers, wood warblers and redstarts return to the Elan Valley p.312 and Gilfach Farm p.302.

May sees the return of the swallows and martins. With them the hobbies are back from Africa to feed on the now emerging dragonflies. For a brief few days large numbers of these beautiful falcons gather over wetland reserves before dispersing to nest and raise their young. See College Lakes p.190, Lakenheath Fen p.242 and Otmoor p.176.

Kingfishers have changed from their autumn and winter locations and are now found on smaller streams and tributaries where they can find a suitable nest hole in a sandy bank. See Slimbridge p.160.

Fox cubs appear from dens. Seabirds are busy nest building at Bempton Cliffs p.132, Skomer p.320, Lundy, p.290, Farne Isles p.110 and Shetland Isles p.66. Bonxies and puffins are nest building in the Shetlands, stoats have kits at Mount Grace Priory p.128 and dolphins play close to the shore at Chanonry Point p.46.

By the end of May the first broods of dippers may already have fledged as summer rolls on, find them on Exmoor p.274 and the Lake District p.120.

SUMMER: June to September

Light is at a premium and the hours of daylight are longer giving increased opportunities.

The vegetation is high and lush making wildlife harder to spot but there is more of it around with summer migrant birds returned and putting their energies into raising the next generation. Reed beds are alive with reed and sedge warblers feeding their young and possibly the young of cuckoos. Otmoor p.176, Wicken Fen p.238, Lakenheath p.242, Strumpshaw Fen p.256, Sculthorpe Moor p.258 and Titchwell Marsh p.262.

Roe deer rut in June and groups of young bucks can be seen chasing each other in the summer meadows. See Foxholes p.170 and Chimney Meadows p.172.

Young swallows and martins fledge in June and can be seen on wires and tree tops as they learn the skills of flight. Hedgehogs are active on warm evenings. Young kestrels are learning to hunt. Your Local Patch p.340. Young animals are more naive and provide opportunities for photographers and predators such as sparrowhawks alike. Dumfries and Galloway Sparrowhawk Hide p.96.

Little owls are noisy as their young fledge in June/July, their cat-like calls at dusk and dawn reveal their presence. Richmond Park p.218 or Your Local Patch p.340.

In July young peregrines are fledging and learning to fly, Avon Gorge p.200 and wildflowers abound in the meadows, College Lakes p.190.

Osprey young fledge and learn to hunt their own food in time for their return to Africa. Aviemore Ospreys p.48. The first ospreys are leaving Scotland by mid August and can be seen briefly as they visit wetland reserves in England and Wales. Ham Wall & Shapwick Heath p.272.

Puffins spend much of the year at sea, nest building begins in May but the adults won't be bringing in sand eels until June, and by August they and the pufflings have returned to sea and are out of the photographer's reach. Shetland p.66, Farne Isles p.110, Lundy p.290 and Skomer p.320.

August sees the heather turning purple on the moors as a backdrop for red grouse. Cairngorm Mountain p.52 and the Peak District p.140. Young barn owls fledge, gannets are now fully fledged at Bass Rock p.88 and dolphins follow the salmon run at Chanonry Point p.46.

In September young kingfishers leave riverbank nest sites and move to lakes and ponds. Upton Warren p.166, Lackford Lakes p.248, Strumpshaw Fen p.256 and Sculthorpe Moor p.258.

September is a good time to see bearded tits as they change from eating insects to feeding on reed seeds. Leighton Moss p.126, Lakenheath Fen p.242, Minsmere p.250 and Strumpshaw Fen p.256.

As the leaves turn and the berry crops ripen the summer may seem all too short but warm Septembers can prolong the season. Look out for common lizards basking making the most of the last of the summer warmth. London Wetland Centre p.224.

The fallow deer rut begins in the Forest of Dean p.154, New Forest p.202 and Richmond Park p.218. Migrant birds such as wryneck appear as they migrate south. Rare and Migrant Birds p.326. Red squirrels gather food in the Lake District p.120, Formby p.138 and Brownsea Island p.206. Wild boar are present in large numbers in the Forest of Dean p.154 and juvenile hobbies congregate before migrating, College Lake p.190, Lakenheath Fen p.242 and Strumpshaw Fen p.256.

Wildlife Seasonal Highlights

AUTUMN: October, November

Autumn is a great time of year for soft golden light and colour. The sun is getting lower in the sky, temperatures begin to fall and you don't have to be quite such an early bird to catch the worm.

Cooler temperatures create morning mists which can be both difficult and creative. Leaves, grasses and bracken change colour to russet browns and reds enriching the backdrop to one of the most exciting events of the wildlife photographers year: the red deer rut. See Richmond Park p.218 and Exmoor p.274.

Wild boar also rut at this time of year and they can be more visible and audible as they gather in groups in the Forest of Dean p.154.

Starlings begin to roost in huge numbers known as murmurations creating fantastic patterns in the sky at many different sites across the country including Gretna Green p.92, Leighton Moss p.126, Ham Wall and Shapwick Heath p.272.

On the coast huge numbers of knot and golden plover amass in the estuaries to create amazing aerial displays to photograph. Snettisham p.268.

Visit Mull for otters and eagles, p.28. Fieldfares and redwings start moving south. Migrant birds like hoopoe occasionally turn up as they get blown off course, see Rare and Migratory Birds p.326.

Short-eared owls appear in southern overwintering spots and Bewicks swans start to arrive at Slimbridge p.160.

As the trees are stripped of leaves it gets considerably easier to find and photograph red squirrels in deciduous woodland. Lake District p.120.

The autumn berries provide a nutritious crop for migrant fieldfares and redwings. Small flocks start to appear in Scotland at the start of November before moving further down the country as the temperatures drop.

In late autumn grey seals are hauling out from the sea to have their pups. This is the best time to photograph these large mammals gathered in large groups on the sometimes frozen ground. Donna Nook p.146.

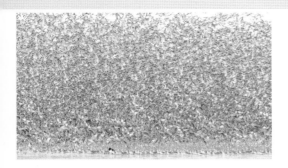

Winter is the time for two of the country's great wildlife spectacles: flocks of knot and golden plover are spectacular in the estuaries, and at dawn and dusk in mid winter at Snettisham p.268 thousands of pink-footed geese fly in V-formation. Also catch the avocets on the estuary at Exmouth p.280.

In January it's a good time to catch garden birds on feeders such as goldfinches, siskins, brambling and redpoll, see Garden Wildlife p.338. Starling murmurations are ongoing throughout winter.

WINTER: December, January, February

Winter used to be my least favourite season but as a wildlife photographer this can be the most interesting and dramatic. I love to head to Scotland and the Highlands for wildlife encounters in this harshest of seasons. The prospect of snow offers new exciting challenges with dramatic backdrops and the chance of catching species like stoats, ptarmigan and mountain hares in winter pelage. Cairngorm Mountain p.52.

Cold weather in the north and in Europe brings short-eared owls, sometimes in large numbers, being driven further south to winter on southern marshes such as Wicken Fen p.238. Likewise a waxwing winter will bring flocks of these exotic looking birds further south in search of ripe berries.

Frozen water seems to improve the chances of catching the elusive bittern out on thin ice at Minsmere p.250, whilst cold weather also improves your chances of seeing barn owls out in daylight hours. Lakenheath Fen p.242 and Titchwell Marsh p.262.

Winter migrant robins feed in gardens whilst whooper swans congregate at Martin Mere p.134 and the entire population of Svalbard's barnacle geese gather at Caerlaverock p.104.

In February Dartford warblers are singing on warm days at Arne p.210 and Dunwich Heath p.254. Adders emerge at Greenham Common p.196 and Braunton Burrows p.284. Skylarks are singing and hen harriers can be seen at the southern wetland reserves of Cley Marshes p.260 and Titchwell Marsh p.262. Brown hares begin boxing at Otmoor p.176. It's a good time to see bittern at Lakenheath Fen p.242 and Minsmere p.250. Crested tits come to feeders at the Crested Tit Hide p.62. Peregrine falcon males display to females in the Avon Gorge p.200 and the Pembrokeshire Coast p.314. Look for capercaillie in the Scottish Highlands before lekking begins, see Rare and Migrant Birds p.326.

By late February the bluebell's green shoots are already up and promising the spring and you will be out looking for those mad March hares again.

Locations Overview

Scotland – Introduction

Wow! It is for good reason that the book starts off with this fantastic part of the country. The Highlands and Islands create some of the most pristine wilderness in the UK ranging from the rugged coastline to the Caledonian forests and mountain highlands. Within these fabulous habitats exist some of the rarest and most exciting of the UK's wildlife.

In the clean ocean waters here we find grey and common seals and at Chanonry Point the amazing sight of dolphins feeding close to the shore.

The Scottish islands are a great example of how wildlife thrives in areas of low population where urbanisation and large scale agriculture have not influenced the landscape. Of these islands the Isle of Mull stands out as a jewel amongst the best of the locations. Here eagles soar and otters thrive on the coastline, the existence of these apex predators indicates that all is well with the entire ecosystem.

Moving into the heart of the country there still remains areas of pristine wilderness represented by remnants of the Caledonian pine forest. A beautiful landscape of gnarled pines where red squirrels and crested tits can be found, together with that fabulous elusive mustelid the pine marten and if you are really lucky the incredible and rare capercaillie.

The Highlands dominate the landscape towards the centre of the country and the rugged mountain ranges here offer a further habitat where mountain hares stand out white against the spring heather and golden eagles soar over remote valleys. The steep terrain is an exciting and invigorating place to go, made all the better by rare and exotic-looking species like the ptarmigan. These birds are only found in the mountains where the snow can lie all year and the views here are simply spectacular.

SCOTLAND

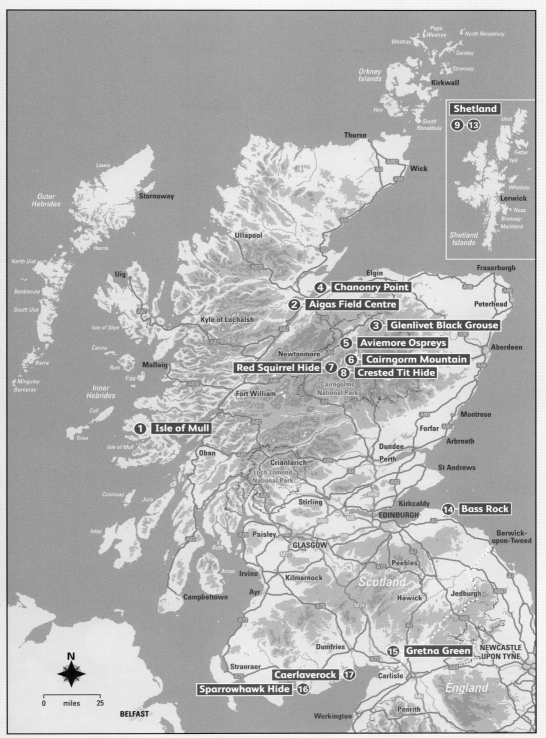

① **Isle of Mull**
② **Aigas Field Centre**
③ **Glenlivet Black Grouse**
④ **Chanonry Point**
⑤ **Aviemore Ospreys**
⑥ **Cairngorm Mountain**
⑦ **Red Squirrel Hide**
⑧ **Crested Tit Hide**
⑨ ⑬ **Shetland**
⑭ **Bass Rock**
⑮ **Gretna Green**
⑯ **Sparrowhawk Hide**
⑰ **Caerlaverock**

Contains Ordnance Survey data © Crown Copyright and database right (2016)

Mother and cub otter crossing the stream
Nikon D4, 300mm + 2 x converter at 600mm, ISO 2500, 1/1000 sec at f/5.6

Mull lies off the west coast of mainland Scotland and is easily reached via a short ferry trip from Oban. Home to otters, the recently reintroduced white-tailed eagle, hen harriers and marine mammals such as orca and dolphins, this is a must visit wildlife destination. The wild landscape and dramatic light make it a photographer's dream.

Otter (*Lutra lutra*)

For many the otter is perhaps the most exciting and interesting wild British mammal to photograph. Until recently the otter was one of the UK's rarest creatures. Even now with increased numbers a close encounter with this secretive mammal is always a privilege and a joy.

General conservation policies and improvements in water quality mean the otter is now making a comeback after being persecuted for years. Recently in Thetford, Cambridgeshire individual otters became very confiding allowing some fantastic photos of their behaviour. Sadly these individuals were killed. Though otters still frequent the River Thet it is an indication of the fragility of these animals, encounters should never be taken for granted.

Where to go

Most of Mull's coastline offers the chance to see otters. The best way to find them is to drive, cycle or walk slowly around any of the numerous sea lochs on an incoming tide and watch for the tell tale motion of the hunting otter out at sea. A tip of a tail disappearing under the water is typical. Loch na Keal is a good place to start with plenty of lay-bys to pull over and scan the ocean. Do not forget your binoculars: these are the one essential piece of equipment when looking for otters.

Technique and ethics

There are some key pieces of knowledge and considerations before photographing otters in the wild.

Despite frequenting the saltwater sea lochs as well as inland freshwater, Mull's otters are not sea otters. They need to come ashore frequently and also need to wash in fresh water after immersion in salt water. Never obstruct an otter from coming ashore where it needs to wash and dry off its coat.

Mull's otters are famous and unfortunately some people have given photographers a bad name by literally pursuing them whilst out at sea. If the otter remains at sea too long it will become distressed and too cold. The wellbeing of the wildlife is always paramount.

The first signs of an otter here are usually a bobbing head or the disappearing tail often far out at sea. As a photographer you will want to get as close as possible. It is important to resist the temptation to approach in crouched fashion out towards the loch shore. Otters are elusive and wary and will be aware of your presence long before you spot them. The best technique is to be quiet, be patient and do not move while the animal is above water. As with much wildlife let the subject come to you rather than trying to sneak up on it.

The otter will at some point need to come ashore, possibly to eat its prey of crab or small fish and it is far better to try and anticipate this than creep up towards an animal that will quickly disappear if alarmed.

For further advice on otters on Mull contact Mull Otter group: **www.mullottergroup.co.uk**

Mull Magic offers walks to watch otters from a safe distance: **www.mullmagic.com, Tel: 01688 301213**

Otter eating a butterfish. Nikon D4, 500mm + 1.4 x converter at 700mm, ISO 2500, 1/1250 sec at f/10

Mountains, sea and clouds: Mull's dramatic coast. Canon EOS 1DS mark ii, 100-400mm at 100mm, ISO 1600, 1/1000 sec at f/14

Otter eating a crab in an unusually calm and sunlit sea. Nikon D4, 300mm + 2 x converter at 600mm, ISO 800, 1/1600 sec at f/6.3

Below: Otter portrait. Nikon D4, 300mm + 2 x converter at 600mm, ISO 800, 1/1600 sec at f/6.3

How To Get Here

Ferry from Oban (Scottish mainland) to Craignuire (on Mull). Caledonian Macbrayne: **www.calmac.co.uk** (Book well in advance)

Oban Port postcode: PA34 4DB

Map: OS Landranger (1:50000) 47: (Tobermory & North Mull), 48: (Iona & West Mull) and 49: (Oban & East Mull)

Accessibility

Most of Mull's sea lochs are accessible by road. Tarmac roads with lay-bys offer easy access with views of the loch shores, getting closer to the water may require careful negotiation of rocky ground, marshland and bogs. Walking or cycling is preferable: the quieter you are and the more time you spend by the water the better your chances.

Best Time of Year/Day

Anytime is a good time to be on Mull. If you are combining your trip with a visit to see the sea eagles be aware the eagle boat trips do not run through the winter months. Try to avoid the main holiday times when noise and dog walkers reduce your opportunities.

Where Else To See

White-tailed eagles can be seen generally in the Western Isles of Scotland. For Otters: the Shetland isles: Yell p.72, Isle of Skye, Minsmere p.250, Leighton Moss p.126, Thetford in Norfolk.

The story behind the picture

Right: This otter which used to frequent the shore line near the Craignuire Ferry terminal was sadly run over a few months after this photo was taken. I had spent over an hour watching him from a prone position on the shore line. By watching the bubble trails that appear on the surface you can predict the position he will surface to eat small crabs and fish. Eventually catching a larger crab he came ashore to dry off and eat his main catch.

Below: Shaking sea water from his fur, this was my first big encounter with a wild otter. Having seen him swimming out in the sea loch I lay concealed behind a rock until he swam within a few metres to haul out and eat the crab. A fast shutter speed caught the water droplets spraying out as the otter dried off. What makes the picture for me is the whip of water at the very tip of his tail and the tones of the rocks and seaweed in the background.

Technique

For much of the time the otter may be in the water, this is a difficult scenario for autofocus that will want to pick up waves on the surface rather than the animal. Use a single focus point or try manual focus and anticipate where the animal will surface. In the water the reflective surface, especially on a sunny day, can cause the camera to underexpose the animal. Use exposure compensation of plus 1 to compensate for this and photograph in RAW format so you can adjust the exposure on your computer when you get home.

Shoot prone from the shore using a bean bag rather than a tripod which would make you more visible on the skyline.

Right: Surfacing with a crab.
Nikon D4, 300mm + 2 x converter at 600mm,
ISO 800, 1/1600 sec at f/5.6

Below: Otter shaking off sea water
Canon EOS 1DS mark ii, 100-400mm at
400mm, ISO 3200, 1/2000 sec at f/6.3

Below right: Closeup with butterfish.
Nikon D4, 500mm + 1.4 x converter at
700mm, ISO 2500, 1/1250 sec at f/10

White-tailed eagle *(Haliaeetus albicilla)*

The white-tailed eagle was reintroduced to the UK in the 1970s and is a well know conservation success. With a wing span of up to 245cm (8ft) this is the largest British bird of prey. There are now estimated to be between 37 and 44 breeding pairs scattered along the west coast of Scotland. A reintroduction program is now also taking place in eastern Scotland.

The massive hooked beak and grasping talons combined with the enormous wingspan make for a dramatic image. Note that Mull is home to a large number of buzzards which look similar from a distance, after your first encounter however the size difference becomes an obvious distinguishing factor. It is said the white-tailed eagle in the sky resembles flying barn doors.

Where to find them.

The white-tailed eagle can be encountered almost anywhere around the island. One almost guaranteed viewing point being the lay-by beside Loch na Keal at Killiechronan. The eagles frequently perch high (and too far away for a decent photograph) in the tops of the conifer plantation but often make low sorties out over the Loch. Mull Magic offer eagle walks and close-up encounters are almost certain if you book a trip with Mull charters on the Lady Jayne. Again book this well in advance and note the boats don't go out in the autumn and winter months.

Sea eagle banking against a grey sky. Nikon D4, 300mm + 2 x converter at 600mm, ISO 1600, 1/2000 sec at f/11

Incoming swoop: Nikon D4, 300mm + 2 x converter at 600mm, ISO 1600, 1/2000 sec at f/16

Approach swoop against the coastal backdrop. Nikon D4, 300mm + 2 x converter at 600mm, ISO 1600, 1/2500 sec at f/5.6

Technique

All the shots on these pages were taken from a boat trip on the Lady Jane with Mull Charters (**www.mullcharters.com**). The bottom right shot of the eagle about to grab a fish is the classic shot everyone wants to capture but it could be anywhere. By including some background to a shot gives more of a sense of place for the local environment.

When photographing from a boat it is preferable to be hand holding for example a 300mm lens with a 2 x converter. As the boat is moving a tripod is not much use and makes it tricky to get over head shots. Set the camera to a fast shutter speed, if the light is poor then a high ISO will be needed as well. Shooting against the sky have at least 9 and preferably 21 focal points active (if your camera has that option) and be in continuous tracking mode (see technique section). Focus on the bird from afar and keep following it as it swoops in and away shooting continuously. Even with a high frame per second camera you may only get one shot with talons outstretched. You might get three dives from the eagles per boat trip so there's a chance to learn from any mistakes. It's always good to work out your settings beforehand though.

Below: The classic: talons ready. Nikon D4, 300mm + 2 x converter at 600mm, ISO 1600, 1/2500 sec at f/8

The chances are you haven't come to Mull for a day trip. It's a big island with lots of different terrain, there are plenty of other photogenic wildlife besides the otters and eagles to entertain the wildlife photographer.

Buzzard *(Buteo buteo)*

Drive anywhere on the island and you are likely to spot buzzards. A common bird of prey, buzzards are largely carrion feeders and will sometimes mob sea eagles for their catch. Distinguishable from eagles by size and frequency, they can often be photographed from the roadside using a vehicle as a hide.

Oystercatcher *(Haematopus ostralegus)*

Drive around any of the sea loch shorelines and you will often hear a piping call before catching a flash of the dramatic black and white plumage of the oystercatcher. A common sight if you are out looking for otters, they are one of the most photogenic of our coastal birds. Oystercatchers are difficult to approach especially during the breeding season (when you should avoid walking on the gravel beaches where they nest). Shooting from a car can be the best way to get close so make sure you have a lens mount for a vehicle or carry a bean bag to support the lens on the car door frame.

Oystercatcher on the shores of Loch Spelve. Nikon D4, 300mm + 2 x converter at 600mm, ISO 400, 1/2000 sec at f/5.6

Above: Buzzard on fence line. Canon EOS 1DS mark ii, 100-400mm at 400mm, ISO 1600, 1/2000 sec at f/5.6

American mink (*Neovison vison*)

The American mink is not a species you should really see in this country, this member of the mustelid family was released into the UK. Its impact on native populations of water vole and bird life has been massive and concentrated efforts are being made to eradicate the species from Mull. It makes a fantastic subject though. This individual was spotted hunting the shoreline early one misty morning. This black subject with a black background on a grey day needed a high ISO.

American mink. Nikon D4, 300mm + 2 x converter at 600mm, ISO 10000, 1/1000 sec at f/5.6

Wheatear (*Oenanthe oenanthe*)

A handsome little bird, the wheatear is widespread on the Isle of Mull. In the image below taken in August the legendary Mull light shows off the male's slate grey back against a sea loch backdrop. Hand held as a spur of the moment shot, these are often the best of wildlife encounters.

Male wheatear, a handsome little bird. Nikon D4, 300mm + 2 x converter at 600mm, ISO 800, 1/1250 sec at f/9

Aigas Field Centre is based near Beauly in the Scottish highlands and is the highland home of the naturalist and author Sir John Lister-Kaye. As such this is not open to the public and visits need to be booked either as part of one of the many courses (which include photography) or alternatively as a tailor made visit including accommodation. The estate is home to an array of wildlife including red squirrels, reintroduced beaver, captive Scottish wildcat and the elusive pine martens.

Pine Marten *(Martes martes)*

Pine martens are rare, and largely but not entirely, nocturnal. A member of the weasel family they are known to feed on a mixed diet of small mammals, carrion, eggs, birds, insects and fruits. They are fast and agile enough to capture squirrels in their favoured habitat of conifer and mixed woodlands.

The recovery of the European pine marten is credited with helping to reduce the population of invasive grey squirrels in the UK and Ireland.

They are known to regularly visit areas where they have been encouraged with food; strawberry jam and peanut butter are apparently favourites.

Sightings even at regularly stocked food points are not guaranteed and very long hours of patient waiting in a hide is the only practical way to photograph this beautiful and endangered mammal.

What to expect

There are two hide options at Aigas for photographing the pine martens. The first is only available by pre-booking with the excellent, friendly and knowledgeable staff. Photographically this is not the best option as you need to shoot through the glass windows; not ideal if it's raining. Likely you will not be alone so other people's noise may interfere with your chances of a sighting even though the staff take great care in explaining the necessity for silence. The sighting success rate is very good however with pine martens seen most nights.

The photographs on this page were all taken through glass and in low light and it is a huge thrill to even catch a glimpse of this beautiful wild creature with its deep brown coat and peach-coloured bib.

The baited spots here are not especially natural or photogenic so look for opportunities when the marten is in open places or on the more natural tree trunks.

Pine Marten in long summer grasses. Nikon D4, 70 -200mm at 200mm, ISO 4000, 1/800 sec at f/2.8

Opposite: Pine marten on silver birch trunk. Nikon D4, 70 -200mm at 200mm, ISO 4000, 1/800 sec at f/2.8

Aigas photo hide

The other and best option at Aigas is the Campbell Photo Hide, named after wildlife photographer Laurie Campbell. The hide featured in BBC Springwatch in 2012. The area in front of the hide is illuminated giving side lighting to the animals. pine martens tend to visit between midnight and three in the morning so be prepared for a long vigil. Other regular night time visitors are badgers and by day you get red squirrels, woodpeckers and jays. A camera trap records when the bait spot is visited, the activity log in the hide gives an idea when the animals have been visiting recently but keep in mind this does change from day to day.

The animals here are used to flash and even the sound of a camera shutter but they are sensitive to movement and even the light from the camera's LCD can alert them to your presence. The pine martens can appear quickly and quietly and be gone again in a short time. It is possible to avoid using flash by relying on the hide lights and by using a high ISO setting.

Also at Aigas

Aigas have a captive group of Scottish wildcats. These are here as part of a sensitively controlled breeding programme designed to allow the reintroduction of the species in selected places.

The wildcat is endangered due to persecution, loss of habitat and most significantly due to inbreeding with feral cats. The DNA of these few captive animals is therefore vital in preserving the species. Some areas of Scotland such as the Ardnamurchan peninsula are being designated for their release and here feral cats are being controlled and neutered to prevent future inbreeding. It was not the intention to include captive animals in this book but their plight is important and the Ardnamurchan peninsula could hopefully be the place to to see a wild Scottish wildcat in the near future.

Technique

Low light means a high ISO is necessary to keep the shutter speed high enough to avoid motion blur especially as pine martens are fast moving animals, only occasionally pausing to look up and pose for a shot.

The second option to photograph the pine martens at Aigas is the purpose built photography hide. This does not need to be booked as such if you are a resident but it makes sense to ask the staff if you can use it on a certain night. Occasionally preplanned visits may be arranged for groups of people and ideally you want to get the spot to yourself for the minimum possible disturbance.

Below: Scottish wildcat (captive). Nikon D4, 300mm + 2 x converter at 600mm, ISO 5000, 1/1000 sec at f/5.6

*Pine marten from photohide at midnight using the hide lights only.
Nikon D4, 70 -200mm at 200mm, ISO 10000, 1/400 sec at f/2.8*

*Juvenile great spotted woodpecker in a Scots pine at Loch Garten.
Nikon D4, 300mm + 2 x at 600mm, ISO 5000, 1/1000 sec at f/5.6*

*Red squirrel portrait. Photographed at Glenmore. Nikon D4, 300mm
+ 2 x converter at 600mm, ISO 1250, 1/1250 sec at f/9*

How To Get Here

Aigas is located off the A831, 6 miles south west of Beauly, 15 miles west from Inverness. Guests on courses can be collected from Inverness train station.

Car parking Lat/Long: 57.443920, -4.559627
OS Co-ordinate: NH 464 421
Nearest Postcode: IV4 7AD

Accessibility

Courses at Aigas are popular and it is wise to book well in advance. The helpful staff will advise of the best arrangements to suit your plans. It is possible to arrange bespoke trips that allow use of the hides without being on a course. Tel: 01463 782443. www.aigas.co.uk Access involves forest trails with a short uphill walk from the main centre with minibus transport to the lower hide.

Best Time of Year/Day

Any time of year is good.

Where Else To See

Pine Martens are increasing in numbers as are the places you may potentially see them. They are being reintroduced into parts of Wales and potentially the North of England too. Their habits and shy nature make them very difficult to spot. See also:

www.naturephotographyhides.co.uk

www.speysidewildlife.co.uk

Scottish wildcats are rare and elusive and you are unlikely to see one in the wild.

A pair of black grouse size each other up on the Glenlivet Estate, Scottish highlands.
Nikon D800E, 500mm, ISO 5000, 1/500 sec at f/5.6

Deep in the Scottish highlands close to the small village of Tomnavoulin is the opportunity to photograph a black grouse lek on the Glenlivet Estate. This is a pay-for hide experience in a wild part of the country. You are required to stay overnight in a pop up camouflage photography hide and therefore require some familiarity with overnight camping in somewhat less than luxurious conditions.

What to expect

Ensure you have good equipment for an all night stay in a hide: a good quality warm sleeping bag, sleeping mat, torch, food and drink, warm and waterproof clothing and waterproof bivvy bag are recommended. The guide meets you at the tourist information office in Tomnavoulin and you are taken by landrover to the location on the moors. Here expect a short night's sleep with an amazing amount of bird sound including snipe drumming, curlew and lapwing calling through the night. Obviously not an experience for everyone but an adventure in itself.

The black grouse arrive at the lek from around 5am and activity continues until around 8am. The site is grassy and has lots of tussocks which can be frustrating and give slightly obstructed views. Here you have the chance to site a movable pop-up tent hide to suit your lens focal range and preferred angle. You need to balance your priorities here between a flat place to sleep and a good spot to view the birds.

Black grouse (Tetrao tetrix)

This is a red list species and very rare in the UK. The black males are a great photographic subject with striking plumage and great action shot opportunities. The well camouflaged females (grey hens) are shy and difficult to spot in the low light.

Technique

Here on the Glenlivet Estate the large game birds are oblivious to the photographer in the hide and perform their courtship display within a few metres. A good prime lens with low light capabilities (300mm f/2.8) is ideal but a zoom lens has its advantages as the birds are at varying distances from the hide. Action between the birds is frequent so watch especially for aggressive behaviour and the amusing vertical jumps and fluttering of wings. The birds are flighty and sporadically may take off and disappear, usually to return a few moments later.

Light can be difficult here with the action starting around 5am. Start with a high ISO but be patient and reduce the ISO level as light levels increase.

Black grouse calling.
Nikon D4, 300mm, ISO 5000, 1/400 sec at f/6.3

How To Get Here

The Glenlivet Estate is 53 miles south east from Inverness and 34 miles north east from Aviemore on the northern edge of the Cairngorm National Park.

Glenlivet Wildlife, Easter Corrie, Tomnavoulin, Moray, Scotland, AB37 9JB. Tel: 01807 590241.
Book via: **www.glenlivet-wildlife.co.uk**
Other black grouse hide: **www.naturephotographyhides.co.uk**

Car parking Lat/Long: 57.318307, -3.327570
OS Co-ordinate: NJ 201 261
Nearest Postcode: AB37 9JB

Accessibility

Access is by rough landrover track then a short walk across moorland. The camping is on rough ground, not one for those who like their creature comforts.

Best Time of Year/Day

Spring (April through to May) is best, just after first light.

Where Else To See

Ruabon Moor, Worlds End p.298, North Pennines p.116.

Above: close combat at the lek.
Nikon D4,300mm, ISO 5000, 1/400 sec at f/6.3

Below: A fine set of tail feathers.
Nikon D800E, 500mm, ISO 4000, 1/400 sec at f/8

'Scoopy' and the salmon. The dolphin logged as Trailscoop catches a salmon. Nikon D4, 500mm, ISO 1000, 1/1250 sec at f/10

Close to the city of Inverness by the village of Fortrose the River Ness meets the sea at Chanonry Point. The 18th century fortress of Fort George forms the backdrop to this location where bottlenose dolphins offer a spectacular wildlife encounter as they hunt for salmon running up-river. This is also a great show for non photographers and a good one to show children a special wildlife event.

Bottlenose dolphin (*Tursiops truncatus*)

The bottlenose dolphin is a surprisingly large sea mammal, especially to see at such close quarters. At Chanonry Point the waters run deep very close to the shore creating enough depth for these large animals to come within a few metres of spectators.

Present all year round they are best spotted in midsummer when they hunt for the salmon running up the River Ness. Different groups of dolphin frequent the narrow strip ranging from individuals to mothers with single calves and pods of three or more adults.

Tall tails: A dolphin show her flukes as she dives deep. Nikon D4, 500mm + 1.4 x converter at 700mm, ISO 1250, 1/1600 sec at f/9

Technique

Opinion differs on the best time of day to see the dolphins. Many suggest that a couple of hours before high tide is good. The incoming tide coupled with the water running out to sea creates a patch of choppy water just off the point where the dolphins actively feed.

The first views are likely to be dorsal fins rising and disappearing and it requires time and patience and lots of empty frames to get a focused shot especially of a head coming towards you. After a while you can get used to their habits and get better at predicting the areas where they are likely to surface. A group is easier than an individual as focusing on one while it disappears will frequently capture the next individual surfacing slightly behind the lead animal. This is particularly so with a mother and calf.

Set the camera to a fast shutter speed, a medium aperture (f/8) and limited number of active focal points (see Technique section). The size of lens depends on the areas the dolphins are frequenting so there can be advantages to both a large telephoto and a smaller prime or zoom lens.

In addition to shooting from the shore there is an option to take boat trips from the neighbouring village of Avoch. These can often but not necessarily get you very close encounters where a small point and shoot camera can achieve good shots.

How To Get Here

Chanonry Point is on the north side of the Moray Firth, 14 miles east from Inverness, just beyond the village of Fortrose on the Black Isle. At the east end of Fortrose turn right, signed for Chanonry Point. Continue to parking at the end of the road. Walk along the beach if the tide is out or a path behind the lighthouse.

Car parking Lat/Long: 57.573789, -4.094210
OS Co-ordinate: NH 748 556
Nearest Postcode: IV10 8SD (1km)

Boat trips leave from the Harbour Office, Pierhead, Avoch, Inverness IV9 8PT. Phone to book: 01381 622383

Accessibility

Car parking can be busy here. A short level path leads behind the lighthouse to a viewing area. To get close to the water requires crossing the narrow steep pebble beach. But wider views can be had by staying higher on the level ground (with picnic benches).

Best Time of Year/Day

June through to August is rumoured to be the best time of year coinciding with the all important salmon run. Opinions vary on the best time of day; they can be seen any time (and sometimes not at all). Usually the best time is at the start of the incoming tide when the dolphins start to chase the fish into the estuary.

Dolphin calf following alongside his mother.
Nikon D4, 500mm, ISO 1600, 1/2000 sec at f/11

Dolphins showing off at Chanonry Point.
Nikon D4, 500mm, ISO 1000, 1/800 sec at f/14

High in the Scottish Highlands at the top of the Great Glen is the town of Aviemore. Known to many as a winter ski resort it lies in a wild landscape of mountain, forest and rivers and lochs. Nearby Loch Garten is famous for the RSPB's success in setting up and protecting a man-made nest site in the 1950s and thus re-establishing the fabulous osprey as a British breeding bird. The surrounding landscape includes ancient Caledonian pine forest: home to red squirrels, capercaillie and crested tits.

Location

The RSPB visitor centre at Loch Garten has a well appointed viewing point for the osprey nest. From a photographer's point of view the distance to the nest is far from ideal. Many of the local lochs now support their own breeding pairs of ospreys and the shores of Loch Awe, Loch of the Lowes, Loch Lomond and Loch Insh are a better bet for unobstructed and sometimes close encounters with these spectacular birds. Nest sites are of course protected by law from disturbance and photographers need to keep a good distance.

Having located a likely fishing spot find a place to photograph that is hidden by overhead trees. The osprey's visual acuity is incredible and they prefer to fish alone.

There are at least two well known hides that require prebooking and a not inconsiderable fee which allow you to get close to fishing ospreys. Though these might seem expensive the costs are justified as they offer magnificent opportunties for action shots of the spectacular dive, splash down and the emergence with a large fish grasped in the talons. This is the recommended option for up close action shots as seen on these pages.

Osprey *(Pandion halleatus)*

The osprey is a migrant to Britain returning here from Africa in the spring to nest and raise its young in time to return back to Africa for the winter. The birds usually leave Scotland in late August through September and are frequently seen at various wetland reserves throughout southern England in September. The young birds raised here in Scotland need to be fledged, fit and fully experienced at catching their own food before the long flight back to Africa.

When fishing, the birds will typically circle over the water, locate the target and stoop at high speed before the plunge, talon first, into the water.

Incoming osprey, straight towards the camera. Nikon D4, 500mm + 1.4 x converter at 700mm, ISO 1600, 1/1000 sec at f/7.1

Osprey with precariously held trout. Nikon D4, 300mm + 2 x converter at 600mm, ISO 1600, 1/1600 sec at f/7.1

How To Get Here

Aviemore sits just off the A9, 84 miles north of Perth and 30 miles south of Inverness. Citylink and Megabus coaches stop at Aviemore from Inverness travelling south and from Edinburgh and Glasgow going north. It is also possible to arrive by train.

Two photography hides are located near Aviemore. Call well in advance to book a hide place:

Aviemore Ospreys. Gordon McLeod: Tel: 07735 388 808
Emai: info@aviemoreospreys.co.uk

Rothiemurchus Estate. Tel: 01479 812345
Emai: info@rothie.net

Accessibility

Some hides are off road and sunken, contact the photography hides directly for feasibility of wheelchair access.

Best Time of Year/Day

Only in summer, May to late August and, in my experience, best in August just before the birds return South.

Where Else To See

Loch Insh – a nest site close to the road.

Loch of the Lowes – near Dunkeld, 16 miles north of Perth. A Scottish Wildlife Trust site with observation hide 150m from nest.

Bassenthwaite Lake, Lake District. **www.ospreywatch.co.uk**

Rutland water, Leicestershire. The local fish farm here now provides photography hides at two locations: www.rivergwashtroutfarm.com Tel: 01780 482 822

Cors Dyfi Nature Reserve, near Machynlleth, Wales.

Technique

Ospreys tend to fish in the early hours of the morning typically between 5am and 7:30 am, plan to arrive at a hide at 4:30am. You may have to wait a further hour before the light is bright enough to get a quality shot. For the first strikes even an ISO of 3200 may not be sufficiently high to capture the subject.

The paid for hide used for these shots was hand dug into the ground and the restricted room inside means a tripod is not practical. The shooting angle means that a large telephoto lens would be quite difficult to catch the overhead shots. A 300mm lens with or without a converter works very well and a beanbag will help to steady the camera.

The osprey will normally circle overhead a few times before selecting the moment and spot for its dive. The dive is fast and steep and capturing the stoop requires a shutter speed in the region of 1/2000th of a second.

As with any fast moving bird it is best to focus on the subject well before it comes in, half pressing the shutter and allowing the autofocus tracking to keep the moving subject in focus, only fire the shutter at the key points.

Once the stoop begins you have to be really fast to keep up with the falling bird and a bit of guess work is involved in predicting the point of entry.

It is most likely that you will miss the entry into the water but focus on the splash down and be ready for the bird to emerge from the water. Depending on the experience of the bird it can sometimes be completely submerged with only a wing tip visible above the surface. Assuming the bird is successful, it will now try to get airborne again with the fish hooked on its enormous talons. As it struggles into the air the more experienced birds will rearrange the fish so it lies head forward and is thus more aerodynamic.

Depending on the time of year, weather and good luck, there could be as many as ten or more attempted dives in the morning so you have time to hone your skills. As the dawn rises don't forget to keep checking your ISO as the available light increases rapidly.

Make sure you are not so zoomed in and intent on the bird that you miss the opportunity of a reflection shot.

Occasionally in gaps between ospreys there may be visits from other local birds such as the redstart.

Below: Incoming osprey with birch clad mountains backdrop: Nikon D4, 300mm + 2 x at 600mm, ISO 1600, 1/1250 sec at f/8

Opposite: The Osprey Blue XD with reflection. Nikon D4, 300mm + 2 x converter at 600mm, ISO 1600, 1/1250 sec at f/13

A few miles drive out of the town of Aviemore is the dramatic and beautiful Cairngorm mountain range. This is a wild and wonderful landscape popular in winter with skiers, climbers and wildlife. It is also one of the most fantastic and inspiring places you can travel to in search of British wildlife.

Mountain Hare *(Lepus timidus)*

The mountain hare is superbly adapted to life in the highlands where the harsh winters produce hostile conditions for the survival of a small mammal. The coat is beautifully thick and a light grey in summer when it blends perfectly with the local granite boulders. In winter the coat turns a pure white and provides excellent camouflage against the snow covered ground.

Other adaptions to the cold include smaller ears (compared to the brown hare), a smaller body size and huge furry feet which allow it to run at speed across the snow. In spring they inhabit the lower slopes of the mountain around the snow line and this is the best time to find them whilst their coats still stand out white against the rock and heather clad slopes. Camouflage is the hares' primary defence against the threat of golden eagles and this means they have the habit of sitting still and motionless in the hope of going unnoticed.

Mountain hare hiding out in granite boulders. Nikon D4, 300mm + 2 x converter at 600mm, ISO 500, 1/1600 sec at f/10

Once disturbed however the second line of defence is speed, hares can move incredibly fast across this rugged terrain. It is worth knowing that they will nearly always run uphill to escape predators.

Technique

Having carried all your equipment up the slopes there are two options open to you: trek around slowly and quietly searching the boulders and snowfields with binoculars or find a suitable spot, sit still and quiet and wait.

The second option usually pays dividends, there are plenty of hare and ptarmigan (see next page) here but they have seen you struggling up the hill a long time ago and will be sitting low and silent in their favourite hiding places. If you sit still they will grow in confidence and emerge to feed and if the weather is favourable bask in the sunshine.

A long telephoto lens is ideal as the subjects are likely to be distant. Once spotted however a slow approach can be rewarding using fieldcraft to stay low and quiet and use boulders to stay below the skyline.

Don't forget binoculars to scan the boulder piles.

Stay late to get the evening sunlight but know your return route and allow time to get down; once the sun sets the temperatures fall quickly. Bring a head torch. Once back in Aviemore after a day in the mountains there is little better than going over your day's work with a wee dram in front of a roaring fire.

Moon over Cairngorm Mountain.
Nikon D4, 300mm, ISO 500, 1/1600 sec at f/10

Mountain hare showing off his huge snow shoes. Nikon D4, 300mm + 2 x converter at 600mm, ISO 500, 1/1600 sec at f/10

How To Get Here

Cairngorm mountain is in the Scottish Highlands,127 miles north of Edinburgh and 30 miles south of Inverness. Aviemore is only 9 miles from Cairngorm Mountain which is is well connected to the road, rail and bus networks.

From the south end of Aviemore follow the B970 signposted with a brown sign for Cairngorm Mountain Railway. Drive through Glenmore Forest, past Loch Morlich and up to the Cairngorm ski station. There are lower and upper car parks and both offer trails leading up the mountain.

Information info@cairngormmountain.org

Car parking Lat/Long: 57.134060, -3.670761
OS Co-ordinate: NH 989 060
Nearest Postcode: PH221RB

Accessibility

This is one of the least accessible of all the sites in this book. Familiarity with a mountain environment is recommended. Check the weather forecast and local conditions at the information office in Aviemore before setting off.

This is not a location for everyone: the terrain is steep and potentially dangerous and in the winter especially can be extremely cold and icy. Equip yourself for mountaineering with warm clothing, waterproofs, walking boots and depending on snow conditions you may consider using skis, snowshoes or crampons. If in any doubt consider hiring a local guide as the footpaths disappear in winter under snow,

The Cairngorm Mountain Railway, Tel: 01479 861261, offers easier access to the top of the hill (open mountain terrain) from where ptarmigan can sometimes be seen.

Best Time of Year/Day

The best time is early spring before the snow fully melts but when temperatures are on the up. Keep a close eye on the weather forecast in February onwards and time a visit when the light is good and the hares and ptarmigan are still wearing their winter coats.

Where Else To See

Mountain Hare: Peak District p.140, Findhorn Valley, Isle of Mull p.28, Flanders Moss between Stirling and Aberfoyle

Ptarmigan: Most of the Cairngorm peaks including Carn Ban Mor offer possible locations for Ptarmigan but the short approach makes Cairngorm Mountain by far the easiest to try.

Displaying male ptarmigan with his hen in the background: Note the fabulous feathery feet.
Nikon D4, 300mm + 2 x converter at 600mm, ISO 250, 1/1250 sec at f/8

Ptarmigan (*Lagopus mutus*)

This splendid bird inhabits the high mountain areas of the Cairngorms. In winter the plumage turns from a perfectly camouflaged mottled grey to this superb white colouration. Like the mountain hares they are easily spotted in a warm spell in spring when the white plumage stands out dramatically against the heather and boulders of the lower slopes. In spring the birds are beginning courtship rituals and make themselves obvious by calling loudly and perching on prominent vantage points from which they can proclaim their territory and protect their females from other males.

It is useful to be able to tell the difference between the ptarmigan's low territorial call and the louder alarm calls of the red grouse that also inhabit these slopes.

The male bird is distinguishable by the red eyebrow and slightly larger size and is likely to be the one most visible.

The hen bird is nonetheless very photogenic. The feet of the ptarmigan are feathered to protect from the cold and it is worth making sure you have these in the frame to get an overall picture of the character of this mountain-dwelling species.

Right: Male ptarmigan strutting his stuff. Nikon D4, 300mm + 2 x converter at 600mm, ISO 500, 1/1600 sec at f/8

Below: Male ptarmigan taking off. Nikon D4, 300mm + 2 x converter at 600mm, ISO 800, 1/1250 sec at f/10

Where to look

Park in the car parks for the ski lift. If you park in the lower car park a narrow rough path leads up the ridge past an old abandoned drag lift. Up on the ridge is a good spot to look and is quieter with generally fewer walkers and skiers around. Look for signs in the snow like the three-pronged footprints (below) and feather patterns left from take off flight (above).

Technique

Once you have located a calling bird it is likely that he will make himself more conspicuous and be joined by his female or other males wanting to claim his territory. Camera settings will depend on the available light; with a clear blue sky the bright sun and reflective snow allow much lower ISO settings than you would normally expect. A tripod would be good for a long lens if you can manage to carry it up here but alternatively a bean bag to rest on a boulder would do.

On your way up the hill from the car park have your camera ready for unexpected encounters with mountain hares and grouse.

Above: Male ptarmigan. Nikon D4, 300mm + 2 x converter at 600mm, ISO 250, 1/1250 sec at f/9

Below: Female ptarmigan. Nikon D4, 300mm + 2 x converter at 600mm, ISO 250, 1/1250 sec at f/8

Red Squirrel descending a Scots pine tree.
Nikon D800E, 300mm, ISO 1600, 1/1250 sec at f/10

There are many good places to photograph red squirrels and crested tits in the Scottish Highlands. A prime location is the Abernethy Forest, a remnant of the Caledonian Forest located in Strathspey close to Loch Garten Osprey Centre. However in order to more or less guarantee seeing the species and to save a lot of hours setting up your own red squirrel jumping shots, the hide at Northshots is the place to go.

What to expect

The red squirrel jumping hide is set up in a beautiful patch of coniferous forest close to Aviemore. You need to book the hide well in advance. It is possible to arrange a combined day with squirrels in the morning and crested tits in the afternoon. Bear in mind that would amount to a long time sitting in a hide.

The squirrel hide is small and set just above ground level, ideal for photographing but somewhat cramped for a three hour session. There are a number of set ups available including a reflection pool which needs to be booked separately. It's a great place to be, various birds visit the hide including crested tits and great spotted woodpeckers. Typically the squirrels are already waiting in the trees for your arrival and it doesn't take long before you hear the scratchy sound of little claws descending the pine bark.

Red squirrel (*Sciurus vulgaris*)

A more charismatic and photogenic little mammal you really couldn't ask for. Here in the Caledonian forests the red squirrel is far away from the introduced disease-carrying grey squirrels and flourishes on a diet of pine cone seeds and, in this case, the hazel nuts provided at the hide.

Technique

There are a couple of 'usual' scenarios here: the squirrel descends the pine tree making for a good natural habitat shot (see previous double page). The squirrel then may approach the jump set up or more often than not will appear up close in the hide window. Ideally it would be good to have a couple of cameras with different lenses, one set up for the jump and one for the close up face in the hide window that the squirrels love to do.

The feed stations at the jumping squirrel hide are set up on logs so that it is easier for a squirrel to jump between logs rather than descend to the ground. The best method to catch the jumping action is to be focused on the piece of wood you hope the animal will use to take off from. Of course you don't know this for sure and sometimes the squirrels go in different directions. A bean bag is better than a tripod to allow rapid position changes.

Squirrel with hazelnut.
Nikon D4, 300mm, ISO 1250, 1/1250 sec at f/6.3

A bit of a nut case. The fast shutter catches a discarded nut shell.
Nikon D800E, 300mm, ISO 800, 1/1250 sec at f/7.1

How To Get Here

Both this and the crested tit hides are run by Northshots who are based in Glenfeshie in the heart of the Cairngorm National Park. To book a hide day call: 01540651352 or contact via:

www.northshots.com

Northshots have accommodation or they will arrange to meet you on site, a short drive from Aviemore.

Accessibility

This involves a short but rough walk through the woods from a parking spot on a forest track, the hide is low and narrow and probably not ideal for wheelchairs. Check with Northshots to see if they can accommodate you.

Best Time of Year/Day

Early morning is best for squirrel activity, with little action from late morning. All year round is good for squirrels, winter is great for snow shots.

Where Else To See

Red squirrels: Lake District p.120, Formby p.138, Brownsea Island p.206, Dumfries and Galloway Sparrowhawk hide p.96, Isle of White, RSPB Loch Garten, Red Squirrel Trail Dalbeattie in Dumfries and Galloway.

Crested tits: RSPB Loch Garten, Glen Affric National Nature Reserve, Loch an Eilein, Scottish Highlands.

Top Tips for a Jumping Shot

Focus on the piece of wood you expect the squirrel to approach. Watch the animal closely – he will probably pause before leaping so resist the temptation to shoot until he crouches to leap. If your camera has autotracking this can work well. Use burst mode/continuous shooting set for the fastest frame rate during the jump to give you the most choice of shots.

Autofocus can and will try and lock out on the background or moving twigs. Do not be afraid of using manual focus and having the aperture closed down (i.e. a high f/ stop of around f/8).

Jumping red squirrel.
Nikon D800E, 300mm, ISO 800, 1/1250 sec at f/6.3

This is again a Northshots pay-for hide (see previous pages Red Squirrel Jumping Hide information section) but provides some excellent opportunities to photograph these birds so typical of the Caledonian pine forest habitat. It is possible to combine a visit to both this and the squirrel hide in one day. You may well have already had a chance to photograph these smart little birds from the squirrel hide but here they are in closer proximity. This hide is roomier and it is suitable for setting up a tripod.

Crested tit *(Lophophanes cristatus)*

This is a specialist bird of the Caledonian pine forests, it feeds on seeds and is often drawn to bird feeders. The 'punk Mohican' crest is characteristic making it quite distinct from other species. Other good places to look are the Abernethy Forest and on the RSPB feeders beside the osprey hide viewpoint at Loch Garten.

The hide attracts a large number of other woodland birds including chaffinch, greenfinch, goldfinch, great tit, coal tit, tree creeper and great spotted woodpecker. These small woodland birds are fairly common but with the well set up perches here it means you stand a chance of getting some quality shots with an uncluttered backdrop.

Technique

There is a lot of luck regarding light at any location, especially in the UK. Good and bright conditions means you can use lower ISO settings for the ultimate in quality. A long lens (600mm) is ideal and the images on these pages are more or less full frame. The lens should be tripod mounted for comfort and stability.

A reasonably high shutter speed is necessary with a long focal length, especially as the birds are fast moving. I was happy with 1/800th of a second, but a slower shutter speed could be used to create wing blur to give an impression of motion.

Concentrate hard on keeping the feeders out of shot as this always looks unnatural. The birds are surprisingly fast and do not sit still for long, only resting briefly on the lichen covered perch before flitting away or onto the feeder. The opportunity may be available to set up the perch on the other side of the hide to get backlit shots however full sun allows for lower ISOs for brightly coloured crisp images.

It's good to arrange a visit to coincide with a good fall of snow to get the classic crested tit amongst snow covered pines shot.

Below: Crested tit (Lophophanes cristatus). Nikon D800E, 300mm + 2 x converter at 600mm, ISO 320, 1/800 sec at f/6.3

Great tit (Parus major). Nikon D800E, 300mm + 2 x converter at 600mm, ISO 400, 1/800 sec at f/8

Coal tit (Periparus ater). Nikon D800E, 300mm + 2 x converter at 600mm, ISO 320, 1/800 sec at f/8

Chaffinch (Fringilla coelebs). Nikon D800E, 300mm + 2 x converter at 600mm, ISO 320, 1/1000 sec at f/5.6

Crested tit (Lophophanes cristatus). Nikon D800E, 300mm + 2 x converter at 600mm, ISO 320, 1/800 sec at f/6.3

Common seals, Lerwick. Nikon D4, 300mm + 2 x converter at 600mm, ISO 1000, 1/1250 sec at f/5.6

The sub-arctic archipelago of the Shetland Isles is composed of over one hundred islands and is arguably the richest area in the UK for unique species and wildlife generally. The relative ease of getting to and around the islands belies their remote location.

Set amongst some of the richest fishing grounds in Europe means it's no surprise that over a million sea birds set up home on the islands' cliffs during the summer season. The Shetlands are also home to the highest density of otters in Europe. The rich diversity of habitat attracts an equally diverse range of species It's a wildlife photographer's dream location.

Sumburgh Head lighthouse.
Nikon D800E, 17-35mm at 32mm, ISO 320, 1/320 at f/18

Sumburgh Head

If arriving by air at Sumburgh airport this headland is a couple of miles south of the airport and is likely to be the first port of call for anyone in search of wildlife on the Island. Sumburgh Head is a well known point for seabirds especially puffins, fulmars, and guillemots. Park in the obvious car parks on the headland and walk up towards the lighthouse. Follow the coast as closely as possible as looking down the cliff face is the place to spot the birds. Typically you will see fulmars coming in from the sea along the first section walking up from the car park but look closely on the thrift covered slopes for puffins going in and out of their burrows. Up at the lighthouse look out over the wall to the east for puffins. Also returning downhill from the lighthouse another cliff or gully frequented by the puffins faces out to the west side of the island.

Angry fulmar in flight. Nikon D4, 300mm + 2 x converter at 600mm, ISO 2500, 1/1000 sec at f/8

Fulmar (*Fulmarus glacialis*)

Probably the first bird you will see on arrival is the fascinating fulmar. To some this may look like 'just a seagull' however look closer at this ocean wanderer. The beak is specialised with a tubular structure on the top mandible which excretes salt. Fulmars are a member of the petrel family and are also known to expel a noxious oily substance used largely for defending itself and its nest from predators. Spending much of its life on the open ocean, they return to cliff faces such as Sumburgh Head to nest. Seen especially in the spring and summer often riding the updraughts along the cliff edge when they can be photographed easily as they cruise by at eye level. Think white bird against a dark background and shoot in RAW. Check your exposure and use plus or minus exposure compensation to avoid over or under-exposing the white bird.

Right: View on arrival at Sumburgh Airport from a window seat.
Nikon D800E, 17-35mm at 22 mm, ISO800, 1/320 at f/18

Puffin coming in to land: Sumburgh Head.
Nikon D4, 300mm, ISO 400, 1/1000 sec at f/6.3

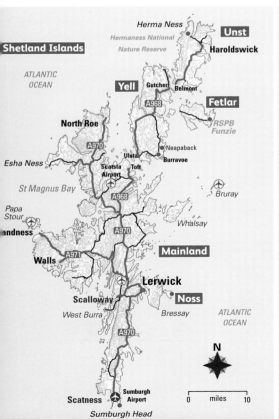

How To Get Here

There are several options for getting to the Shetlands. The quickest and easiest being by air, there are regular flights from Aberdeen airport which is served by most major UK airports.

Alternatively an overnight ferry leaves Aberdeen giving you the ability to bring your own vehicle. For a similar cost you can easily hire a car on the island.

For Sumburgh Head exit the airport and follow the road to the left, signposted for Sumburgh Farm.

Car parking Lat/Long: 59.857763, -1.271766
OS Co-ordinate: HU 408 083
Nearest Postcode: ZE3 9JN (1km)

Accessibility

Sumburgh Head has a steep tarmac road to walk up from the car park. This brings you close to some viewpoints. Higher viewpoints have decked walkways. Wheelchair access is limited due to the topography.

Best Time of Year/Day

The summer breeding season sees the cliffs teeming with birds. The weather can be very rough in the winter months.

Puffin (Fratercula arctica)

Most people come to Sumburgh Head to look for puffins. There are better places to photograph them on the islands (see Shetland Islands: Unst) and in the UK (see Wales: Skomer). However this is a great place to catch them with the pink sea thrift backdrop and this is one of the easiest places to get to involving only a short uphill walk from the car park.

Technique (Puffins)

The big factor to contend with is the weather. The exposed headland here is prone to mist, low cloud and strong winds. In misty conditions try a little fill flash and consider that the local weather varies massively; while mist lingers here the other side of the island may well be in glorious sunshine. Use the wind to your advantage, the uplift on the sea cliff causes the incoming birds some difficulty and they may pause longer than usual adjusting their landing before touch down and disappearing into their burrows. Time your visit carefully for puffins, they are only here from May and will have returned to sea by August. See section on Unst for more information.

Puffin landing, Sumburgh Head.
Nikon D4, 300mm, ISO 400, 1/1250 sec at f/5.6

Common seal (Phoca vitulina)

Seals are common around the mainland coast of Shetland, either hauled out on the beaches or heads bobbing like buoys just offshore.

Both grey seals and common seals are found in Shetland and unlike most of the rest of the UK the common seal is more common than the grey.

The difference between the species is quite distinct when you see the two together. Common seals have rounder faces and shorter snouts and frequently have a mottled coat which blends beautifully with the local granite bedrock and boulders.

Technique (Seals)

The seals here are reasonably obliging and no great skill is needed to get within decent range. Their body language is easy to interpret so stay at a distance where they are aware of you but not looking too anxious.

A medium aperture of around f/8 is good when the seals are on land to ensure they are entirely in focus. A sharply focussed eye is critical. Move the focus point if you want the seal's head off centre. In the water use predictive focus and pan (follow) the seal as it swims, keeping the active focus point on the head or eye.

With a bright sea you may need to use exposure compensation to get the seal correctly exposed, check your preview display on the back of the camera.

Common seal swimming in a calm sea. Nikon D4, 300mm + 2 x converter at 600mm, ISO 1000, 1/1250 sec at f/13

Common seal posing for a photograph. Nikon D4, 300mm + 2 x converter at 600mm, ISO 800, 1/1000 sec at f/9

Shetland pony landscape. Nikon D800E, 70-200mm at 200 mm, ISO 640, 1/400 at f/7.1

Shags are often found around the coast, this is a juvenile. Nikon D800E, 300mm + 2 x converter at 600mm, ISO 800, 1/1000 sec at f/7.1

Sand tombolo, West Burra, Shetland.
Nikon D800E, 17-35mm at 35mm, ISO 640, 1/400 at f/14

Mother and cub in the sea loch. Nikon D4, 300mm + 2 x converter at 600mm, ISO 800, 1/1250 sec at f/6.3

A short hop on the ferry from the northern tip of the mainland lies the island of Yell. Widely regarded as one of the best spots in the UK to find otters with the additional attraction of not so widely known sea bird colonies.

Otters *(Lutra lutra)*

Having already covered these fantastic animals in the section on Mull, the Shetland Island otters are similar if not even more confiding. The crystal clear waters around Shetland sometimes afford clearer views in the water and the nature of the beaches and shoreline sometimes offers an easier place to hide and better vantage points.

Where to look

Otters are all around the coast of Yell and the other islands as well. You need good luck and a good pair of binoculars to find an otter. Good places to start are around the ferry terminals. Otters are frequently seen in these surprisingly noisy and busy locations, especially when landing on Yell at Ulsta but also on Fetlar and the small pedestrian ferry to Unst. On Yell try around the boat harbour at Burravoe where otters sometimes hang around the jetty. Look for sign of otters: crab shells on the shore line and stones marked with spraint (otter faeces) are useful guides.

By far the best way of course is to ask others you meet and especially locals if they have seen otters recently.

If you are still struggling for that elusive encounter try booking with a local guide, see info in grey box.

Story behind the pictures

The encounter on these pages was with a mother otter and her two almost fully grown cubs, taken from a low cliff around 2.5 metres above the water. I found myself at times too close but was afraid of changing the lens in case the noise alerted them to my presence. The click of my camera shutter, even in 'quiet mode,' made the mother swimming out at sea pause and turn in the water. You can see her path through the incredibly calm sea in the photo below. Meanwhile the two cubs were ashore eating the remains of a fish she had caught earlier. The young animals were even more unafraid of the click of the shutter and though alert were tantalisingly close for a few minutes before moving back into the sea and on up the shoreline.

I had spent a few days searching for otters in the early morning and evening and was thrilled with this encounter just after midday.

Mother otter stopped mid paddle. Nikon D4, 300mm + 2 x converter at 600mm, ISO 400, 1/1250 sec at f/5.6

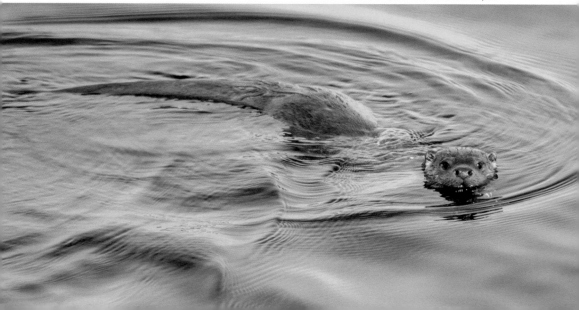

Young otter, looking for more supper. Nikon D4, 300mm + 2 x converter at 600mm, ISO 400, 1/1250 sec at f/5.6

How To Get Here

Shetland Ferries. For a newcomer to the Islands the inter island ferries can be a bit of a mystery. Rest assured that the ferries run very regularly and very efficiently. If you are here for a few days your carefully worked out itinerary is likely to change according to the weather and what you find. Some islands may be more productive and others less so. Have a rough schedule in your head but be prepared to change it at the last minute. It's a good idea to book a ferry if it's very important to catch the plane back or last ferry back to the hotel for example but otherwise I find it easier to turn up and roll on as needed. If the ferry is full it won't be too long before the next one and you can spend time exploring the coast for otter signs or with a bacon butty and coffee in the cafe.

Yell is accessed by a 20 minute ferry journey from Toft at the north end of the mainland: Toft to Ulsta boats run typically every half hour. **www.shetland.gov.uk/ferries**

Shetland Nature are a specialist local company offering wildlife guiding and tours with an excellent record and sound ethos:

www.shetlandnature.net

Accessibility

Coastal paths and shorelines require fitness and good walking equipment, paths can be rough and intersected with peat gullies. For otters you need to spend time on the shore so be aware of tide times and keep an eye on the rising water, don't get cut off.

Best Time of Year/Day

Otters live here year round but summer is best when the long days provide plenty of light.

Where Else To See

Otters can be seen throughout the Shetland Isles, also the Isle of Mull p.28, Isle of Skye, Minsmere p.250, Leighton Moss p.126, Strumpshaw Fen p.256.

Black guillemot *(Cepphus grylle)*

This striking sea bird is found mostly along the northern and western coasts of the UK and is a speciality of the Shetland Isles. Their smart black and white pattern is dramatically offset with the vivid red mouthparts visible when they call. Black guillemots favour the rockier sea cliff locations and congregate in smaller numbers than common guillemots that nest in much larger colonies. Both species are usually difficult to get close to due to the nature of their habitat.

Where to look

On Yell there is a spectacular small reserve called Neapaback meaning 'steep hill ending in a precipice.' This is accessed by a short but unmarked walk from the small harbour at Burravoe. The harbour itself may well have fulmars and terns flying around and if you are lucky perhaps an otter on the jetty. Walk directly from here across the grassland to reach the coast again and follow the steep track alongside the cliff ledge. In summer the sea thrift is in flower and the fulmars rise stiff winged on uplifting air currents soaring at eye level across the cliff face. Scattered on the grass you may well find the remains of puffins and shearwaters killed by gulls and bonxies (Great skuas).

The cliffs at Neapaback are full of fulmars and higher up on the grassier slopes are puffin burrows. The black guillemots tend to be found lower down on the cliffs nearer the beach. They can also be found on the island of Noss p.82.

Technique

Approach with caution as the cliffs here are in places unfenced. A long lens on a tripod would be best. The stationary birds on the cliffs are an easy enough target but make sure you are focussing on the eye. With a shallow depth of field on a close-up bird focus is critical, the autofocus may want to pick up on the beak and leave the all important eye out of focus. If in doubt close the aperture down to f/8. You can do this by pushing the ISO higher until the aperture is small enough.

Sometimes your composition calls for a vertical shot. Tracking is harder when holding the camera in this position so consider shooting in normal landscape orientation and cropping later.

Black guillemot calling, Neapaback. Nikon D800E, 300mm + 2 x converter at 600mm, ISO 640, 1/1250 sec at f/5.6

Close up puffin portrait. Nikon D4, 300mm + 2 x converter at 600mm, ISO 400, 1/1250 sec at f/5.6

Fulmar coming in from the sea. Nikon D4, 300mm + 2 x converter at 600mm, ISO 640, 1/1250 sec at f/6.3

Black guillemot calling. Nikon D800E, 300mm + 2 x converter at 600mm, ISO 640, 1/1250 sec at f/8

Unst is the most northerly of the Shetland Isles and perhaps the most obvious destination for seeing and photographing the dramatic great skuas or bonxies as they are known locally. At the northern point of the Island is Hermaness National Nature Reserve, a large area of moorland ending in spectacular cliffs with views of the dramatic coastline and lighthouse at Muckle Flugga.

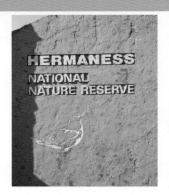

Where to look

Below the car park is a visitor centre in the old lighthouse keeper's shore station and it is a good idea to get a map and advice from here. The path across open moorland is marked reasonably in places by a boardwalk but there are few signs and this is a large space. Walking off the path is not advised, there's lots of bog here. There are no facilities or food or drink beyond the car park so go prepared. Consider travelling with lightweight camera kit.

Great skua 'Bonxie' *(Stercorarius skua)*

The great skua is a speciality bird of the Shetlands. They are large predatory birds not dissimilar to a large brown gull, the skua is aggressive and dramatic as a subject. They are easily located on Hermaness where you will see lone birds standing on tussocks marking their territory. Displays of extended wings emphasise their claimed nest sites and any invading neighbour will be seen off by loud calling and dive bombing. This famously includes humans so you are advised to keep to the paths to avoid being attacked. In any case you are likely to experience close fly-bys as you walk the long trail out to the coast. Bonxies are known as pirates due to their habit of mugging other birds for food. They are also predatory, killing smaller species such as puffins and shearwaters as well as stealing eggs from the cliff faces.

Technique

This is a large bird so ensure a reasonably small aperture such as f/8 to get the whole bird in focus in flight towards you. Bonxies are easy to approach but it's better to keep your distance, a long lens is recommended.

Great skua displaying. Nikon D4, 300mm + 2 x converter at 600mm, ISO 1600, 1/1600 sec at f/7.1

Below left: Geat skua landing. Nikon D4, 300mm + 2 x converter at 600mm, ISO 1600, 1/1600 sec at f/5.6

Incoming bonxie. Nikon D4, 300mm + 2 x converter at 600mm, ISO 1600, 1/1600 sec at f/7.1

How To Get Here

There is a regular ferry from Gutcher on Yell to Belmont on Unst. Booking is advisable at busy times but not usually necessary for the 10 minute ferry. Tel: 01595 745804

An easy ferry trip across from the Island of Yell takes you to Belmont at the southern tip of Unst. Here a red bus cafe and a welcoming sign greet you. A car is recommended to get around Unst but it's possible with a bike too. The winding road leads north over open moorland to the town of Baltasound and further north still the road is signposted for Hermaness. Here the road ends in a small carpark where a gated footpath leads on to the coastline.

Accessibility

The track at Hermaness is initially very steep and rugged followed by a long trail across peat moorland some of which is a boardwalk. This is rugged walking terrain. Bonxies can be seen early on the trail and the walk to the coast is around 2 to 2.5 km. Take a map from the information box at the gate.

Best Time of Year/Day

Spring and summer are the best for bird numbers and daylight.

Where Else To See

Bonxies are found throughout the Shetland Isles.

For a small island Unst simply flourishes with wildlife. Besides the bonxies the following species are prevalent:

Arctic tern *(Sterna paradisaea)*

A delicate sea bird differing from the common tern most noticeably by the all red bill (i.e. no black tip). They are frequently seen around the coastline especially the ferry landing points. It's always good to capture wildlife within its local setting. The colourful ropes, bollard and chain add interest to the image below.

See also the Farne Isles p.110.

Gannet *(Morus bassanus)*

Featured elsewhere in the book but here the huge colonies are in a particularly dramatic setting. From a position on top of the cliff opposite the Muckle Flugga lighthouse watch the gannets leaving the gannetry and returning with nesting materials at eye level.

Puffin *(Fratercula arctica)*

Featured also on the following pages, the puffins here can be difficult to photograph especially if you do not have a head for heights. The nest holes are located on the top of very high cliffs and to get close requires extreme caution.

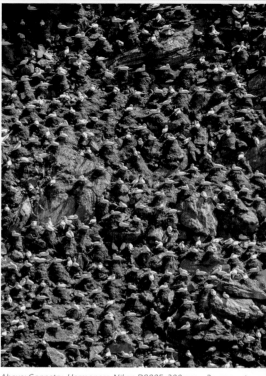

Above: Gannetry, Hermaness. Nikon D800E, 300mm + 2 x converter at 600mm, ISO 640, 1/1000 sec at f/7.1

Arctic tern on bollard and ropes. Nikon D4, 300mm + 2 x converter at 600mm, ISO 400, 1/1250 sec at f/9

Muckle Flugga Lighthouse in the mist.
Nikon D800E, 70-200mm at 150mm, ISO 250, 1/250 sec at f/13

Redshank *(Tringa totanus)*

So named because of its obvious red-orange legs. Look out for these all over the Shetlands but especially on Unst. In the early mornings they frequently perch on fence posts along the roadside between Baltasound and Hermaness.

The roadside fields are good places to keep an eye out for other moorland birds including snipe and curlew,WW which also call and display from roadside fence posts. Drive slowly and look for opportune lay-bys from which to take your shot using the car as a hide, but park safely with consideration for the locals.

Redshank on fence post. Nikon D4, 300mm + 2 x converter at 600mm, ISO 800, 1/1250 sec at f/6.3

Puffin on the edge. Nikon D4, 300mm + 2 x converter at 600mm, ISO 640, 1/1250 sec at f/6.3

Fetlar feels more remote and less populated than the other Isles. Described as the most fertile of the islands it has a long history of farming and the bird life here reflects this. Loch Funzie in the north has a small RSPB reserve and is well know amongst birders as a breeding place for rare red phalaropes and red-throated divers.

Red-throated diver (Gavia stellata)

Also found on a few other remote lochs in the Shetlands this is a superbly photogenic bird. At Loch Funzie they are difficult to approach and frequently keep a wary distance out in the middle of the water where they are too far out for a shot. Early morning is best for these secretive birds and lying prone on the shore is the best way to get a close encounter, this creates a low profile which the birds do not shy away from but also gives a low shooting angle putting you near eye level with the birds.

Eider ducks (Somateria mollissima)

A sea-going duck famed for their insulating feathers, eiders are iconic birds of the Scottish coastline. The male's black and white plumage is striking. In this image (facing page bottom left) the islands and mist in

Red throated diver. Photographed Isle of Bressay. Nikon D4, 300mm + 2 x converter at 600mm, ISO 1600, 1/1000 sec at f/5.6

the background help create atmosphere. In addition the bird is calling to try and attract a mate and establish his territory over other males close by. See also the Farne Isles p.110.

Starling (Sturnus vulgaris)

Starlings are evident throughout the Islands during the summer months when they are nesting and raising young here. The many abandoned stone outbuildings and stone walls provide great nest sites and the farm land provides plentiful food. In winter these birds will move further south to form large flocks (see Gretna Green and Leighton Moss pages). Sometimes seen as a common drab bird a bit of sunlight shows off the amazing irridescent plumage. The feeding behaviour here also helps give the photograph interest (facing page middle).

Wheatear (Oenanthe oenanthe)

A fairly common species on the Shetlands, seen perched on the tumbledown walls from where they fly down to pick up insects in the grass. The male has the smart slate grey back and black bandit mask. The Shetland stone walls are a feature of the landscape here and make an excellent subject to include in a wider habitat shot.

Male wheatear on stone wall. Nikon D4, 300mm + 2 x converter at 600mm, ISO 1600, 1/1000 sec at f/5.6

Red throated diver displaying. Photographed Isle of Bressay Nikon D4, 300mm + 2 x converter at 600mm, ISO 2000, 1/1000 sec at f/5.6

How To Get Here

Inter-island ferries from Gutcher (on Yell)and Belmont (Unst) are less regular than some of the other ferries so it is worth booking in advance: 01595745804

From the ferry terminal follow the road east to Loch of Funzie. The RSPB hide is a short walk around the side of the small loch.

Continue past the Loch down to the bay at Funzie. Park on the left by the cattle grid and scan the ocean for a chance of seeing eider ducks.

Accessibility

Narrow tarmac roads lead to the main bays and lochs. Follow the B9088 to a rough car park by Loch Funzie. Getting close to the water's edge requires a short walk over rough moorland. Or continue on foot on tarmac around the shore and then across a rough moorland footpath (signposted) to the RSPB hide.

Best Time of Year/Day

Spring and summer offer long hours of daylight and the greatest numbers of birds. Fetlar is one of the Shetland's most easterly islands which makes it one of the first points of landfall for exhausted migrating birds in spring and autumn, including some rare species. In autumn you can see the arrival of overwintering wildfowl such as goldeneyes, tufted ducks, wigeons, teals and whooper swans.

Where Else To See

Shetland is the UK stronghold for red-throated divers with other populations on Orkney, the Outer Hebrides and the northern part of the Scottish mainland.

Starlings feeding young. Nikon D800E, 300mm + 2 x converter at 600mm, ISO 400, 1/1250 sec at f/6.3

Male eiders calling. Nikon D800E, 300mm + 2 x converter at 600mm, ISO 400, 1/1000 sec at f/13

The whole of the island of Noss is a National Nature Reserve run by Scottish Natural Heritage. In 1851 Noss had a population of 20 but has had no permanent inhabitants since 1939. The island has an area of 1.3 square miles with a high point of 181m (594ft) at the Noup of Noss.

The only human residents now are wardens who stay here during the summer. Access around the island is by foot only, a circuit taking around 4 hours. The spectacular gannetry on the Noup of Noss, close access to puffin colonies and a wide range of other seabirds make this a must visit destination for any wildlife photographer.

On the island

The wardens give a short informative talk on the wildlife and then leave you free to explore. Take heed of the very real danger of crevasses and cliffs. A low protecting wall runs around some of the cliff tops but is incomplete, it's not a good place to trip over. Watch also where you are walking as puffin burrows are plentiful on the cliff top.

The horizontally bedded sandstone cliffs have weathered, forming ledges which are home to 45,000 guillemots, 8,600 pairs of gannets and 5,000 pairs of fulmars. There are also shags, kittiwakes, razorbills, fulmars and great skuas. Otters are often seen around the island.

Puffin *(Fratercula arctica)*

Covered elsewhere in the book, see Unst p.76, Farne Isles p.110 and Skomer p.320, this sharp-dressed bird with the colourful bill is found here sometimes at very close quarters affording extraordinarily close views. Timing is critical with puffins as they spend most of their lives at sea. Puffins come ashore during the short breeding season when they nest in burrows in the sea cliffs.

The small inflatable ferry crossing to Noss. Nikon D800E, 17-35mm at 17 mm, ISO 800, 1/250 at f/14

A group of puffins hanging out: wide angle. Nikon D800E, 17-35mm at 35 mm, ISO 640, 1/320 at f/11

Technique

There are several different kinds of shot to look for with puffins: gathering nest material, courtship, bill rubbing, group shots with habitats, action shots coming into land and the classic sand eel shot (see Skomer). Timing of the visit will dictate whether you can get nest material gathering early in the summer or sand eel shots when they are feeding young.

The shot above uses a wide angle lens to get a group portrait with much of the surrounding landscape. In contrast to the bill rubbing shot, right, with a 300mm focal length to zoom in on this special behaviour.

Incoming flight shots require a fast telephoto lens and good tracking skills. Locate close to where the puffins seem to be landing and pre-set your focus point to a good distance, say 20 metres away. Focus on the incoming bird as soon as it becomes visible: this is a small bird travelling fast and needs good reactions or lots of attempts to follow the subject in to its landing. A recommended lens for this would be a 300mm f/2.8, capable of reacting quickly even in low light and maintain a fix on a fast moving subject coming towards the lens.

How To Get Here

An hourly car ferry departs from Lerwick to the Isle of Bressay from where a short drive or cycle ride takes you to the car park on the east side of the island. From here walk down the steep rough track to the small jetty. The wardens on the island keep a watch for waiting passengers and bring across the small inflatable boat to take you to the island for a small charge.

The tiny Noss ferry operates only in summer from May to the end of August except Mondays and Thursdays. In bad weather a red flag is flown on the island if it is closed. It is always best to call the Noss Ferry Line 0800 107 7818 before a visit.

Accessibility

From the car park the track down to the small boat crossing is steep and rough. The small boat requires some agility to board. The island itself has only vague footpath access; this is rough and in places pitted with puffin burrows and crevasses. Danger of high unprotected cliff faces.

Best Time of Year/Day

The boats only run between May and the end of August.

Where Else To See

Bempton Cliffs p.132, Lundy p.290 and Skomer p.320.

Puffin couple bill rubbing.
Nikon D4, 300mm, ISO 500, 1/1000 sec at f/6.3

Also on Noss

Although Noss is a small island there is much to see and photograph within the few hours walk round the coast. Otters are frequently seen in the sound from the ferry crossing to Noss. Thousands of gannets and other birds flying around the 500ft cliffs of the Noup of Noss are a spectacular sight.

An anti-clockwise circuit from the warden's information point takes you to Feaddaness at the southern tip. This is the best spot to photograph puffins close up. From here to the Noup of Noss the cliff face is a huge gannetry, a 500ft seabird skyscraper home to thousands of birds. The views of sea birds en masse is spectacular.

North from the Noup of Noss the cliffs have colonies of guillemots clinging to ledges on the vertical cliffs. You will need a long lens and a head for heights to get close-ups but there are plenty of possibilities for wide shots of the birds on the cliffs and guano-covered ledges.

Around Whiggie Ness fulmars nest amongst beautiful wildflowers adding colour to photos. From here you are looking straight across a ravine at the nests. Watch out for crevasses.

The northern edge of the island is more rugged and though you are less likely to see puffins here this is a good spot for black guillemots and little plover. Ravens also nest on the north side of the island, listen out for their *cronk cronk* call as they barrel roll overhead and chase fulmars for the fish they are bringing back to the youngsters in the nest.

A long lens and a head for heights are useful. Nikon D800E, 17-35mm at 20 mm, ISO 800, 1/400 at f/13

Gannetry on the east side of the island: note the two figures on the cliff top for scale. Nikon D800E, 70-200mm at 70 mm, ISO 800, 1/640 at f/6.3

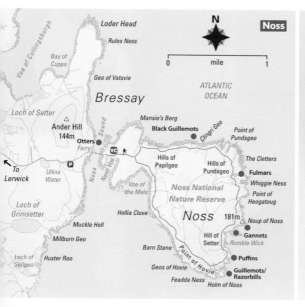

Raven harassing a fulmar. Photographed on Shetland Mainland Nikon D4, 300mm + 2 x converter at 600mm, ISO 1600, 1/1250 sec at f/14

Ringed plover. A small ground nesting bird usually quite difficult to get close to is found here on the open moorland where they nest. The adult birds will call loudly and feign injury if you are too close to their nest site. Try lying prone on the ground to reduce their nervousness and to steady a hand-held camera. Being eye level to any creature makes a better picture.

Nikon D800E, 300mm + 2 x converter at 600mm, ISO 800, 1/1250 sec at f/5.6

Guillemot colonies nest far out of reach on steep cliff faces. The central crack in the rock face makes an interesting focal point for a wide landscape shot.

Nikon D4, 70-200mm at 165mm, ISO 800, 1/400 at f/10

A group of fulmar nest with their surrounding 'garden' makes for an interesting habitat shot. Try using a group of three or five (instead of two or four) to create a more interesting balanced image.

Nikon D4, 70-200mm at 200 mm, ISO 800, 1/400 at f/10

Gannet showing off to his mate on Bass Rock.
Nikon D800E, 500mm, ISO 800, 1/1250 sec at f/10

Bass Rock in August, white with thousands of birds.
Nikon D800E, 17-35 @ 17mm, ISO 640, 1/500 sec at f/11

Bass Rock, also known as 'the Bass,' is an ancient plug of volcanic rock lying in the Firth of Forth approximately 1.2 miles from the town of North Berwick in Scotland. The rock is uninhabited except for a colony of around 150 thousand gannets, the largest single-rock gannetry in the world. The rock appears white as if snow clad due to the huge numbers of these large white seabirds.

What to expect

A variety of boat trips are available from the Scottish Seabird Centre at North Berwick. These all pass close to the Bass but only one organised trip is permitted to land.

The Bass Rock landing gives the best opportunity for photography allowing around 4 hours on the island in very close proximity to these spectacular birds. The boat ride is short but can be wet from ocean spray; make sure your kit is in protective bags and take waterproof clothing even on clear sunny days.

Landings are dictated by the ocean swell, getting off a moving boat onto solid land is at best precarious, even on calm days. A level of physical fitness and agility is required to ensure a safe landing. Conditions mean landing trips are prone to cancellation and bookings may be postponed for a few weeks.

When landing on the island listen to advice and keep both hands free. A short but steep climb follows which takes you about two thirds of the way up the rock where you are surrounded by birds. Everywhere is covered in guano (bird droppings) so ideally have a cover for camera equipment and anything else you have with you. The birds are unlikely to give way to passing humans and will peck at your legs with their very sharp beaks as you try to pass, wearing shorts is not advisable.

Left: Surrounded! The Star Trek landing party feeling birds have taken over this small planet.
Nikon D800E, 17-35 @ 35mm, ISO 1000, 1/1250 sec at f/11

Right: Courtship ritual, sky pointing.
Nikon D800E, 500mm, ISO 1000, 1/1250 sec at f/11

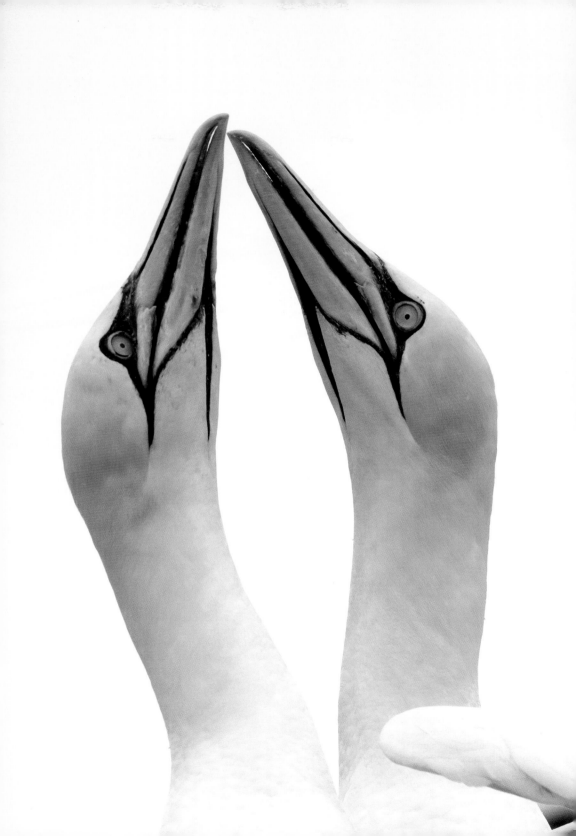

Gannet (*Morus bassanus*)

This is a large seabird, a little bigger than a herring gull with a very large wingspan allowing it to soar for hours over the ocean. Present here in large numbers to breed from May to October most of the population then move south as far as Africa for the winter.

Famous for their habit of diving arrow-like into the water from height to spear fish in the waters below, these are a stunning bird to photograph. In summer plumage the adults have a yellow to orange tinge to the head and back of the neck contrasting with the dramatic blue ring around the eye set in a black background.

The courtship or pair bonding rituals between these birds are beautiful to watch and photograph. Pairs reunited after sojourns out to sea will bill rub, preen and skypoint in synchronicity. Skypointing from one individual often precedes a controlled fall from the ledge into the air to join the mass of birds wheeling around.

Early spring is a good time to witness courtship and nesting behaviour, the adults bring in seaweed and feathers to build a rough and ready nest for the eggs. Gannets use this collection of material in a further display, showing it off proudly to their partner and tossing it in the air to demonstrate their success.

Technique

There are a huge variety of opportunities here from aerial shots of the birds in the sky, wide angle landscape shots, close-ups and portraits. Take as much camera kit as you can reasonably carry. A tripod is essential for big lenses. This is a white bird sometimes in a blue or grey sky and sometimes against dark rock so pay attention to exposures, use compensation and always shoot in RAW. The mass of birds means it is often difficult to get a clear shot with an uncluttered background so look for pairs out on prominent outcrops with a clear sea or sky background. Light can be difficult here so try to find a position with the sun behind you. For in-flight shots look for a spot below the rock face where birds are using updraught to hang in one place.

Above: Eye eye.
Nikon D800E, 300mm, ISO 800, 1/250 sec at f/11

Right top: Sky full of birds.
Nikon D4, 300mm, ISO 500, 1/1800 sec at f/14

Right bottom: Gannet showing off his nesting material.
Nikon D4, 300mm, ISO 500, 1/1800 sec at f/14

How To Get Here

Bass Rock is accessed from North Berwick which is situated 25 miles east of Edinburgh on the outer part of the Firth of Forth.

Various boats visit Bass Rock for close encounters with birds on the cliffs but only the Scottish Seabird Centre trips can land on the rock. Trips run from April to September. Book well in advance but be prepared for cancellations due to ocean swell.

The Scottish Seabird Centre is located at the harbour in North Berwick: **www.seabird.org. Tel: 01620 890202**

Car Park Lat/Long: 56.060517, -2.717474
OS Co-ordinate: NT 554 856
Nearest Postcode. EH39 4SS

Note: some boats also depart from Dunbar (further south).

Accessibility

A good level of fitness and mobility is essential for the landing trips. If in doubt please call and ask for advice before booking.

Best Time of Year/Day

There are gannets here all year round but the landing boat trips only run from April to September.

Where Else To See

Shetland Isles : Unst p.76, Noss p.82, Bempton Cliffs p.132.

This is a wildlife spectacle that will enthrall anyone with a sense of nature's spirit. In the autumn and winter tens of thousands of starlings gather here to feed on the arable farmland during the day. Each evening just around sunset they get together to perform a spectacular aerial ballet. The birds fly so close together it blackens the sky. The murmuration continually changes shape creating incredible aerial sculptures before at some unseen signal the birds descend as one to roost.

Starling murmuration

The individual starling is a fairly non-descript bird unless viewed closely in good light when its plumage shines with irridescence. Gathered *en masse* here however with a backdrop of the Lake District mountains and a spectacular sunset they can create some amazing photographic opportunities.

Technique

Aim to get to Gretna Green and Rigg (most recent display location) at least an hour before sunset in order to first of all find the birds and then to enjoy the whole show. Check your local sunset times. The best displays tend to be on clear evenings so check the forecast or

As many as 100 000 birds can come together most evenings. Nikon D4, 500mm + 1.4 x converter at 700mm, ISO 2500, 1/800 sec at f/5.6

keep your eye on the weather during the day. Early in the season it can be common for the birds to go straight to roost, especially if it is cloudy and raining or very windy. So be prepared for some disappointment.

Find a good location

The site of the murmuration can move so it is not always possible to be specific about their exact location, the final roost site can also change on a daily basis. In the past the birds have roosted in the small forest near the police station in Gretna. In recent years however the roost site has been near the village of Rigg, a few miles west of Gretna. Ask around, the locals have a love-hate relationship with starlings depending on how much they have been affected by the droppings.

Once in the general area keep an eye out for groups of starlings, as evening progresses the groups congregate and coalesce for a grand finale.

Above: Having a whale of a time. Nikon D800E, 17-35mm at 35mm, ISO 2500, 1/250 sec at f/2.8

*The murmuration morphs with the Lake district fells as a backdrop.
Nikon D800E, 17-35mm at 35mm, ISO 2500, 1/250 sec at f/2.8*

As the murmuration moves quite fast tripods are a hindrance. A monopod can work but hand-held is best. Camera settings revolve around freezing the bird's movement and reducing blur. The swirling masses take on many forms and shapes and are too fast to predict so fire away and look for the best images later.

The most dramatic displays tend to occur close to roosting time which means it will be getting quite dark. You will usually need an ISO of 1000+ to allow shutter speeds of 1/125 and preferably higher to capture sharp images. Apertures should be set at the widest (smallest number eg f/2.8) to allow suitably fast shutter speeds at the lowest ISO.

Another effective creative technique is to deliberately blur the murmuration with the camera on a tripod. Using a shutter speed of around 1/15th of a second or slower will result in intentionally blurred birds, creating a sense of movement. A long lens works well especially with an in focus static object like a tree or pylon in the frame as well. A bit of trial and error is involved here.

Some of the best shots are taken from afar capturing the rapidly changing formations. A point and shoot camera can also achieve good results.

Murmurations in general are often accompanied by attacks from raptors, including sparrowhawks, peregrines and marsh harriers so keep one eye out for these. Once the birds have dropped down to roost do not assume it is all over as a passing predator can cause them to rise again and repeat the performance.

How To Get Here

Gretna is at Junction 45 of the M6. Follow the B7076 to Gretna Gateway in the centre of Gretna Green. Turn left at the roundabout by the filling station and follow the B721 for 2.4 miles to the village of Rigg. At the west end of the village look for the white painted village hall on the left. There are lay-bys here and a few options of side roads to walk down. Be aware of local priority for parking and do not obstruct access.

Rigg Village Hall Lat/Long: 54.990621, -3.112139
OS Co-ordinate: NY 290 668
Nearest Postcode. DG16 5JE

Best Time of Year/Day

November to February is best but murmurations can occur from September right through the winter. The birds get together around an hour before sunset. Arrive well before dusk to find a good vantage point. Be aware the point of roost can move day to day. Clear evenings are best and with a bonus chance of some sunset colour.

Accessibility

Murmurations can be enjoyed from a long way away. A long lens from the roadside is a good option.

Where Else To See Murmurations

RSPB Leighton Moss, Lancashire – See p.126
Martin Mere Local Nature Reserve, Lancashire – See p.134
North Pier Blackpool, Lancashire
Hornsea Mere, Humberside
Runcorn Bridge, Cheshire
Middleton Moor/Cavendish Mill, Derbyshire
RSPB Minsmere, Suffolk – See p.250
Sizewell, Suffolk
Suffolk Wildlife Trust Lackford Lakes
RSPB – Otmoor, Oxfordshire – See p.176
Swindon Sewage Works, Wiltshire
Brighton's West Pier, Sussex
Hinton near Slimbridge, Gloucestershire
Weston-super-Mare Sewage Treatment Works
RSPB Ham Wall/Avalon Marshes, Somerset – See p.272
Westhay Moor Nature Reserve, Somerset
Okehampton Camp, Devon
Slapton Ley National Nature Reserve, Devon
RSPB Marazion Marsh, Cornwall
Camrose, Pembrokeshire, Wales
Kenfig National Nature Reserve, Glamorgan
Aberystwyth Pier, Ceredigion

A male sparrowhawk watches for danger as feathers float away on the breeze.
Nikon D800E, 500mm, ISO 1600, 1/250 sec at f/8

Deep in the county of Dumfries and Galloway is a fabulous pay-for private hide set up for photographing sparrowhawks. This is a beautiful location in mixed woodland based around a feeding station that attracts a large number and variety of woodland birds. Ideal conditions for this top predator.

As with any wildlife you are not guaranteed to see the main attraction, but the supporting cast offers enough entertainment for a wildlife photographer should the star not appear. (See story behind the pictures).

Sparrowhawk *(Accipter nissus)*

The sparrowhawk is a stunningly attractive, agile and deadly bird of prey. In many ways the bird world's equivalent of the stoat in the mammal world; it is widespread, unpredictable, fast and often seen in random encounters rather than pre-planned arrangement. They are opportunistic and can turn up almost anywhere at anytime of the day. Most reserves and wild places with woodland are good places to encounter this predator. Listen out for the alarm calls of other birds especially the blackbird which can alert you to a sparrowhawk's presence.

The female is larger than the male and is brown-backed with light barring on the chest plumage. The male has a slate grey back and the barring on the chest is almost orange-brown. Both have fierce yellow eyes that make

them a dramatic photographic subject. This bird is much smaller than the large and slower buzzard (which also visits ths spot). Sparrowhawks are speciality hunters of small birds , typically in woodland and hedgerows and increasingly common in gardens. The female is large enough to take a wood pigeon.

These raptors are supremely adapted with incredible eyesight and the ability to fly at speed through woodland passing effortlessly through tangled undergrowth with lightening quick manoevrability. This makes them difficult to photograph unless perched. Often a perched photo opportunity arrives after a hit on a prey species.

Technique

Extreme patience and silence may be required. The bird will arrive silently and unanounced but will be spooked by movement of a lens or any noises from the hide. Once feeding the hawk will probably stay and finish its meal. The hide set up here works well with a bean bag rest and/or a small tripod which will tuck in under the window ledge. A 300mm lens will just about be big enough but a 500mm or larger is better. A reflection hide is also available here and this will need a lens of 300mm or less as the bird will be very close indeed. Use a fast shutter speed (1/1000th) or more to freeze the action and, if light allows, an aperture of f/8 will ensure most or all of the bird is in sharp focus.

Sparrowhawk plucking his meal.
Nikon D800E, 500mm, ISO 1600, 1/250 sec at f/8

Eye of a predator: Sparrowhawk portrait.
Nikon D800E, 500mm, ISO 1600, 1/250 sec at f/8

Story behind the pictures

In researching this book I had for a long time planned to visit this hide. Photographs on the internet show a superb slate grey male sparrowhawk perched in full sun on a mossy log with clouds of feathers from some unfortunate songbird drifting on the breeze as he plucks his prey a few metres from the lucky photographer.

I duly booked the hide and arrived in sub-zero conditions at the tranquil woodland location and sat patiently for a whole day in numbing cold. I was entertained by good light and an array of subjects including buzzard, great spotted woodpecker, jay and nuthatch plus many common or garden birds visiting the feeders, but alas no sparrowhawk. I revisited the site on three more occasions and saw the bird fly in and out in a fleeting blur of stunning beauty causing the small birds to scatter in panic and my heart to beat faster but still with no picture to take home or show in this book.

One day I was accompanied by a fellow photographer who had visited previously and got the shots and was surprised to hear of and witness a 'no show'. On the positive side from my point of view I thought this would help to illustrate that the game is not easy and you can have good and bad luck and that paying for a hide day will not necessarily get you the shot you dreamed of. It makes the goal somehow more exciting and interesting and I hoped to return and try again to get that image.

The post script to this of course is that I did return and was lucky. The jinx was lifted and the photos now give me so much more pleasure than they may have done if I had just turned up, saw the bird and got the photo.

How To Get Here

This private hide is run by Alan McFayden at Scottish Photography Hides and is located in Dumfries and Galloway in the Scottish Borders. Tel: 0744 7454525. **www.photographyhides.co.uk**

Accessibility

Access to the hide involves a short steep walk on a rough forest trail. Check with operator for disabled access.

Best Time of Year/Day

Sparrowhawks can be seen here all year round.

Where Else To See

Sparrowhawks have made an imprerssive comeback after their decline in the 1950s and 1960s due to pesticides. They can be found all over the country. But where? It's impossible to predict but try: Otmoor RSPB reserve p.176, Elan Valley p.312, or your (or a friend or neighbour's) garden.

Bird feeders for song and garden birds also attract sparrowhawks to prey on them, so feeding garden birds may attract sparrowhawks.

Buzzard (Buteo buteo) a dramatic and powerful looking raptor.
Nikon D4, 500mm, ISO 1600, 1/800 sec at f/4

Also at the sparrowhawk hide

Buzzard *(Buteo buteo)*

As with many birds of prey the once rare buzzard is making a strong comeback in the UK. It is a stunning raptor especially at close quarters. Thought largely to be a carrion feeder buzzards do take live prey. Here they have been attracted to the food left out for the sparrowhawk and make a spectacular subject even if the sparrowhawk does not show. Buzzards have a distinct mewing call and will often be heard if not seen from the hide. The birds will frequently perch on branches far back in the woodland offering the chance of distant habitat shots before they swoop in to the perch.

Technique

The hide is effectively a wooden shed with narrow windows and limited view; a bean bag is almost essential to rest on the wooden ledge and support the lens (between 300mm and 500mm being ideal).

A 500mm lens is great for close ups of the raptors on the perches, but a smaller lens is good for pictures of the whole bird with prey and also for the smaller woodland birds that come into feeders closer to the hide. If the hide is not fully occupied and you are fortunate enough to have two camera bodies it is worth having two different set-ups: one for close-ups and the other for wider angle or closer action.

Always keep one eye on the surrounding woodland for birds waiting to come in to the perches.

Reflection Hide

The reflection hide offers the chance to photograph a wide range of woodland birds especially the jay, great spotted woodpecker, nuthatch and chaffinch with the bonus of a reflection. Red squirrels are commonly seen here too.

Red squirrel reflection.
Nikon D800E, 300mm, ISO 1600, 1/800 sec at f/5

Buzzard landing. Nikon D4, 500mm, ISO 1000, 1/640 sec at f/4.5

Habitat shot: Buzzard perched up in silver birch trees.
Nikon D4, 500mm, ISO 1600, 1/500 sec at f/4

Young jay from the reflection hide.
Nikon D800E, 300mm, ISO 1600, 1/800 sec at f/5

Also at the sparrowhawk hide:

Great spotted woodpecker
(Dendrocopos major)

This broad leaved woodland specialist is both extremely photogenic and a common visitor to the feeders here. Seeming to prefer to feed on the fat offered it is a fairly easy subject to capture posing on the various trunks. Be careful to use single or only a limited number of focal points so you pick up on the eye rather than the tree trunk. The male has a striking red almost vermillion patch on the back of his head which makes him the preferred subject for a photograph.

Jay (Garrulus glandarius)

A stunningly beautiful member of the crow family with the fabulous blue wing patch and light blue eyes. This is an intelligent bird and wary but easily drawn to its favourite food of peanuts.

Male great spotted woodpecker in some beautiful light.
Nikon D4, 500mm, ISO 800, 1/640 sec at f/8

Sunlight catches the blue eye of the Jay perched on a frosty branch.
Nikon D4, 500mm, ISO 1000, 1/640 sec at f/5

Nuthatch. Much like a mini woodpecker, the Nuthatch is common here and relatively easy to attract to the feeders, seeming to favour sunflower seeds. A jaunty little bird with lots of attitude you have to be quite fast and accurate to pick him out in a nice pose without focussing on the tree trunk.

Nikon D4, 500mm, ISO 800, 1/640 sec at f/4

Chaffinches arguing. Even the commonest birds can make for an interesting photograph. Interaction between two male chaffinches requires a fast shutter speed but low light in the woodland can be an issue. Getting the shutter speed just right creates some wing blur to show motion but the eye remains sharply focused.

Nikon D4, 500mm, ISO 2000, 1/500 sec at f/4

Great spotted woodpecker on lichen covered branch. The photogenic perches here covered in lichens and moss all help to create a strong image especially given a touch of winter light.

Nikon D4, 500mm, ISO 1600, 1/800 sec at f/6.3

Caerlaverock is a National Nature Reserve on the shores of the Solway Firth in Dumfries and Galloway. The reserve is internationally renowned for its overwintering wildfowl. Virtually the entire Norwegian Svalbard population of up to 40,000 barnacle geese overwinter here alongside large numbers of migratory whooper swans. The BBC program Autumnwatch visited in 2015.

You can visit Caerlaverock all year round. It is well appointed with a good network of paths, raised boardwalks, a viewing platform, picnic areas, cycle racks and viewing hide. Nearby there is a Wildfowl and Wetland Trust Reserve with well appointed hides and facilities.

Where to look

The reserve itself is a great place to view whooper swans and other wildfowl. Barnacle geese however are quite mobile, roosting out on the Solway estuary and flying inland at dawn to feed on farmland during the day. The WWT reserve is only open during daylight hours starting from 10 a.m. It is still worth arriving at dawn and parking up in the nearby car park to watch the skeins of geese coming in from the coast. They may well land in a nearby field from where they can be photographed from the roadside.

Skeins of geese fly in ahead of the rising sun. Nikon D4, 500mm + 1.4 x converter at 700mm, ISO 2500, 1/500 sec at f/11

Barnacle Goose *(Branta leucopsis)*

One of the smaller of the UK geese, they are an easy bird to distinguish being significantly black and white with grey wings and usually seen in large sociable flocks. The birds wintering here on the Solway represent the entire population that breeds in Svalbard during the summer.

Technique

If you are lucky enough to find a flock feeding in the fields and a suitable place to park then use the car as a hide and take your photos from there. Getting out of the car or approaching on foot will send the whole flock skywards and away.

A pair of Barnacle Geese coming in from the Solway. Nikon D4, 500mm + 1.4 x converter at 700mm, ISO 1600, 1/800 sec at f/13

If the flock lands in a far corner of a field be patient as they will graze their way across a field unless disturbed. As always allow the wildlife to come to you rather than trying to approach it.

Portrait of the handsome barnacle goose. Photographed at Regent's Park. Nikon D4, 500mm + 1.4 x converter at 700mm, ISO 320, 1/1000 sec at f/5.6

How To Get Here

Caerlaverock is situated in south west Scotland on the north side of the Solway Firth, 9 miles south of Dumfries.
Lat/Long: 54.976347, -3.483820
OS Co-ordinate: NY 051 656
Nearest Postcode. DG1 4UF

Arriving early before the centre is open follow the narrow roads westwards to the small carpark by the farm from where you may see the geese fly in.

Accessibility

Access around the WWT reserve is good with reasonably level grit tracks and purpose built hides.

Best Time of Year/Day

From October tens of thousands of wild barnacle geese and hundreds of whooper swans arrive to spend the winter here, leaving again in April.

Where Else To See

The island of Islay (Loch Gruinart) is the winter home for birds from the Greenland population of barnacle geese.

Left: Flock of Barnacle geese leave the fields. Nikon D4, 500mm + 1.4 x converter at 700mm, ISO 1600, 1/800 sec at f/11

Northern England – Introduction

The North of England is of course the best part of England. The wildlife benefits from large areas of relatively unpopulated land including the Lake District and the large areas of upland moors of the high Pennines.

The Lake District is stunningly beautiful offering picturesque mountains, lakes and rivers worthy of a visit in their own right, it's a landscape photographers dream. The deciduous wooded valleys have remained isolated long enough to protect a good population of red squirrels as well as summer migratory birds like pied flycatchers and redstarts and the fresh water habitats are becoming repopulated by otters and ospreys.

The north English coastline is hugely varied in character; at Bempton in the east the sheer limestone cliffs are home to colonies of sea birds soaring on uplifting sea breezes. On the west coast the salt marsh and mud at Martin Mere is an overwintering site for spectacular flocks of winter swans and the reedbeds of Leighton Moss create a habitat for bittern, marsh harriers and bearded tits. Over on the Lincolnshire coast the wide mud and sand beaches at Donna Nook afford a home to a large and noisy colony of grey seals who haul out in winter to give birth to their white-furred pups.

Inland man-made habitats such as the Cromford Canal offer homes to water voles and little grebes; a great example of wildlife finding a place to exist in a once industrial landscape.

On the edge of the North York Moors the magnificent remains of Mount Grace Priory hide a magical secret: families of stoats live in the ruins, making use of old human habitation.

There are fewer island habitats here but the rocky outcrops of the Farne Isles offer some of the most spectacular sea bird colonies in the country where puffins, shags, guillemots and razorbills can all be seen at incredibly close quarters.

NORTHERN ENGLAND

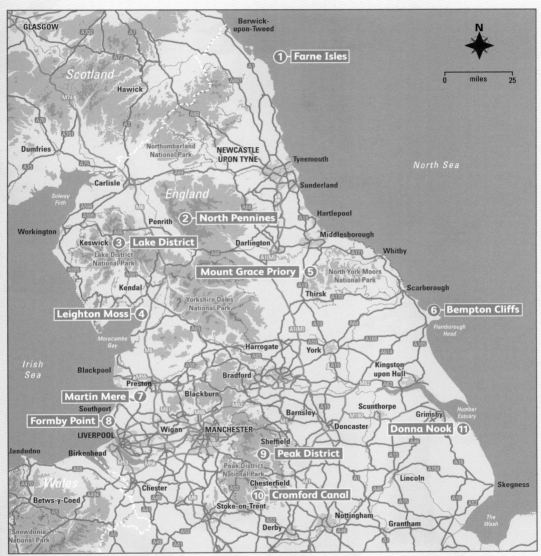

GLASGOW
Berwick-upon-Tweed
① Farne Isles

N

0 miles 25

Scotland
Hawick
M74
A702
A7
A72
A1
A697
A76
A68
A701
Dumfries
Northumberland National Park
NEWCASTLE UPON TYNE
Tynemouth
North Sea
A75
A69
Carlisle
England
Sunderland
Workington
A596
M6
② North Pennines
Hartlepool
A19
A595
Penrith
Middlesbrough
A66
Darlington
Whitby
③ Lake District
Keswick
A1(M)
A171
Lake District National Park
A66
A19
Mount Grace Priory ⑤
North York Moors National Park
Scarborough
A591
Kendal
Thirsk
A170
A65
Yorkshire Dales National Park
A1(M)
A19
A64
⑥ Bempton Cliffs
Leighton Moss ④
Flamborough Head
Morecambe Bay
M6
Harrogate
A59
A166
A165
Irish Sea
Blackpool
M55
Bradford
York
A19
Kingston upon Hull
Preston
A59
A614
Martin Mere ⑦
Blackburn
M62
A63
Southport
M61
M62
Barnsley
Scunthorpe
Grimsby
Humber Estuary
Formby Point ⑧
Wigan
M66
A1
M180
Donna Nook ⑪
LIVERPOOL
MANCHESTER
Doncaster
Sheffield
A15
Llandudno
Birkenhead
M60
⑨ Peak District
A16
A55
M53
M56
Peak District National Park
Lincoln
A153
Skegness
Wales
A470
Chester
Chesterfield
M1
A46
A52
Betws-y-Coed
A494
M6
⑩ Cromford Canal
A15
A16
A5
Stoke-on-Trent
A53
Nottingham
Grantham
The Wash
Snowdonia National Park
A49
A41
Derby
A52
A46
A1

Contains Ordnance Survey data © Crown Copyright and database right (2016)

Puffin take off: Farne Isles.
Nikon D4, 300mm, ISO 640, 1/1000 sec at f/11

Lying off the North East coast of England the Farne islands are a superb wildife destination. Sir David Attenborough describes the islands as his favourite wildlife site in the UK. The thousands of sea birds found here range from the large and impressive shag to the small, comical and colourful puffin. The birds here are wonderfully unafraid of human visitors and the islands offer close up views.

Also present in significant numbers are guillemots, razorbills, eider duck and the notoriously aggressive arctic terns. With grey seals almost guaranteed it makes for a superb day out for the wildlife photographer or indeed for anybody who likes wildlife and doesn't mind boats.

What To Expect

There are several different trip options available from several operators. Depending on time available the all day trip to both Staple Island and Inner Farne is recommended. This needs booking in advance and you will need food, drink and all weather clothing as there are no facilities on the islands. The boat leaves from Seahouses harbour. Allow some time before the boat leaves to find parking. Park at the harbour or a few hundred metres away by the public toilets. It's worth having time to spare as the harbour can be a great place to photograph eider ducks and swallows. It's a short trip across to Staple Island, sometimes via a grey seal colony where they can be seen on outlying rocks.

Above: Male and female eider duck, Seahouses harbour.
Nikon D4, 500mm, ISO 500, 1/1000 sec at f/7.1

Opposite top: Female eider duck: Seahouses harbour.
Nikon D4, 500mm, ISO 500, 1/1000 sec at f/7.1

Opposite middle: Bamburgh Castle from the boat.
Nikon D4, 500mm, ISO 500, 1/1000 sec at f/8

Opposite below: Grey seals greeting the boat.
Nikon D4, 300mm, ISO 500, 1/1600 sec at f/6.3

Below: Grey seal colony.
Nikon D4, 300mm, ISO 500, 1/1600 sec at f/6.3

Staple Island is the first stop on the all day trip but can be visited on its own. This is a small and rocky outcrop thronging with puffins, guillemots, razorbills and also provides opportunities to see shags at very close quarters, nesting in some places within touching distance of the loosely roped off paths.

What To Expect

The boat coming in to the landing may well approach rafts of guillemots floating on the sea by the cliffs. Have your camera ready to capture their take off. Once on the island there is a fairly limited area to access but an incredible array of photographic subjects. Most of the birds are obvious enough: shags often nest very close to the walkways. Head to the point for views of the large guillemot and razorbill colonies, or to the north western edge for puffins and more guillemots.

Technique

There are a huge variety of photographic opportunities here. A zoom lens or a wide selection of lenses is a good idea. You do not have to walk far so bring what you can carry. A 500mm is useful for very close portraits, a 300mm great for flight shots and a wide angle-lens for habitat and group shots.

Shag preening in good light showing the green gloss of the plumage. Nikon D4, 300mm, ISO 800, 1/1250 sec at f/7.1

The shag's green eye and tufty crest feathers stand out against a blue sky. Nikon D800E, 500mm, ISO 640, 1/1000 sec at f/7.1

Above : Portrait of a shag. Nikon D800E, 300mm + 1.4 x converter at 420mm, ISO 800, 1/800 sec at f/4.5

Shag *(Phalacrocorax aristotelis)*

Similar to but smaller than a cormorant this is a large bird with distinctive crest feathers and glossy green plumage in the breeding season. Its plumage requires the right angle of light to bring out its best so check your position in relation to the sun and look at different birds for the best subject and light.

Below: Guillemot colony with shag as a focal point, Staple Island. Nikon D800E, 17-35mm at 17mm, ISO 640, 1/500 sec at f/11

Rafts of guillemots on the waves and colony perched on the sea cliffs. View approaching Staple Island by boat.
Nikon D4, 17-35mm at 32mm, ISO 640, 1/1000 sec at f/8

How To Get Here

The Farne Isles are a group of 15 or so islands located within 4 miles of the Northumberland coast near the coastal villages of Bamburgh and Seahouses which are 55 miles north of Newcastle and 95 miles from Edinburgh.

Boat operators leave from the small port of Seahouses and there are several options, some visiting several islands. Recommended is an all day trip to Staple Island and Inner Farne.

Booking in advance is advised, although you can buy a ticket on the day. Billy Shiel's Farne Island Boat Trips are the best established – they have seven boats – and booking details can be found at www.farne-islands.com. You can book special all day bird watching tours which give you 2 hours on each island. Look at all options on the website when planning your trip.

Seahouses Car Park Lat/Long: 55.581410, -1.656123
OS Co-ordinate: NU 218 320
Nearest Postcode. NE68 7SL (100m)

Accessibility

The islands are rough outcrops of rock and require some sure-footedness and confidence on rough terrain. Bring waterproofs, a good pair of boots, a packed lunch and a drink.

Best Time of Year/Day

May and June are best for nesting birds especially the must-see arctic terns on Inner Farne.

Guillemot *(Uria aalge)*

See also Skomer p.320.

Large mixed flocks of common and bridled guillemot populate the guano-covered cliffs and float in rafts surrounding Staple Island. From the boat there are great opportunities to catch the birds in flight as they struggle to take off from the waves. Use a fast shutter speed to allow for the movement of the boat, the movement of the birds and hand holding the equipment. A tripod is of no use on the boat.

The large crowds of birds on the sea cliffs also make for good group shots.

Arctic tern *(Sterna paradisaea)*

The arctic tern colony on the island of Inner Farne is legendary. On leaving the boat ensure you are wearing a hat or hood as the terns are very aggressive defending their nests that lie inches away from the main access track. Consider wearing light gloves as waving your pink finger can also receive the tern's sharp-beaked attention.

Also known as sea swallows these are beautiful birds to photograph especially in flight and interacting with people and other birds. Arctic terns are incredible long distance migrants spending the winter in the Antarctic (yes the Antarctic). So allow them a little respect even if they do manage a painful peck to your head or fingers.

Technique

A wide-angle lens is a great idea to capture the action as terns bombard other visitors. Also good for capturing landscape shots on these beautiful islands. The birds are very close and a 300mm lens works well for close ups and also for flight shots.

Following the steps up to and around the chapel gets you to the best place to see the terns. Further round the small island there are large colonies of puffins, this is a good place to photograph puffins in flight. Position yourself downwind and wait for them to take off as they venture out to sea for sand eels. A stiff breeze is a help as they can be surprisingly fast on calm days.

Keep an eye out for the small colony of sandwich terns that nest here, these have a black crest and a yellow tip to their black beak.

Eider ducks nest here and are amazingly well camouflaged, again often quite close to the marked track. Look for yellow marker sticks that indicate the positions of the nesting birds. Mothers with newly fledged black ducklings have to be wary and aggressive towards the predatory gulls which hang around looking for undefended fledglings.

At the furthest point of the island shags can be found, some very close to the marked trail.

Don't forget your hat: an Arctic tern attacks a visitor.
Nikon D800E, 17-35mm at 35mm, ISO 1000, 1/1250 sec at f/13

The Arctic tern: note the sharp all-red beak.
Nikon D4, 300mm, ISO 800, 1/1000 sec at f/8

Arctic tern passes a sand eel to his mate.
Nikon D4, 300mm, ISO 800, 1/1250 sec at f/10

The North Pennines Area of Outstanding Natural Beauty is a fabulous and little visited area of moorland in the centre of Northern England. On spring mornings the high moor is absolutely thronging with drumming snipe, the high cries of peewits (lapwing), the haunting call of the curlew and the spectacle of lekking black grouse. All this can be seen from the roadside and from rough footpaths that have permitted access across the peat moorland.

Where to look

Head for the highest points of the moorland, around the Langdon Beck Hotel in Teesdale is a great place to start. The road to St John's Chapel has plenty of lay-bys which serve as good spots to scan the moors for birds.

Curlew *(Numenius arquata)*

Notable for its amazing down curved beak the curlew generally winters on coastlines but returns to moorland such as this in spring to breed. Recognisable from afar especially by the evocative piping call synonymous with misty windswept moors. It is very similar to the rarer whimbrel which has a lighter eye stripe and shorter bill.

Lapwing *(Vanellus vanellus)*

A striking bird especially at close quarters when the green and violet colouration becomes evident on the shoulders. From afar lapwings appear black and white and are especially photogenic in flight. In spring males give spectacular territorial flights attracting females and rival males on the wing. The common name peewit comes from its clear and obvious call.

Black grouse *(Tetrao tetrix)*

There is only a relatively small population of black grouse in the North Pennines but the advantage here (as at World's End) is that they can be seen and photographed from the roadside. Also the females (grey hens) seem more prominent here.

See also Glenlivet Black Grouse Hide p.42 and Ruabon Moor, World's End p.298.

Technique

Binoculars are important to scan the moorland and locate the birds. As mentioned above you don't even have to stray from the car for good shots. Take care in choosing an appropriate pull in spot so as not to obstruct the road or get bogged down in the soft ground off the road. A bean bag or car door mount is a good idea when using longer lenses.

Much of the moorland is Access Land where you can wander anywhere, as well as having footpaths across the moors.. Get hold of an OS map and compass and know how to use them before setting off across the moors. Weather here can be inclement. As these images show, mist and rain are not uncommon so appropriate footwear and weather-poof outdoor gear is advised.

Black grouse displaying in the rain on the Teasdale Moors. Nikon D800E, 500mm + 1.4 x converter at 700mm, ISO 2500, 1/800 sec at f/7.1

Below: Female red grouse hunkered down in the mist. Nikon D4, 500mm + 1.4 x converter at 700mm, ISO 1600, 1/1250 sec at f/5.6

Lapwing close up. Nikon D4, 500mm + 1.4 x converter at 700mm, ISO 2500, 1/800 sec at f/7.1

Above: Curlew striding out on the misty moorland. Nikon D4, 500mm + 1.4 x converter at 700mm, ISO 2500, 1/1250 sec at f/5.6

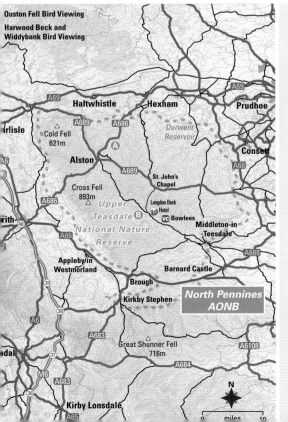

How to get here:

A good base is the Langdon Beck Hotel which is located on the B6277 11.6 miles south east from Alston and 17 miles north west from Barnard Castle. From the Langdon Beck Hotel drive north west for 0.4 miles. Turn right towards St John's Chapel and start looking.

Langdon Beck Hotel Lat/Long: 54.675962, -2.2293239
OS Co-ordinate: NY 853 312
Nearest Postcode. DL12 0XP

Accessibility

Many opportunities are available from the roadside. Footpaths are well marked but are across peat moorland, requiring good outdoor equipment. It's likely to be wet, uneven and muddy.

Best Time of Year/Day

Black grouse lekking displays are at their peak in early spring.

Best black grouse-watching practice:

Arrive before daybreak. A vehicle stopping in daylight can disturb the birds. Stay in your vehicle and watch quietly through binoculars and telescopes. Don't start the engine until lekking has wound down, usually about two hours after dawn.

Excuse the crumbs. Nikon D3X, 300mm + 2 x converter at 600mm, ISO 3200, 1/1250 sec at f/5.6

The Lake District National Park encompasses a compact area characterised by incredibly beautiful landscapes of mountain, woodland, moor, and of course lakes and rivers. Much of the area is managed by the National Trust and it is worth considering membership to avoid car park charges. Whilst being a popular holiday destination it is still possible to find quiet spots to photograph the wildlife.

The beauty of the landscape here is outstanding and nowhere in the UK equals its compact diversity from a photographer's point of view.

Red squirrel (Sciurius vulgaris)

The red squirrel is a top wildlife photographic subject. The population of red squirrels in Britain is estimated at around 140,000 compared to over 2.5 million greys. In the Lake District they remain a species of broad leaved woodland as oppposed to the conifer plantations they tend to inhabit elsewhere in the UK. This makes a far more interesting backdrop.

Where to look

Red squirrels inhabit most of the woodland areas around the Lakes; the Borrowdale valley, Aira Force near Ullswater, the Ennerdale Valley and also around Haweswater and Thirlmere are good spots to try. Squirrels are easily drawn to bird feeders especially if stocked with hazelnuts or peanuts although the feeders themselves are an unnatural feature if left in shot. Feeding spots include the red squirrel trail at Swirls car park above Thirlmere, Whinlatter Forest and the Haweswater Hotel.

In the Lake District a tough strategy is in action to control grey squirrels and thus protect the reds from the squirrel pox borne by the greys. For now at least this appears to be working but the red squirrel remains an endangered denizen of the woodland.

Technique

Squirrels are usually a fairly easy subject as they are often more interested in food and other squirrels than human activity. Be still and quiet and use a camouflaged pop up hide if you need to get really close. Light can be an issue in broad leaved woodland. A high ISO will normally be required and slower shutter speeds than usual assuming the subject sits still long enough. In sunny conditions the dappled light is very contrasty which is problematic unless you can get the squirrel in direct sunlight. A bright but overcast day is best in terms of reducing high contrast in the forest.

Surprised to see a photographer. Nikon D4, 300mm + 2 x converter at 600mm, ISO 2500, 1/1250 sec at f/7.1

Keeping an eye on things. Nikon D4, 300mm + 2 x converter at 600mm, ISO 1600, 1/1000 sec at f/8

*Right: Grey squirrel v red : An unusual encounter.
Nikon D3X, 300mm, ISO 3200, 1/1250 sec at f/2.8*

How To Get Here

The Lake District is accessed from the M6 motorway. From the M6 motorway head towards Keswick or Ambleside for a good central base.

Where To See Red Squirrels

The Swirls. Woodland by the A591 on the east side of Thirlmere.
Car parking Lat/Long: 54.542506, -3.059240
OS Co-ordinate: NY316168
Nearest Postcode: CA12 4TW (1.5km)

Dodd Wood, Keswick. Red squirrels are usually seen near the osprey viewing point uphill from the car park. Pay and display car park by the Old Sawmill Tearoom on the A591 on the east side of Bassenthwaite Lake, north of Keswick.
Parking Lat/Long: 54.642850, -3.1868505
OS Co-ordinate: NY235281
Nearest Postcode. CA12 4QE (100m)

Forestry Commission Whinlatter Forest Park. Ask staff the best spots to explore.
Pay and display car park Lat/Long: 54.609342, -3.2270515
OS Co-ordinate: NY208244
Nearest Postcode. CA12 5TW (300m)

Haweswater Hotel, Guerness Wood, Haweswater. Red squirrels visit the gardens of the hotel and live in the adjacent woodland.
Haweswater Hotel Lat/Long: 54.517728, -2.799774
OS Co-ordinate: NY483138
Nearest Postcode. CA10 2RP (3km)

Dippers and grey wagtails are widespread in the Lake District and are found by streams and rivers. Try the Borrowdale and Duddon Valleys, and the River Rothay and River Brathay near Ambleside.

Accessibility

These locations are mostly roadside or along good to uneven paths with rougher ground by the rivers.

Best Time of Year/Day

As with most mammals, early morning and evening are best though at key times of year they can be active all day. For example in autumn squirrels are visible collecting and stashing their stores in readiness for winter. Late spring is good when vegetation is low and the trees are still bare of leaves for better light.

Dippers and wagtails (next pages) are present all year round. Late summer will see the juveniles learning to feed themselves which offers more opportunities.

Dipper *(Cinclus cinclus)*

The fast flowing streams that run into and out of the numerous lakes are the perfect habitat for this specialist water bird. The smart black and tan plumage is offset with the bright white bib.

Dippers are characteristically perched on an obvious stone midstream or seen in low flight skimmming up or downstream. When perched the dipper bobs up and down (as many water's edge birds do). This behaviour can be folllowed by periods of up to 30 seconds diving underwater, and sorties under stream banks searching for insect prey. Their habits make the dipper easy enough to find but often quick to lose again. They tend to favour territorial sections of stream and are here all year round.

Grey Wagtail *(Motacilla cinerea)*

The same waters that feed the dippers are nearly always also home to the grey wagtail. These are a much more exotic looking species with the flash of yellow on the tail and underparts. The greys have the longest tails of all wagtails. The alarm call is loud and carries well above the rush of water so familiarise yourself with this before going in search of this pretty bird. Often found quite high up on the fellside streams in the summer, they move to lowland areas in the winter.

Young grey wagtail close up. Nikon D4, 300mm + 2 x converter at 600mm, ISO 800, 1/1000 sec at f/8

Where to look

Almost all the fast flowing streams here are dipper and grey wagtail territory. Grey wagtails usually nest close to the water in crevices or hollows lined with grass, moss and twigs. Alongside streams is an ideal place to find their main diet of midges and ants, along with tadpoles and water snails.

Technique

Both species are highly mobile but territorial. This means that as soon as they see you they will fly up or down stream but probably not too far away. It works well to spot the birds at a distance and approach slowly and cautiously. If the bird sees you first and flies off, find some cover and await its return. Quite often whilst waiting for one species the other may appear on the same stretch.

Top tip

Photographing in wooded river valleys is often very contrasty and the camera may have difficulty coping with both the bright highlights and dark shadows. Try to choose a bright but overcast day, spot meter off the subject if possible and use exposure compensation to correctly expose the subject. Shoot in RAW to give the best chance of recovering tonal range later if necessary.

Dipper in the middle of the fast flowing Lakeland stream.
Nikon D800E, 300mm, ISO 3200, 1/640 sec at f/2.8

Dipper: portrait photographed at Exmoor. Nikon D4, 300mm + 2 x
converter at 600mm, ISO 10000, 1/1250 sec at f/5.6

Bottom: Lake District stream Borrowdale.
Nikon D3X, 17-35mm at 24mm, ISO 50, 0.6 sec at f/22

Below: Reflection of grey wagtail. Nikon D4, 300mm + 2 x converter
at 600mm, ISO 800, 1/1000 sec at f/5.6

Starling murmuration against sunset sky photographed at Otmoor.
Nikon D800E, 70-200mm at 70mm, ISO 1250, 1/1800 sec at f/2.8.

Leighton Moss is the largest reed bed in North West England, it is managed by the RSPB and in recent years was host to the BBC's Autumn Watch programme.

This is a large and popular reserve with great hides overlooking the main viewpoints. The enthusiastically staffed visitor centre has good facilities including a large cafe serving Chris Packhams' favourite: lemon drizzle cake.

Starling *(Sternus vulgaris)*

Starlings are resident in the UK all year round and also breed here, however in autumn and winter the UK resident population is massively increased by migrants from Northern Europe.

In the evenings congregating starlings amass in huge numbers prior to roosting and this get together is known as a murmuration. The mass of birds fly together as one and drift and reaccumulate forming mesmerising displays and patterns in the sky. This swirling mass of life, often at close proximity is a sight and sound to behold, and a great oppportunity for the photographer. See also Gretna Green p.92 for a list of other significant murmurations around the country and Ham Wall p.272.

Technique

Keep an eye on the weather and try and choose an evening promising a clear sky as a back drop.

There are several ways to approach photographing a murmuration. Generally the sought after image is a distinct pattern in the sky showing the incredible numbers and beautiful shapes the flock forms. Depending on how close you can get a medium to wide angle lens is best. Better to go too wide then crop in later than to miss part of the formation shape.

Alternatively use a longer lens (300mm and up) to close in on a section of the flock and show the dense numbers and proximity in which they fly. A longer lens alongside a wide aperture (small f/ number) will reduce the depth of field, this can be used to good effect, see photo opposite at bottom right.

Where to look

Pick up a trail map from the visitor centre and ask the staff advice on recent murmuration locations. As these move from day to day it is not always possible to be in the right place. From the visitor centre there is a short walk back up the road to join the main trail that goes down to the Public Hide. Depending on where the birds roost this trail is often a good spot to start from.

Grey heron on a grey day at Leighton Moss. Nikon D4, 300mm + 2 x converter at 600mm, ISO 1600, 1/1250 sec at f/5.6

Starling murmuration at Leighton Moss with sunset colours. Nikon D4, 17-35mm at 35mm, ISO 400, 1/400 sec at f/7.1

Below: Close up the sound and spectacle is mesmerising. Nikon D4, 300mm + 2 x conv at 600mm, ISO 5000, 1/1000 sec at f/5.6

Murmuration against blue sky. Nikon D800E, 300mm, ISO 800, 1/1600 sec at f/4.5

Also at Leighton Moss

The BBC chose Leighton Moss in 2013 and 2014 to host Autumn Watch for good reason. Amongst many other species otters, kingfishers, bearded tits, bittern, red deer and marsh harriers are all possible sightings here.

The Public Hide is a good spot to see herons hunting close by with plenty of teal and other waterfowl in the foreground and is also a great place to photograph dragonflies in summer. The Lower Hide is good for otters, though these can be frustratingly far off, and marsh harriers frequently hunt the far edges of the pools. In autumn bearded tits visit the grit trays just off the track near the Public Hide. Red deer are commonly seen at the Grizedale Hide.

A short side trip takes you to the hides overlooking the estuary from where you can see waterfowl and waders including flocks of godwit feeding on the mud flats.

How To Get Here

Leighton Moss is situated west of the M6 motorway 4 miles from Carnforth in Lancashire. Exit at junction 35. Follow brown RSPB signs to the visitor centre car park near Silverdale Railway Station.

Car Park Lat/Long: 54.16814,-2.80107
OS Co-ordinate: SD 478 750
Nearest Postcode: LA5 0SW

There are other hides overlooking Morecambe Bay just west of Leighton Moss and at Hest Bank (LA2 6EA). Details are available at the RSPB Leighton Moss visitor centre.

Accessibility

The reserve is open from dawn to dusk and the visitor centre is open 9.30 am to 5 pm (4.30 pm in December and January, closed 25 December). RSPB members free, £7 for others. There is a network of mainly level paths which are wheelchair accessible. The paths can be muddy. Maps are available from the visitor centre.

Best Time of Year/Day

The best time for murmurations is late October until late March. Arrive two hours before sunset to find a good vantage point. The point of roost can move day to day.

Mount Grace Priory is located close to Northallerton within the North York Moors National Park. This is a superb location for both wildlife and landscape photography.

Built in 1398 the ruins of the medieval Carthusian monastery stand in honey-coloured sandstone amongst black shadows and a backdrop of deciduous woodland. The foreground of neatly mown lawns and, in spring, ranks of yellow daffodils is home to plenty of rabbits which are of course the favoured prey of the priory's most famous residents: the stoats.

Stoat (Mustela erminea)

This small, handsome, swift, carnivorous mammal is often confused with weasels but is larger and with a black tip to the tail. These superb little mustelids are perhaps one of the most difficult of British wild animals to photograph. Lightning quick and far smaller than you might imagine they are opportunistic predators and almost impossible to predict.

Stoats are widespread throughout the UK, they can and do turn up when least expected, typically making a fast run across a road or track and quickly vanishing in the undergrowth. They prey on rodents and especially rabbits which can be up to six times their size so the best chance to locate them is first looking for large rabbit warrens.

In the Cotswolds, Lake District and elsewhere in the country stoats love stone walls where they can hide, squeezing into amazingly small cracks. Here at Mount Grace they seem to love the small underground drainage channels which crisscross the ruins allowing them to disappear and reappear in different areas at high speed. They are present all year round but June is a great time to see them as they are feeding young kits and are more active in daylight hours.

Stoats at Mount Grace Priory became more famous when they starred in a David Attenborough documentary *Stoats in the Priory.*' They also featured in *The Life of Mammals* series.

Technique

Good luck or lots of patience are required. Good field craft is needed if specifically out looking for stoats. In any case whilst wandering around just be ready with camera settings locked onto a fast shutter speed, a single focus point activated and predictive focus, see Technique section p.354.

Top tip

Stoats are constantly on the move, it's worth practising making a good 'squeak' so you can at least make him pause momentarily in his tracks. A small block of polystyrene on a piece of glass is rumoured to work well.

Mount Grace Priory in spring. Nikon D800E, 17-35mm at 25mm, ISO 160, 1/200 sec at f/10

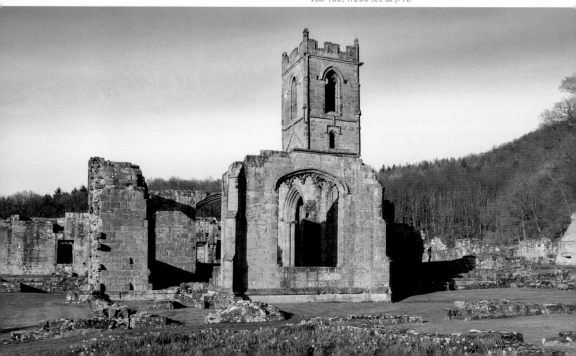

*Stoat in the forget-me-nots at Mount Grace Priory.
Nikon D4, 500mm, ISO 800, 1/1250 sec at f/8*

*Rabbits breed like rabbits. Nikon D4, 300mm + 2 x converter at
600mm, ISO 1600, 1/1600 sec at f/6.3*

How To Get Here

Mount Grace Priory is situated just off the A19, six miles north
west of the town of North Allerton and 12 miles south west of
Middlesbrough, within the North York Moors National Park.

Priory Car Park Lat/Long: 54.379570, -1.3105488
OS Co-ordinate: SE 448 984
Nearest Postcode: DL6 3JG

Accessibility

Owned by the National Trust and managed by English Heritage.
Members of those organisations get free entry. This is a location
for all, with mobility parking spaces and good paths suitable
for wheelchairs.

Check for opening times and also for event days. Limited opening
in the winter, summer usually open 10am–4pm daily Thursday to
Sunday. There is a footpath which goes by the Priory and into
Mount Grace Woods.

Best Time of Year/Day

Summer mornings are best, especially June and July.

Gannet (Morus bassanus) : Cruising the updraughts at Bempton cliffs.
Nikon D4, 300mm + 2 x converter at 600mm, ISO 400, 1/1600 sec at f/9

This stunning clifftop RSPB reserve lying on the North Yorkshire coast is an exhilarating and dramatic spot to photograph nesting sea birds in spring. Kittiwakes, gannets, razorbills and puffins are present here in huge numbers creating a cacophany of sound and flying with easy grace on the uplifting breeze above the dark sea far below. The clifftop path leads from the RSPB information office along the cliff edge, a vivid foreground of pink campion flowers adds to the assault on the senses.

Kittiwake (Rissa tridactyla)

Probably the most obvious of the seabirds here, the kittiwake is a small delicate-looking gull with black wing tips and a yellow bill. These are numerous on the first cliff faces you come to and often in flight over the sea and close overhead as you follow the cliff top path.

Gannet (Morus bassanus)

Gannets are large and elegant seagoing birds and a rewarding subject for the photographer, see also Bass Rock p.88. On the sea cliffs they act out their complex courtship display including sky pointing, bill rubbing and presentation of nesting material (usually seaweed). They have a dark yellow colouration to the head, pure white plumage with black tipped wings, fantastic green stripes on the large webbed feet and to top it all a sky blue outer ring to the eye. The younger immature birds are marked with black patches on their backs making them even more spectacular against a dark turquoise sea.

Kittiwake asleep on the edge. Nikon D4, 300mm + 2 x converter at 600mm, ISO 640, 1/1000 sec at f/9

Technique

There will be a dizzying array of birds flying in and around the cliff faces. Spot a bird as far out to sea as possible and track it in using autofocus as it arrives at the nest. Exposure can be difficult with essentially white sea birds against either a dark sea or bright cliff background, check your images on the screen and be prepared to use exposure compensation. Shoot in RAW to allow for adjustment later.

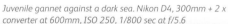

Juvenile gannet against a dark sea. Nikon D4, 300mm + 2 x converter at 600mm, ISO 250, 1/800 sec at f/5.6

Below pink campion glowing in evening sunlight. Nikon D800E, 70-200mm at 155mm, ISO 1000, 1/200 sec at f/9

An early start is needed to get a prime position. Nikon D800E, 17-35mm at 17mm, ISO 640, 1/250 sec at f/8

Top: Bempton cliffs in late golden evening sunlight. Nikon D800E, 17-35mm at 20mm, ISO 1000, 1/200 sec at f/10

Right: Gannet incoming with nesting material. Nikon D800E, 300mm + 2 x converter at 600mm, ISO 320, 1/1000 sec at f/8

How To Get Here

Bempton Cliffs are on the Yorkshire coast south of Scarborough, 4 miles north of Bridlington. The car park and visitor centre for RSPB Bempton Cliffs are a mile down a minor road – turn north at the White Horse Pub – from Bempton village.

There are six viewing stations at the cliffs all within a kilometre of the visitor centre with the option for exploration along the cliff top path.

RSPB Bempton Cliffs Car Park and Visitor Centre
Lat/Long: 54.14609,-0.16889
OS map co-ordinate: TA197738
Nearest Parking Postcode: YO15 1JF (800m)

Accessibility

The paths are well maintained and level to the viewing platforms overlooking the cliffs.

Best Time of Year/Day

Spring (April–June) is the best time when the seabirds return and begin nest building and courtship displays. After this the breeding season is in full swing and in summer there are a quarter of a million seabirds at Bempton with eggs and chicks. In autumn most of the seabirds depart.

Above: Gannet courtship display. Nikon D800E, 300mm + 2 x converter at 600mm, ISO 320, 1/1000 sec at f/9

Martin Mere used to be the largest body of fresh water in England. The lake formed in a depression left after the retreat of glacial ice at the end of the last Ice Age. The lake has long since been mostly drained but the area remains a large and, from a wildlife point of view, important area of marshland.

Martin Mere is now a Wildfowl and Wetland Trust Reserve, it is situated near Ormskirk on the Lancashire coast in North West England. The reserve is internationally important for overwintering wildfowl especially the spectacular whooper swans but also geese such as the greylag and ducks including shelduck and wigeon.

What to Expect

This is a well-appointed reserve with plenty of facilities. The most important consideration here is timing to make the best of the weather and the birds. There are eleven hides and each offers different opportunities. One of the best hides for sightings of the swans is Raines Observatory. This hide is glass fronted and therefore difficult to get a decent shot especially on a wet day.

The swans spend much of their time feeding out on the mud and swimming in the main lagoon known as the Mere. The Hale Hide further along is good for shots of incoming and outgoing whoopers and the Ron Barker Hide at the end of the trail can be good for barn owl, godwits and kestrels.

For the main event though make sure you are in position at feeding time at the Swan Link Hide. From here hundreds of whoopers and other wildfowl gather in close proximity. The number of birds and the interaction between them is a spectacle to see and photograph and is well worth a visit to brighten up any grey winter day.

Whooper swan *(Cygnus cygnus)*

The whooper is a large swan similar to but larger than the Bewicks, see Slimbridge p.160. At between 140 to 165 cm (55–65 in) long and with a wing span of 205 to 275 cm (81–108 in), it is considered to be one of the heaviest flying birds. Whoopers have a more angular head and more yellow than black on their bill (Bewicks have more black than yellow). Like the Bewicks this is a migratory species which, apart from a few northern individuals, only visits in the winter months. Whooper swans are especially spectacular in flight.

Below: Winter whoopers on the wing at Martin Mere. Nikon D4, 500mm + 1.4 x converter at 700mm, ISO 2000, 1/1000 sec at f/14

Right: Whooper swan profiles. Nikon D4, 500mm, ISO 1600, 1/640 sec at f/6.3

Also at Martin Mere

Besides the whooper swans expect to see other wildfowl including geese, shelduck, wigeon and mallard. The common or garden mallard might not be everybody's choice photographic subject but with so much going on, here is a chance to try different creative techniques. Try using a wide aperture to create a shallow depth of field thus focusing on one subject in a crowd. Slow shutter speeds will result in intentional blur to give an impression of motion, this can be very effective when a flock takes off or whilst tracking birds in flight.

Technique

Allow plenty of time to be at the Swan Link Hide for feeding time (October to March at 3pm).

The angle of the sun is important and it's worth moving far down the hide to make sure the sun is as far behind you as possible. There is not much room to swing a large telephoto lens so take it off the tripod and rest on a bean bag on the windows. Some windows have a better field of view than others. The feeding moves over to the Raines Observatory at 3:30pm but the glass windows there obscure the view.

The feeding frenzy as hundred of swans and ducks gather on the shore and in the shallows to gobble grain is well worth witnessing and provides plenty of photo opportunities as they squabble amongst themselves.

Intentional blur: slow exposure flock of whoopers.
Nikon D4, 500mm, ISO250, 1/13 sec at f/22

How To Get Here

Martin Mere is located south west of Preston and east of Southport, off the A59, just north of the village of Burscough. There is free parking at the visitor centre.

Martin Mere Wetland Centre Lat/Long: 53.622771, -2.866600
OS map co-ordinate: SD 427 143
Nearest Parking Postcode: L40 0TA (90m)

Address: Fish Lane, Burscough, Lancashire
Phone: 01704 895181

Accessibility

The Wetland Centre is accessible to all with flat level paths and is fully accessible to wheelchair users. There is a visitor centre and restaurant. Maps and advice from friendly staff are available.

The centre is open all year except 25 December. The car park and visitor centre is open 9:30am to 4:30pm from 4 November to 29 March, and 9:30am to 6:00pm from 30 March to 2 November. There is a public footpath that traverses the wetland.

www.wwt.org.uk

Best Time of Year/Day

Late autumn and winter is the best time to visit when the reserve is home to many migratory species. Northerly winds help migrating birds to travel south so it's worth waiting until after the first cold spells.

Mallards in the mix.
Nikon D4, 500mm, ISO 1600, 1/250 sec at f/4

Wet male kestrel, Ron Barker Hide. Nikon D4, 500mm + 1.4 x
converter at 700mm, ISO 2000, 1/1000 sec at f/14

Below: Whooper swan argument.
Nikon D4, 500mm, ISO 1600, 1/640 sec at f/6.3

Formby Point is a small but attractive area of pine forest and sand dunes within easy reach of the city of Liverpool. This is famously home to a small and isolated population of red squirrels. In the woods you will also find a variety of birds including jays and woodpeckers and the sand dunes are well known for rare natterjack toads.

What To Expect

A beautiful pine woodland that can be a little busy at times for wildlife photography. Time your visit carefully, it's best to avoid sunny weekends.

Red squirrels (*Sciurius vulgaris*)

The red squirrels though accustomed to human disturbance are still elusive and require a quiet and subtle approach. There are feeding stations located around the red squirrel walk and these are the most likely places to see them. See also Red Squirrel Jumping Hide p.60, Lake District p.120 and Brownsea Island p.206.

Jay (*Garrulus glandarius*)

Jays are usually a difficult bird to photograph. Members of the crow family, they are extremely intelligent and often wary of human presence. Here this is definitely not the case and their intelligence has taught them that people bring food, usually intended for the squirrels. They are a striking bird with almost pink plumage and a vivid blue wing patch. The eye has a light blue outer ring. Though shy, jays are noisy which often gives their location away.

Technique

Light is at a premium in this shady evergreen woodland, a high ISO is often necessary to maintain a fast enough shutter speed especially if hand holding a large lens.

Avoiding the crowds here is the key to a successful photography trip. Try early morning and mid-week. Find a quiet corner near a feed station and remain still and quiet. It is amazing how the woods can come to life if you are patient, quiet and still. A hazelnut or two left in appropriate spots may help draw in the star attractions.

Jay in the shaded woods at Formby. Nikon D4, 300mm + 2 x converter at 600mm, ISO 3200, 1/1250 sec at f/5.6

Red squirrel on the move through the Scots pines.
Nikon D4, 300mm, ISO 1600, 1/1000 sec at f/2.8

Light filtering through the Scots pines at Formby.
Nikon D800E, 17-35mm at 35mm, ISO 2500, 1/200 sec at f/10

How to get here :

Formby Point is situated next to the town of Formby north of Liverpool. Parking is at the end of Victoria Road and is free to National Trust members. The car park is open from 9am until 4.30pm all year.

National Trust Formby Point Lat/Long: 53.565651, -3.0962884
OS map co-ordinate: SD 274 082
Nearest Parking Postcode: L37 1YD (300m)

Address: Victoria Road, near Formby, Liverpool, L37 1LJ

Phone: 01704 878591

Accessibility

There are good paths through the woodlands, some suitable for wheelchairs. For access to the beach it can be windy and walking through sand dunes is hard work.

www.nationaltrust.org.uk/formby

Best Time of Year/Day

Good at most times of year but avoid sunny weekends and holidays as the area can get busy.

Close up and curious jay. Nikon D4, 300mm + 2 x converter
at 600mm, ISO 3200, 1/1250 sec at f/5.6

The Peak District was the first area in the UK to be designated as a National Park. The northern part, known as the Dark Peak, is largely heather and grass moorland offering an excellent upland habitat for red grouse, mountain hares, short-eared owls and merlin.

Red grouse *(Lagopus lagopus)*

The red grouse is a game bird, reared and released in numbers for hunting in many places of the UK. The upland moor is managed for their benefit including heather burning and feed stations. The grouse are generally wary of people and the first signs of the birds in the area are likely to be the loud indignant calls as they take flight and whir away over the horizon.

Male birds are distinct from the hens in that they have red eyebrows which together with their habit of standing on prominent tussocks and rocks to proclaim their territory makes them easy enough to spot.

Technique

Ideally check out the area in daylight then return the next morning under cover of darkness to stake out a likely position. Either use a camouflage hide or simply hide out in the shelter of one of the Tors.

Red grouse habitat: high in the Peak District.
Nikon D4, 17-35mm at 17mm, ISO 400, 1/400 sec at f/14

It is a better option to be patient and wait for birds to come into a territorial perch than try and walk up on them. If your field craft is good use the terrain to your advantage if you need to get closer. Try lying prone in the heather to achieve a low angle of view as in the bottom image on the opposite page.

If fell walking is not your thing there are sections of the higher roads where grouse feed and claim their territories. Find a lay-by or safe place to park. Use the car as a hide and a bean bag to rest the lens on the window.

Close encounters of the bird kind. Nikon D4, 300mm + 2 x converter at 600mm, ISO 800, 1/1600 sec at f/7.1

Red grouse profile. Nikon D4, 300mm + 2 x converter at 600mm, ISO 1000, 1/1250 sec at f/5.6

How To Get Here

There is much grouse moorland in the Peak District and there are grouse in abundance. The easiest places to access the grouse moorland are at the Eastern Edges above Hathersage. Two good spots are Curbar Gap where you can access the moorland above Curbar and Baslow Edges and for a remoter experience try the Derwent Edges accessed from Cutthroat Bridge.

Curbar Gap, NT Haywood car park
Parking Lat/Long: 53.269436, -1.608036
OS map co-ordinate: SK 262 747
Nearest Parking Postcode: S32 3YR

Cutthroat Bridge Lat/Long: 53.382894, -1.680455
OS map co-ordinate: SK 213 873
Nearest Parking Postcode: S33 0AX

Accessibility

The Peak high moorland reaches up to 2,000ft and is often wet and boggy, mist can make navigation difficult. They are traversed however by good paths. Good waterproof boots are recommended to cope with the wet and rough terrain.

Best Time of Year/Day

Mornings and evenings for the best light. grouse are active all year round but the best times are the Spring and from August (purple heather flowers) through the autumn. Autumn is good for males disputing territory.

Mountain Hare *(Lepus timidus)*

This species is also covered in the Cairngorms, see p.52, however the hares here are living on somewhat different terrain. The climate is less prone to the snow conditions of the Cairngorms and this is an easier place to access.

Like their cousins the brown hare (Lepus europaeus) they are in breeding mode in early spring, the males are chasing females and establishing territories in February and March. Late spring when there is little or no snow on the ground means that the white pelage of the hares stands out in beautiful contrast to the black peat and subtle green mosses and buff coloured grasses.

Where to look

Likely spots to look for them in the Peak District include Kinder Scout, Bleaklow and Derwent Edges. Kinder Scout is a large National Nature Reserve.

In the Peak District the peat moors are intersected by eroded ditches called *groughs*. Hares, unlike rabbits, do not make burrows and instead use the groughs as hiding places on the otherwise very exposed moors.

Technique

This is another example of where binoculars are your second most important piece of kit. Scan the moors for white specks on the horizon and pay special attention to the groughs. Good field skills, see p.352, are required to get close. A low profile and working into the wind ideally with the sun behind you are the most important.

Top tip

A low profile is not only good for getting close but also good for getting down at eye level with the subject. Shooting prone (lying down) requires good waterproof gear and a bean bag instead of a tripod. If hand held keep the shutter speed high to compensate for not having a steady tripod to shoot from.

Also in the Peak District

There are two good locations for red deer: Chatsworth House and Big Moor (see map on previous page).

Misty moorland mountain hare. Nikon D800E, 300mm + 2 x converter at 600mm, ISO 1000, 1/1600 sec at f/5.6

Good field craft can get you close. The alarmed look is characteristic. The hare continued to graze nonchalantly for a half hour photo shoot. Nikon D4, 300mm + 2 x converter at 600mm, ISO 500, 1/1600 sec at f/5.6

Late evening light illuminates the white hare against a black grough. Nikon D4, 300mm + 2 x converter at 600mm, ISO 500, 1/1600 sec at f/5.6

How To Get Here

Bleaklow Moor is the most accessible place to see mountain hares. The start point is at the Snake Pass summit (512m) on the A57 east of Glossop. Park by the small tarn where the Pennine Way crosses. Follow the flagged path north on to the moor. Mountain Hares are common here, but walk for around a mile to get well away from the road and explore the drainages and groughs.

Snake Pass summit Parking Lat/Long: 53.432959, -1.869390
OS map co-ordinate: SK 087 929
Nearest Parking Postcode: SK13 7PQ (3.2km away)

Kinder Scout. The quickest way to access the Kinder Scout Plateau is in the north from the Snake Pass Inn on the Snake Road (A57). Follow Fair Brook for 1.5 miles gently up hill to the plateau.

Snake Pass Inn Parking Lat/Long: 53.411720, -1.832397
OS map co-ordinate: SK 112 905
Nearest Parking Postcode: S33 0AB (2.3km)

Accessibility

As for previous pages, dress for hiking on moorland trails and across wet peat moors. People get lost on the Kinder plateau, you need to be proficient with map and compass. Take extra clothes, food and a hot drink.

Best Time of Year/Day

Mountain hares transition from their summer brown coat to white in November/December until March/April. When there is no snow they are easy to spot. If there is snow cover they do look spectacular, but you have to be alert to spot them.

Built by William Jessop and completed in 1794 the Cromford Canal runs 14.5 miles along the east side of the Derwent Valley and on to Langley Mill. The 6 mile section between Cromford and Ambergate is a Site of Special Scientific Interest and a Local Nature Reserve.

This is a tranquil stretch of waterway and at one time a good location for photographing water voles. The vole population at the time of writing seems diminished or at least less obliging to photographers. The canal however remains a fabulous location for other wildlife especially the charismatic little grebe. The calm water with overhanging trees offers a great opportunity for reflection shots.

Little Grebe *(Tachybaptus ruficollis)*

A small water bird with distinctive russet plumage on the head and neck. Not uncommon and often also seen in parks and on reed bed reserves. It makes a pretty subject to photograph especially with dark reflective water. The birds are easily located, they will dive underwater and resurface some distance away so best approached quietly. Access is easy from the canal footpath so tripods are not a problem, though look for a low angle of view.

Mallard drake reflected in the still black water. Nikon D4, 300mm + 2 x converter at 600mm, ISO 500, 1/1000 sec at f/5.6

Cromford Canal: still waters reflecting the overhanging trees.

How To Get Here

Cromford Canal is in the eastern Derbyshire Dales 12 miles north of Derby. Park at High Peak Junction by the A6, next to the canal, 3 miles south of Matlock. You can explore both north and south along the canal path from here.

High Peak Junction Lat/Long: 53.101007, -1.5310532
OS map co-ordinate: SK 314 560
Nearest Parking Postcode: DE4 5AH

Accessibility

Easy walks along the canal towpath. There is a cafe at High Peak Junction.

Other possible water vole locations close by:

Bar Brook on Big Moor: SK 281 751
Bradwell Brook: SK 173 812
Lathkill Dale, River Wye: SK 203 664

Best Time of Year/Day

Any time of the year, mornings and mid-week are likely to be quieter as this location can be busy at holidays and weekends.

Above: Pair of little grebes. Nikon D4, 300mm + 2 x converter at 600mm, ISO 2500, 1/1000 sec at f/5.6

Below: Water vole photo taken at East Malling. Nikon D4, 500mm, ISO 4000, 1/640 sec at f/4.5

On the Lincolnshire coast between Grimsby and Mablethorpe lies the National Nature Reserve of Donna Nook. This is a sanctuary for grey seals, managed by the Lincolnshire Wildlife Trust. Grey seals are resident here and especially in evidence from late October through to the end of December when they haul out from the sea to give birth to their new white pups often in freezing conditions, but in theory beyond reach of the highest tides.

To reduce disturbance to the seals the mud flats have been fenced off meaning the public is restricted to a limited footpath which at peak times can be very popular.This still allows for some very close up views of the extraordinary sights and sounds of this active colony.

The reserve covers a 10km stretch of coast that is rich in bird life; 47 species of bird breed here and there have been more than 250 species recorded.

Grey Seal (Halichoerus grypus)

The UK is home to some 40 % of the world's population of grey seals. This makes Donna Nook together with other hotspots such as Blakeney Point critical to their survival as a species.

Adult seals are huge, especially the bulls, and can move surprisingly fast across the mud. During the breeding season they are aggressive and fights between males are common. The females too are noisy and aggressive to one another especially in defense of the area surrounding their new born pups. The bond between mother and pup is very evident with gentle whiskery nose touching between mother and pup. The mothers also caress their pups tenderly with their flippers, especially whilst suckling. These behaviours and the undeniable cuteness of the fluffy white pups with their big doe eyes make the whole event unmissable, for photographers and all wildlife enthusiasts.

Right: Grey seal pup calling for his mum. Nikon D800E, 70-200mm at 200mm, ISO 200, 1/800 sec at f/5.6

New-Wborn pups have white fur and are adorable. Nikon D4, 300mm + 2 x at 600mm, ISO 640, 1/1250 sec at f/5.6

Technique

The animals are easy to locate and it is merely a question of selecting the best subjects to photograph. Check the sun position and try to get the light behind you for the best results.

Watch carefully for action further away from the fence, the bulls fighting tends to occur further out on the mud or sand. A long telephoto lens and tripod is useful for the long distance action. Most of the best opportunities can be very close up though so almost any camera and equipment is capable of getting good shots here.

The biggest problem from a photography point of view is the relatively new picket fence which not only obstructs close up views but more importantly casts shadows on any animals lying close up the beach. This is a very popular destination so getting here early allows you a better chance of getting a good viewpoint. Be prepared to move around to look for different kinds of action; from two females bickering over space to the birth of a newborn pup.

"There is one hard and fast rule, whose spirit must be observed at all times. The welfare of the subject is more important than the photograph."
The Nature Photographers' Code of Practice

Below: Greeting between mother and pup. Nikon D4, 300mm + 2 x converter at 600mm, ISO 400, 1/1250 sec at f/6.3

Opposite left: Close up portrait.
Nikon D4, 300mm, ISO 2500, 1/640 sec at f/2.8

Above: Motherly love. Nikon D800E, 70-200mm at 200mm,
ISO 400, 1/1000 sec at f/7.1

Above: Load of old bull.
Nikon D4, 300mm, ISO 2500, 1/640 sec at f/2.8

Above: That's hilarious. Nikon D4, 300mm + 2 x converter at
600mm, ISO 200, 1/1250 sec at f/5.6

How To Get Here

Donna Nook National Nature Reserve on the estuary of the River
Humber is situated 15 miles south of Grimsby and Cleethorpes in
Lincolnshire just north of the village of North Somercoates. The car
park is at Stonebridge adjacent to the dunes and viewing areas.

Donna Nook National Nature Reserve Car Park
Lat/Long: 53.475985, 0.14111638
OS map co-ordinate: TF421998
Nearest Parking Postcode: LN11 7PB (800m)

Accessibility

Access is restricted to a marked sandy footpath through dunes and
in front of the fence to prevent disturbance of the seals. No dogs
allowed. Access would be difficult but not impossible for wheelchairs
with assistance. The area is a bombing range, be aware of red flag
warnings. If there is a frost the minor roads in the area are prone
to black ice, drive cautiously.

Best Time of Year/Day

In late October and November the seals give birth to their pups near
the sand dunes. Early morning and evening light is best. If possible
visit mid-week when the area will be less congested.

Left: Curious cow. Nikon D4, 300mm + 2 x converter at 600mm, ISO
640, 1/1250 sec at f/5.6

Central and Southern England – Introduction

Central and Southern England do not have dramatic mountains or rugged coastlines but the low lying countryside offers a different kind of habitat that is ideal for many species to flourish.

Large areas of arable and dairy farmland mean barn owls, brown hares and roe deer can find a niche that suits them, though the old stone barns and hedgerows they rely on are much reduced.

Wetland reserves managed by charities like the RSPB and the Wildfowl and Wetland Trust create and protect valuable ecosystems, especially reed beds, which otherwise might have been drained and developed. RSPB Otmoor represents a huge conservation success. The mixed meadow and reed bed habitat is home to a huge number of diverse species. Most important are those that rely entirely on this habitat including bitterns, hobbies and the recently reintroduced European crane.

Areas of deciduous and mixed forest remain here as a remnant of the extensive woodland that would have covered most of this part of Britain. Remaining pockets like the New Forest and the Forest of Dean are invaluable as a habitat for woodland specialists like fallow deer and the reintroduced wild boar, one of our most exciting British mammals to meet alone in a forest.

As a more populated area this part of England relies even more on the small pieces of land that remain protected thanks to the work of the Wildlife Trusts. Reserves such as College Lakes and Chimney Meadows are tiny but hugely important refuges for wildlife, both resident, for example roe deer, and for visitors passing through like migrating hobbies.

Down in Dorset the heathland reserve at Arne protects an important heather and gorse heath habitat. Home to endangered reptiles including the smooth snake and adder it is also a year round location for the delightful Dartford warbler.

Offshore from Poole harbour, Brownsea Island maintains a small isolated and very approachable population of red squirrels protected from the squirrel pox carried by their grey American cousins.

CENTRAL AND SOUTHERN ENGLAND

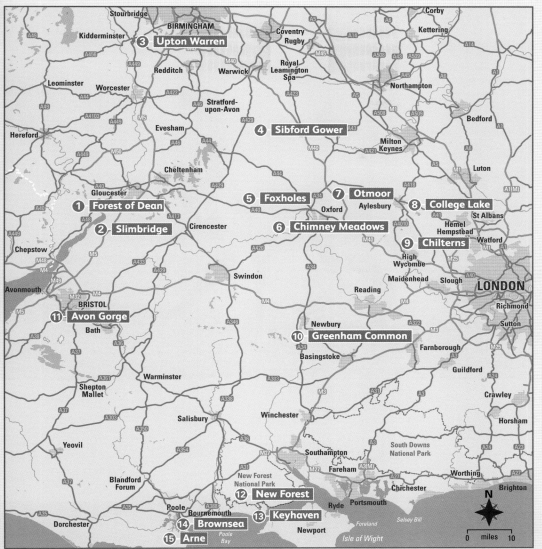

Stourbridge
Kidderminster
BIRMINGHAM
Corby
Kettering
Coventry
Rugby
③ Upton Warren
Redditch
Warwick
Royal
Leamington
Spa
Northampton
Leominster
Worcester
Stratford-
upon-Avon
Bedford
Hereford
Evesham
Cheltenham
Milton
Keynes
Luton
Gloucester
① Forest of Dean
⑤ Foxholes
⑦ Otmoor
Oxford
Aylesbury
⑧ College Lake
St Albans
Hemel
Hempstead
Watford
② Slimbridge
Cirencester
⑥ Chimney Meadows
⑨ Chilterns
Chepstow
Swindon
High
Wycombe
Avonmouth
BRISTOL
Reading
Maidenhead
Slough
LONDON
Richmond
Sutton
⑪ Avon Gorge
Bath
Newbury
⑩ Greenham Common
Farnborough
Guildford
Warminster
Basingstoke
Crawley
Shepton
Mallet
Salisbury
Winchester
Horsham
Yeovil
South Downs
National Park
Worthing
Blandford
Forum
Southampton
New Forest
National Park
Fareham
Chichester
Brighton
Dorchester
Poole
Bournemouth
⑫ New Forest
⑬ Keyhaven
Ryde
Portsmouth
N
⑭ Brownsea
Newport
Foreland
Selsey Bill
⑮ Arne
Poole
Bay
Isle of Wight
0   miles   10

Contains Ordnance Survey data © Crown Copyright and database right (2016)

The Forest of Dean is a large area of more than 110 square kilometres of mostly mixed forest. Lying to the west of the county of Gloucestershire it is managed by the Forestry Commission and is a popular destination. It is famously home to a population of wild boar which were initially escapees from a wild boar farm but also in 2004 an illegal release of around 60 animals. A breeding population is now thriving here.

The forest generally has good trails and well marked footpaths but between these the woodland can be thick and in places impenetrable and the going underfoot boggy. Perfect to hide a wide range of wildlife.

Wild Boar *(Sus scrofa)*

Wild boar are one of the most difficult subjects to locate and photograph included this book. It is possible to be lucky and simply come across a family of boar feeding peacefully by a forest trail on a summer's evening, however like so many creatures, once you go looking for them they become incredibly elusive.

Wild boar trotter print.   Scratching post marked with mud from recent wallow.

Mud wallow surrounded by wild boar prints.

Where to look

Finding wild boar in the forest is all about tracking skills. Firstly choose a location near to signs of wild boar activity. This begins with the upturned ground on the road verges: these are obvious and look like the grass verge has been dug over. At the time of writing the road from Little Dean towards Cannop Ponds is a good example, though due to culling this may change. Take a forest trail as far away from the well populated cycle trails and dog walking routes as you can. Now look for tracks, trails, and wallows. (See images below).

Note the difference between a boar trotter (fatter and rounder) and the slot marks of a fallow deer hoof print. Wallows are quite obvious, these are areas of wet ground or pools where the boar roll around in the mud. They are made more obvious by mud splashes on bracken and trees and the wide marks where boar rub and scratch against tree trunks and saplings.

Technique and timing

Wear camouflaged or dull green/beige clothing. It's best if it's waterproof and a soft fabric so that it is quiet when brushing through undergrowth. Move quietly and slowly through likely places or wait hidden by wallows or obvious recent feeding sites. Field Craft on p.352.

As with most mammals, early morning or late evenings are best. Autumn is a great time to be in the forest and photographs will benefit from the backdrop of rich colours of changing leaves. At this time of year the boar gather together to mate, often accompanied by much activity and squealing which can give them away. The disadvantage at this time of year is that undergrowth is still thick and it is often difficult to get a clear shot unobstructed by long grass or other vegetation.

Spring and early summer can be good as there is less vegetation around and also the piglets will be with the sows making them easier to find and see. The young piglets are born with orange brown stripes making them well camouflaged, and are consequently known as humbugs. These stripes fade through the year and adults are black or grey.

Winter snowfall helps to track the boar, they will also stand out more against a white snowy backdrop.

Warning

Wild boar can be large and at times aggressive. This is particularly so in spring when sows protect their young. They are especially aggressive towards dogs at this time of year. Be extremely careful especially in dense undergrowth. There is good wild boar advice on the Forestry Commission website: www.forestry.gov.uk.

Right: Young wild boar: sniffing the air for trouble. Nikon D4, 300mm + 2 x converter at 600mm, ISO 5000, 1/1000 sec at f/9

Top Tip

Sound is your friend and your enemy. The snorting grunt of feeding wild boar gives them away. The click of a camera shutter or the snap of a dry twig underfoot will send them running for cover.

Equipment

Wild boar are large beasts and it is often possible to get quite close. A 300mm f/2.8 lens is ideal, especially in low light, or with a 2 x converter which will allow you to get a more distant shot. A zoom in the range of around 100 to 400mm would be the most versatile to carry and give you the advantage of zooming out for landscape shots or closing in for a portrait.

Also in the Forest of Dean

Fallow deer *(Darma darma)*

These are common throughout the forest but are shy and elusive. Here there are some melanistic (black) individuals which have an interesting variation on the usual tan spotted hide. Deer will be most frequently encountered crossing the forest tracks. It's always good to have your camera ready and with suitable settings for the

Sow and young boar, the humbug stripes are disappearing. Nikon D4, 300mm + 2 x converter at 600mm, ISO 5000, 1/1000 sec at f/10

conditions you are experiencing. Always anticipate seeing something and having to react very quickly. Choose a shutter speed of around 1/1000th second, an aperture of around f/8 and the corresponding ISO to achieve that speed and aperture. Autofocus should be set on tracking/predictive and a central focus point or cluster of points chosen.

Story behind the photos

This proved to be one of the most difficult projects in the book. After my fourth visit to the forest looking for deer, I followed wild boar tracks into an area of smaller trees and long grass. There, very close by, I spotted a large 'dead deer' under the base of a conifer tree. On approaching closer the 'deer' rose to its feet, grunted and slid off into the shadows. This was my first wild boar encounter but I was so surprised and the animal so close I didn't manage to get a photo.

Staying quiet I explored the area and, hearing grunting and squealing, discovered a group of around eight boar feeding and mating in thick undergrowth: the photographs weren't great, but the excitement of the close encounter with this large potentially dangerous creature more than made up for it. Subsequent visits proved more successful photographically.

A melanistic fallow deer crosses the forest track. Nikon D4, 300mm + 2 x converter at 600mm, ISO 5000, 1/1000 sec at f/5.6

How To Get Here

The Forest of Dean is situated north of Bristol, bordered by the River Wye in the north-west and River Severn in the south. The main routes to the forest are by the M50, M5 and the M4 then the A4136 in the north and the A48 in the south. The main towns to head for are Cinderford in the north east and Parkend in the south, with several other villages and small towns on the edge of the forest.

Cinderford
Lat/Long: 51.824843, -2.500103
OS map co-ordinate: SO656141
Nearest Parking Postcode: GL14 2SD

Parkend
Lat/Long: 51.768238, -2.5568533
OS map co-ordinate: SO616078
Nearest Parking Postcode: GL15 4JA

Map: OS Explorer OL14 Wye Valley & Forest of Dean

Recommended are:

Woorgreens Nature Reserve
Managed by Gloucestershire Wildlife Trust. Parking is in a lay-by off the main B4226 road, just before Kensley Lodge.
Lat/Long: 51.812003, -2.540529
OS map co-ordinate: SO628127
Nearest Parking Postcode: GL14 3HU

Cannop Ponds and Cannop Bridge Marsh
Area of grassland, woodland, marsh and open water south of Speech House Road, two miles east of Coleford. Car park beside B4228.
Lat/Long: 51.794382, -2.567309
OS map co-ordinate: SO609107
Nearest Parking Postcode: GL15 4JS

RSPB Nagshead Woodland.
Lat/Long: 51.774228,-2.571716
OS map co-ordinate: SO606085
Nearest Parking Postcode: GL15 4JQ

Accessibility

The forest covers 42 square miles and is traversed by minor roads with several car parks and lay-bys. There is a good network paths in the forest but once you stray from them the undergrowth can be dense.

Best Time of Year/Day

Spring through autumn. The wild boar sows give birth in the spring. Early morning is good although the boars are active during the day.

Young boar in long summer grass (August). Nikon D4, 300mm + 2 x converter at 600mm, ISO 5000, 1/1000 sec at f/10

A whooper swan coming in to land at Slimbridge WWT.
Nikon D4, 300mm, ISO 800, 1/1000 sec at f/14

The Wildlife and Wetland Trust reserve at Slimbridge in Gloucestershire was founded by Sir Peter Scott, an early pioneer for conservation. Much of the area around the reception building is given over to enclosures for captive birds. Head for the outlying hides looking over the wild wetland areas.

Bewick's swan *(Cygnus columbianus)*

The Bewick's is a migrant swan that overwinters in the UK before heading north for the summer to breed. The timing of your visit is therefore crucial. This is probably the most attractive of the swans being smaller and more elegant in flight. Distinguishing Bewick's from the larger and more common mute swans is easy, mute swans have an orange red bill. Bewick's and whooper swans however are very similar in appearance. The bill pattern is a distinguishing factor and the best method is to look at the yellow area where it joins the black tip at the side of the bill. This is rounded in the Bewick's and comes to a sharp angle on a whooper.

Where to look

The best hide for the Bewick's is the Rushy Hide. This is a small hide and can get full of photographers. There may not be room for tripods at busy times so get there early and take a bean bag to rest on the window. This hide overlooks the Rushy Pond where the swans arrive in the evening and can be seen leaving in the morning. Evening is best as the light is in the right direction.

Technique

A very big telephoto lens is not necessary, there is little room to move it and the field of vision is limited. A 300mm prime lens or a 100 to 400mm lens would work well. A smaller lens such as a 70 to 200mm is also useful for wider angle group shots. Focus on the birds in flight as they appear, sometimes from overhead and behind you. Watch carefully for background buildings and fencing which can spoil the backdrop.

A pair of whooper swans coming in to land at Slimbridge WWT. Nikon D4, 300mm, ISO 800, 1/1000 sec at f/14

Bewick's swans in flight formation at sunset. Nikon D4, 70-200mm at 160mm, ISO 800, 1/800 sec at f/7.1

How To Get Here

Slimbridge Wetland Centre is situated south of Gloucester and Cheltenham, off the M5 motorway on the Severn Estuary. Exit at M5 junctions 13 or 14 and follow the A38 and the Slimbridge brown duck signs to Slimbridge Village and the Centre, just beyond which there is a large free car park.

Lat/Long: 51.741002, -2.4037446
OS map co-ordinate: SO 722 047
Nearest Parking Postcode: GL2 7BT

Phone: 01453 891900

More details at **www.wwt.org.uk**

Accessibility and facilities

The centre is open from 9.30am until 5pm (5.30pm in the summer) all year except Christmas day. Entry is £12 for adults. A WWT reserve membership is recommended to avoid the daily admission charge. The paths are level with good accessibility to the hides for all. There is a cafe and toilets. The Severn Way path traverses around the outskirts of the centre.

Best Time of Year/Day

Early morning and late evening in the winter is the time to photograph the Bewick's swans. The swans roost on the ponds near the hides but feed out in fields during the day.

This is a busy place which is popular with families and school parties, especially at weekends.

Bewick's swan preening. Nikon D4, 300mm + 2 x converter at 600mm, ISO 800, 1/1600 sec at f/13

Also at Slimbridge

A wide variety of waders, waterfowl and other bird life visit Slimbridge. These include lapwing, golden plover, dunlin, barnacle, Canada and white-fronted geese, bittern, teal, wigeon and resident European cranes.

The European cranes usually seen here are part of the Great Crane Project which seeks to re-establish the once native cranes back in the UK. Cranes are bred at Slimbridge for release initially on reserves in Somerset. The breeding birds are marked clearly with muti coloured leg rings which allow easy identification. The birds are an interesting photographic subject especially in spring when they perform their courtship ritual dances. Occasionally wild bred birds visit Slimbridge. See also Lakenheath Fen p.242.

The Rushy Hide is good for pintail as well as the swans. The Robbie Garnett and Martin Smith hides can also be useful especially for large flocks of golden plover, passing curlew, shelduck and sometimes cranes. The Zeiss Hide is occasionally good for bittern and in summer the Kingfisher Hide..... well, you can maybe guess what that is good for.

Pintail Duck *(Anas acuta)*

A very smart and photogenic duck, the male especially is richly marked with a chestnut head, black and grey wing markings and that distinguishing long pin tail.

Black-headed Gull *(Chroicocephalus ridibundus)*

In winter many gulls move inland away from the coast. Here at Slimbridge a large flock of black headed gulls gather and can be seen benefitting from the free food handouts. Watch for the action of a mass feeding frenzy when the wardens feed the birds.

Moorhen *(Gallinula chloropus)*

Never miss an opportunity to take a photograph of even the commonest species. The black skulking moorhen is often ignored but take a closer look at the bright red and yellow bill, this can be quite an exotic looking bird in the right light.

Black-headed gull feeding frenzy. Nikon D800E, 70-200mm at 175mm, ISO 4000, 1/640 sec at f/10

Pintail drake in flight. Nikon D4, 300mm, ISO 800, 1/1000 sec at f/9

Pintail drake portrait.
Nikon D4, 300mm, ISO 1600, 1/1000 sec at f/3.2

Moorhen portrait in sunlight.
Nikon D4, 300mm, ISO 640, 1/800 sec at f/3.2

Juvenile kingfisher on the watch. Upton Warren. Nikon D4, 300mm + 2 x converter at 600mm, ISO 800, 1/1250 sec at f/9

Upton Warren is a small reserve run by the Worcestershire Wildlife Trust. The 26 hectare reserve is split into two distinct areas: the freshwater Moors Pools in the north and the saline pools of the Flashes in the south.

The Flashes attract a variety of specialist birds and plants that require the salt water conditions. The hides at the Flashes provide excellent views of the shallow lagoons where avocets breed alongside common tern, black-headed gull, oystercatcher and redshank. The reeds and surrounding vegetation are also home to reed, sedge and Cetti's warblers and reed bunting.

Kingfisher *(Alcedo atthis)*

This most attractive and colourful of our native birds is high on any photographer's wish list. Here at Upton Warren kingfishers are regular inhabitants of the Moors Pool part of the reserve and can be seen at most times of the year but especially September when the juveniles leave the nest and are learning to fish. This often lasts for a brief few days before the adult birds chase the youngsters off to find habitat of their own.

With kingfishers the bill colouration is key to knowing who you are dealing with. The adult male has an all black bill, the female has a red patch on the lower mandible and the youngsters often have a white tip to the bill (which may be a guide for the adults offering food in a dark burrow).

Technique

Kingfishers generally need a fast shutter speed, in flight a minimum of 1/1600th is recommended to freeze the fast wing beats. However you can reduce this a little to get a litle wing blur giving an impression of motion.

A small aperture of f/8 to f/13 will allow sufficient depth of field to keep both the bird and the perch in focus.

Background and sunlight direction will affect the colours that show in the bird; a bright background of reflective water was used to advantage in some of these images to produce a high key image.

Photographing a relatively dark bird against a bright background means being accurate with the spot meter or using exposure compensation to increase the exposure by one or two stops. You can increase exposure in post processing, especially with RAW files but it's always best to get this as close as possible whilst shooting.

Hide space is limited at Upton Warren at key times so take a bean bag to rest a big lens on if you can't squeeze your tripod in.

Top: Kingfisher alights on a perch at the Moors Pool. Nikon D4, 300mm + 2 x converter at 600mm, ISO 1600, 1/1600 sec at f/13

How to get here

Upton Warren is located south west of Birmingham near the town of Bromsgrove. From junction 5 on the M5 drive north on the A38 through Wychbold toward the village of Upton Warren to a roundabout next to the Upton Warren Sailing Club.

Part of this reserve is known as the Christopher Cadbury Wetland Reserve. The Moors Pool is the water to the north, and the Flashes an area to the south split by the River Salwarpe.

Car parking for the Flashes is at the sailing club, with parking for the Moors Pool at the end of a small lane east of the A38, accessed slightly north just past the Swan Inn. There are hides at the Flashes and more hides on both sides of Moors Pool accessible by paths around the lakes.

Sailing Club Lat/Long: 52.302782, -2.102124
OS map co-ordinate: SO931671
Nearest Parking Postcode: WR9 0DG

Accessibility

There are level access tracks to the hides. Wheelchair access at the Moors has a padlocked barrier. Please contact Worcestershire Wildlife Trust for access. Day permits for non Wildlife Trust members are £3 and can be obtained from the Trust offices at Smite, from onsite volunteers and from the Outdoor Education Centre or in advance from Worcestershire Wildlife Trust by email or post.

Best Time of Year/Day

Spring and summer sees the avocets nesting on the pools at the Flashes. September is good to catch kingfishers at the Moors Pool. More species and seasonal details at **www.worcswildlifetrust.co.uk**

Kingfisher dives for a fish. Nikon D4, 300mm + 2 x converter at 600mm, ISO 800, 1/1250 sec at f/10

Evening sunlight brings out the green colouration. Nikon D4, 300mm + 2 x converter at 600mm, ISO 800, 1/1250 sec at f/5.6

Hidden away in the countryside of Oxfordshire is a little known haven for badgers. The badger watch at Sibford Gower is a private enterprise and booking is required as part of an accommodation deal. Once booked you have free use and unlimited access to the private photography hides.

Subject Badger *(Meles meles)*

The nocturnal badger spends most of its time underground and rarely ventures out in daylight hours. The optimum time to photograph badgers in daylight hours is early morning and dusk in mid summer. For the most part badgers are active at night when their varied diet is largely sustained by earthworms. This is worth bearing in mind as they will be more active on damp nights when earthworms come to the surface.

Badgers have a well known liking for peanuts and these are the usual way to entice these amazing mammals into your field of view.

What to expect

At Sibford Gower there is an amazing set up for viewing badgers. Two main hides are currently in operation: one raised overlooking the sett (which is fairly distant) and a second hide dug in at ground level allowing very close up views of the animals as they search high and low for tasty snacks. The site also includes large and surprisingly high tree trunks on which the badgers readily climb, being lead by their incredible sense of smell.

Technique

Lens choice here is key: ideally have a wide range of lenses as there are many different scenarios to chose from. A large telephoto lens is not necessary for the main action though it could be used for more distant shots during daylight. A 70 to 200mm is ideal for close up shots and is small enough to work within a usable range for a camera-mounted flash. In addition a wide angle lens is useful for close proximity group shots.

The hides are lit by standard light bulbs which create an orange/yelllow cast in photographs. Consequently this is one of the few times I would consider using flash for a nocturnal subject. The badgers here are accustomed to human presence, flashguns and the sound of a camera shutter and should not be unduly bothered..

With artificial light and an auto white balance camera setting the white balance will most likely need adjustment in post processing. Note, partly due to the local earth colouration the badgers are not purely black and white.

As a final option try processing in black and white, this is always effective with a black and white subject.

Below: Midnight rambler. Nikon D4, 70-200mm at 82mm, ISO 2000, 1/250 sec at f/2.8, Nikon flash

Wide angle group shot. Black and white photo. Nikon D4, 17-35mm at 32mm, ISO 4000, 1/250 sec at f/2.8, Nikon flash

Portrait: face to face. Nikon D4, 70-200mm at 145mm, ISO 2000, 1/250 sec at f/2.8, Nikon flash

How To Get Here

Sibford Gower is a village 6.5 miles west of Banbury in Oxfordshire. The Badger Watch hides here are run by Richard and Sandra Butt. To use the hides you must book a stay in their accommodation. Book early, it is popular.

Booking: Call Sandra Butt on 01295 780352.

Address: College Barn Farm, Sibford Gower, Banbury, Oxfordshire, OX15 5RY.
www.badger-watch.com

Other Badger Hides: The Badger Trust promotes the conservation and welfare of badgers. Their website lists badger groups in the UK some who offer badger watches. There is also a directory of where to watch badgers in the UK that include pay-for-hides and nature reserves.
www.badger.org.uk

Best Time of Year/Day

Summer nights from June to August are best.

Foxholes

Foxholes is a broad leaved woodland nature reserve in Oxfordshire with very limited parking and a very rough, effectively off-road access track. This is a great place to see roe deer and spectacular displays of foxgloves and, in spring, carpets of buebells.

Where to look

As at Chimney Meadows, (following pages) the roe deer are shy and are best spotted at dawn and dusk when they emerge from the woodland. Follow the woodland paths to the points where they emerge into surrounding farmland, look for trails with the characteristic slot marks made by the two-toed hoof. The woodland is marked with way markers but keep a bearing on your location as it is easy to get disorientated with few landmarks in the wood. The small carpark has a Berkshire, Buckinghamshire and Oxfordshire Wildlife Trust (BBOWT) notice board showing a trail map.

Foxgloves grow only in the lighter parts of the forest, often where trees have been cleared or fallen. Bluebells are found in the deciduous areas especially under beech trees and will be obvious if you have arrived at the right time of year, see panel opposite.

Roe deer doe amongst the foxgloves.
Nikon D3X, 300mm, ISO 3200, 1/640 sec at f/2.8

Above: Bumblebee on foxglove.
Nikon D3X, 300mm, ISO 3200, 1/320 sec at f/2.8

Above: Roe deer buck scent marking a honeysuckle vine. Nikon D4, 300mm + 2 x converter at 600mm, ISO 2500, 1/1000 sec at f/5.6

Below: Marbled white butterfly on thistles. Nikon D4, 300mm + 2 x converter at 600mm, ISO 800, 1/1250 sec at f/9

How To Get Here

Foxholes is 4 miles north of the village of Burford, off the A424, 25 miles north west of Oxford. Go north on A424 from Burford and take a right turn to Bruern, continue past a crossroads towards Bruern for 2 miles then past a right turn to Shipton-under-Wychwood. Park in the lay-by on left immediately after next left hand turn. Walk down the track to the reserve entrance.

Lat/Long: 51.885302, -1.6266882
OS Co-ordinate: SP257208
Nearest Postcode: OX7 6RW

www.bbowt.org.uk

Accessibility

Paths through a gently sloping woodland. Access and footpaths are often muddy and potholed, wear a good pair of boots.

Best Time of Year/Day

Dawn and dusk is best for the roe deer, all year round.

Bluebells flower between April and May.

The Berkshire, Buckinghamshire and Oxfordshire Wildlife trusts are now combined to form BBOWT. Between them they have some fantastic little nature reserves, many of which are free even to non-members. There are many others worth visiting but as an example Chimney Meadows is a great place to look especially for roe deer and barn owls.

Roe deer *(Capreolus capreolus)*

Timid and shy, the roe deer is perhaps the most attractive of the British deer. Look for these emerging at dusk from the woodland and hedgerows around the field edges, or arrive early morning under cover of darkness to catch them feeding out in the fields from the main hide.

Barn owl *(Tyto alba)*

The elusive and seldom seen hunter of the meadows. Winter is a good time to see them flying in daylight hours. See also Sculthorpe Moor p.258, Titchwell Marsh p.262 and Snettisham p.268.

Above: Skipper butterfly in summer meadow grass. Nikon D3X, 300mm + 2 x converter at 600mm, ISO 1600, 1/1000 sec at f/5.6

Black and white portrait roe deer doe. Nikon D3X, 300mm + 2 x converter at 600mm, ISO 3200, 1/500 sec at f/5.6

How To Get Here

Chimney Meadows is located by the River Thames 4 miles from the village of Bampton, 18 miles west of Oxford. From A420 at the village of Buckland take the road north signposted to Tadpole Bridge and Bampton. Turn right just after Tadpole Bridge and Trout Inn, follow signs to Chimney. Park in the designated small car park and follow the tarmac drive using the path along the field edge to the entrance to the reserve. The access road from either direction is single-track: give way to oncoming traffic and farm vehicles.

Lat/Long: 51.705784, -1.4813089
OS Co-ordinate: SP359009
Postcode: OX18 2EH

www.bbowt.org.uk

Accessibility

Paths through meadows and by wetland, some are suitable for those with limited mobility. There are two bird hides. From the car park it is a long walk down a tarmac road and across the fields to the hides. This route is all good territory for wildlife. Further walks across fields and board walks leads to the canal where potentially kingfishers, otters and water voles can be found.

Best Time of Year/Day

Winter for barn owls, dusk and dawn all year round for roe deer.

Barn owl image from a roadside encounter. Nikon D4, 300mm + 2 x converter at 600mm, ISO 800, 1/1000 sec at f/11

Early summer morning roe buck with twisted horn. Nikon D3X, 300mm + 2 x converter at 600mm, ISO 6400, 1/640 sec at f/5.6

Brown hare legging it across rolling Cotswold fields. Canon EOS 1DS mark ii, 300mm + 2 x converter at 600mm, ISO 800, 1/1250 sec at f/10

Otmoor is an RSPB reserve near Oxford. In winter it's a cold, wild, windswept marshland haunted by elusive hen harriers and in some special years by short-eared owls. In spring and summer Otmoor is alive with dragonflies and insects and the birds that live on them including the spectacular hobby. This is one of those places that you can go and see nothing at all or on some days you see almost everything.

Hobby *(Falco subuteo)*

The hobby is a super fast, aerobatic, beautifully marked little falcon. Hunting dragonflies and occasionally swifts, its speed and agility also make this one of the most difficult birds to keep in the viewfinder. Arriving in this country in spring usually at the same time as the swallows, hobbies can be seen on Otmoor and many other wetland reserves throughout the summer months before heading back south in September.

Technique

Take binoculars to scan the far hedgerows and marshland for the distinctive flight pattern. Watch for a typical falcon shape with rapid wing beats followed by a flurry of action as with outspread wings and outstretched talons the

Above: Hobby on aerial manouvres. Nikon D4, 300mm + 2 x converter at 600mm, ISO 2000, 1/3200 sec at f/13

Below: Hobby with dragonfly. Nikon D4, 300mm + 2 x converter at 600mm, ISO 1600, 1/4000 sec at f/11

Above: Hobby diving down. Nikon D4, 300mm + 2 x converter at 600mm, ISO 2500, 1/2500 sec at f/16

bird snatches a dragonfly from the air. This is then followed by soaring flight as the bird decapitates and eats its prey still on the wing.

Otmoor kestrels have learned to hunt dragonflies in the same way and the flight pattern can be very similar, the kestrel is generally distinctly brown in colour.

Spot the falcon in flight at a distance and while following the bird through the viewfinder wait to take shots at the crucial and closest moments. Angle of sun is really important in these pictures. Ideally the bird needs to be flying towards you to catch the light on the eyes and beak. However this frequently turns into an overhead shot looking straight into the sun and showing only the underparts. Ideally be positioned to take a shot from the side as the bird passes on the wing. The undersides frequently become shadowed and these may need lifting in post production.

Shutter speeds of 1/2000th and higher are ideal for this fast moving falcon. Keep the aperture narrow if possible to perhaps capture the dragonfly in the same frame.

Where to look

Walk from the car park to the five bar gate by the cattle pens. From here the birds can often be seen hunting the far hedgerows or perched on posts in the fields.

Anywhere along the main bridleway and also from the first screen hide are good possibilities. Polarised sunglasses help you spot the birds in a bright sky.

How To Get Here

Otmoor is ten miles north east of Oxford next to the village of Beckley. Take extreme care through the village which has narrow bends and a school. With the Abingdon Arms (OX3 9UU) on your left follow the narrow road down and left to Otmoor Lane. Continue down this lane to the car park at its end. There are no facilities or toilets here.

Lat/Long: 51.809583,-1.173907
OS map co-ordinate: SP570126
Nearest Parking Postcode: OX3 9TD (0.7km)

Accessibility

Otmoor is open 24hrs a day. There is no entrance fee charged though RSPB membership is recommended and donations are welcomed. There are information boards at the car park and you can download a reserve map at www.rspb.org.uk. There is a visitor trail of 1.5 miles, the trail is compacted stone, other paths are unsurfaced. Paths can be muddy and wet especially in winter. Some bridleways go across MOD land and may be restricted: do not enter where red flags are flying.

Best Time of Year/Day

Hobbies: May to October. Hobbies hunting dragonflies are active after midday. Kestrels are seen all year round with September best. Hares all year round with winter being best. The starlings start to murmurate in October through until March.

Hobby homing in on dragonfly. Nikon D4, 300mm + 2 x converter at 600mm, ISO 2500, 1/3200 sec at f/16

Brown Hare (*Lepus europeus*)

Hares are a fairly common species in southern England. With wide emotive eyes and huge black tipped ears they make great photographic subjects. Unlike its smaller cousin the rabbit the hare lives entirely above ground and this makes it an easy subject to locate in the large open fields at Otmoor.

The mad March hare of course refers to their apparent mad behaviour in late winter to early spring when they gather together to vie for the attentions of a mate. The boxing behaviour is now known to be generally an uninterested female fending off the attentions of a male.

Where to look

Follow the bridlepath down to the first large wetland hide, a footpath through the kissing gate leads up to the first screen (now a partially covered hide) and further on to the second screen. Hares are often seen on the footpath here and on top of the bank. If instead you continue along the bridleway the large fields to the right (Big Otmoor) are also a likely spot. This part is protected by a wire netting fence but it is possible to get shots over or through the wire.

Technique

A large focal length is useful to get as close as possible. Hares are not always afraid of people and sometimes exhibit the bizarre behaviour of turning and running straight back towards you. Be prepared for this and crouch down or lay prone to get an eye level shot. The raised banks around the reed bed mean that occasionally the animals may be at eye level anyway and therefore in the perfect position.

A pair of hares in evening light. Nikon D3X, 300mm + 2 x converter at 600mm, ISO 1600, 1/800 sec at f/7.1

A close encounter in winter sunshine. Nikon D3X, 300mm + 2 x converter at 600mm, ISO 1250, 1/800 sec at f/5.6

Brown hare, caught on the hop. Nikon D4, 300mm + 2 x converter at 600mm, ISO 1250, 1/1000 sec at f/6.3

A close up portrait brown hare at Otmoor in winter sunshine. Nikon D3X, 300mm + 2 x converter at 600mm, ISO 1600, 1/800 sec at f/5.6

Kestrel (*Falco tinnunculus*)

The commonest British falcon but recently thought to
be much reduced in numbers nationally, Otmoor is a
great place to find these birds. Characteristic in hovering
flight or hunting from a perched vantage point these
can sometimes be confused with merlins or hobbies,
especially as here the kestrels have copied the dragonfly
hunting flight used by hobbies. The brown tan
colouration is therefore a useful distinguishing factor.
The male has a distinctive slate grey head and tail
feathers the female a brown head and tail.

Where to look

Fairly easily spotted, there are often kestrels perched
on telegraph wires and posts or hovering over the larger
fields. Further along the bridleway past the first wetland
hide an electric fence line is a likely place, especially
for young kestrels learning to hunt.

Technique

A large tripod-mounted telephoto lens is ideal as kestrels
are slower moving than hobbies and can be easily
tracked especially when hovering. Use a fast (1/2000th)
shutter speed to freeze the bird in flight or experiment
with slower shutter speeds to create wing blur to give
a sense of motion.

*Young kestrel perched by the second screen at Otmoor. Nikon D4,
300mm + 2 x converter at 600mm, ISO 1000, 1/1600 sec at f/8*

*Below: Female kestrel or 'wind hover'. Nikon D4, 300mm +
2 x converter at 600mm, ISO 1600, 1/2500 sec at f/9*

*Right: Male kestrel hovering. Nikon D4, 300mm +
2 x converter at 600mm, ISO 800, 1/2500 sec at f/8*

Like all of the reed bed wetland reserves featured in this book Otmoor is host to a large cast of species. Different times of the year see an array of star birds and insects, reptiles and mammals. Spring and early summer is a good time to look out for the following species.

Butterflies

A variety of different species of butterfly are found here including brimstone, comma, common blue and the rare brown hairstreak. The latter are seen on the rough track on the edge of the reserve known as the Roman Road.

Turtle dove *(Streptopelia turtur)*

Once a common farmland bird in the UK the turtle dove is now extremely rare. Look closely at the colourful plumage with distinct turtle shell-like markings. Listen out for the purring call in the hedgerow and watch for the display flight, often perched near the cattle pens.

Red Kite *(Milvus milvus)*

Otmoor is home to quite a few red kites which make themselves highly visible. Often mistaken for the less obliging hen harriers and marsh harriers that occasionally visit the reserve. The kites here have diverged from their usual scavenger role to become opportunist predators, sometimes taking young fledgling birds such as this lapwing chick, see photo top right.

Grass snake coiled in the reeds. Nikon D800E, 300mm + 2 x converter at 600mm, ISO 640, 1/1250 sec at f/8

Toads *(Bufo bufo)*

In spring for a brief few days large numbers of these amphibians emerge from the reeds and ditches to gather for spawning. Groups amass in mating balls. Unlike frogs they have a warty rough looking skin and beautiful copper-coloured eyes.

Dragonflies

The dragonflies at Otmoor are spectacular, the many different species include darters, hawkers and damselflies. A macro lens can yield great results though a long focal length lens is perhaps more versatile and allows you to photograph from a distance.

Grass snakes *(Natrix natrix)*

For a brief spell in spring when the weather is warm and the reeds are not too high grass snakes become visible. A quiet stealthy approach is required. Grass snakes respond both to sound and movement and they will quickly vanish, they are difficult to get close to.

Mute swan *(Cygnus olor)*

Mute swans are widespread and common but they make a great photographic subject. In spring swans conduct an elaborate courtship display including mimicking each others movements and culminating in this fabulous heart shape formed by curved necks and bowed heads. Exposure compensation may be required to cope with this bright white subject.

Mute swan courtship ritual. Nikon D4, 300mm + 2 x converter at 600mm, ISO 500, 1/2000 sec at f/10

Red kite with juvenile lapwing. Nikon D4, 300mm + 2 x converter at 600mm, ISO 1600, 1/2000 sec at f/11

Common blue butterfly warming up on dead grasses. Nikon D4, 300mm + 2 x converter at 600mm, ISO 1000, 1/1600 sec at f/8

Turtle dove. Nikon D4, 300mm + 2 x converter at 600mm, ISO 800, 1/1600 sec at f/8

Common toad taking to the water to breed. Nikon D4, 300mm + 2 x converter at 600mm, ISO 800, 1/1000 sec at f/7.1

Brown hawker. Nikon D3X, 300mm + 2 x converter at 600mm, ISO 1600, 1/2500 sec at f/10

Poppy in a corn field : College Lakes BBOWT reserve. Nikon D4, 300mm + 2 x converter at 600mm, ISO 640, 1/1000 sec at f/8

College Lake is a very attractive little reserve near Tring where over 1000 species have been recorded. Once a chalk quarry the reserve has been managed by BBOWT to produce varied habitats. The ponds are frequented by lapwing and wildfowl with the aerobatic hobby visiting in the summer months. Surrounding meadow areas have been managed for wildflowers and these are well worth a visit in midsummer when the cornflowers are in bloom. The mixed native plant species also attract a fabulous array of butterflies including large numbers of marbled whites.

The reserve has a great visitor centre and facilities including a cafe. Note the reserve is fenced and gated with restricted opening hours.

Wildflowers

It was not my intention to cover flora in this book however this is too good an opportunity to miss when visiting this reserve where possibly the main focus is looking for hobbies. In this case it is worth keeping a long focal length lens on the camera for the birds and using the same for the wildflowers and butterflies. A focal length of 600mm gives a shallow depth of field creating the out of focus effect in the fore and background which emphasises the delicate nature of the subject.

Hobby *(Falco subbuteo)*

The main path leads right round the reserve. Hobbies fly over the lakes from all directions so think about the sun direction then sit and wait in a good location rather than trying to follow these highly mobile falcons.

See also Otmoor p.176.

Cornflowers in a wildflower meadow. Nikon D4, 300mm + 2 x converter at 600mm, ISO 640, 1/1250 sec at f/9

How To Get Here

BBOWT College Lake is located 2 miles north of Tring, 9 miles east of Aylesbury, 13 miles north west of Hemel Hempstead in Buckinghamshire. From Tring take the B488 for a mile to the roundabout. Go right on Bulbourne Road for 0.8 miles over the canal to find the entrance on the left.

Car park Lat/Long: 51.815792, -0.64460456
OS Co-ordinate: SP 935 138
Nearest Postcode: HP23 5QG
Phone: 01442 826774

Accessibility

Opening Times: March–October 9.30am–5pm
November–February 9.30am–4pm

Some wheelchair access, including hides; two mobility Tramper vehicles are avaliable to use – contact: 01442 826774.

Best Time of Year/Day

There is something to photograph year round. Spring and early summer (June and July) are best for wildflowers.

College lakes:
Nikon D800E, ISO250, 24mm, f22, 1/200

Juvenile hobby photographed at Otmoor. Nikon D4, 300mm +
2 x converter at 600mm, ISO 2500, 1/2500 sec at f/14

Pair of red kites in dead tree. Nikon D4, 300mm + 2 x converter at 600mm, ISO 1600, 1/1250 sec at f/5.6

This area of low chalk hills in southern England is easily accessed via the M40 motorway and is well known for the recently reintroduced and highly visible red kite. A good location is thecar park for the National Nature Reserve at Aston Rowant. Any rural footpaths and roads around the towns of Stokenchurch and Watlington are also likely to produce good views.

Red Kite *(Milvus milvus)*

In the 1970s the idea of seeing a wild red kite in the UK was regarded as impossible without visiting the tiny remote population in Wales. This huge conservation success has resulted from a reintroduction programme centered around the Chilterns allowing a population explosion of this colourful and photogenic bird of prey.

Technique

Kites are not difficult to find or to get in the frame. Close encounters can be by chance or careful planning. A pop-up hide is a good way to get close and using raw meat scraps from a butcher or road kill as bait is an easy way to draw the kites in.

A lens up to 400mm is useful as you will need to track the birds with autofocus as they wheel in circles overhead. Maintain a fairly small aperture (f/8 and above) to keep all the bird in focus.

Top tip

Check out Chris's Cafe in Studley Green where they feed the kites most afternoons. Large numbers gather to swoop down into a small carpark to pick up food scraps. It's a good place for a bite to eat for you as well.

Pair of kites in an ash tree. Canon EOS 1 Ds Mark ii , 300mm + 2 x converter at 600mm, ISO 500, 1/1000 sec at f/13

Red kite in cloudy sky, Ibstone Common. Canon 40D, 100-400mm at 400mm, ISO 400, 1/2000 sec at f/7.1

Above: Red kites argue over food.
Nikon D4, 300mm, ISO 1000, 1/1600 sec at f/16

How To Get Here

Aston Rowant is located off M40 between junctions 5 and 6, approx 2 miles west of Stokenchurch. From the M40 turn off at junction 5 for Stokenchurch. Follow the A40 north and after 0.6 miles turn left for the Aston Rowant National Nature Reserve.

Other good places nearby include Ibstone Common, Christmas Common and Watlington Hill.

Aston Rowant car park Lat/Long: 51.663423, -0.94306444
OS Co-ordinate: SU 732 966
Nearest Postcode: HP14 3YL

Accessibility

In Aston Rowant there are two easy-access trails suitable for wheelchair users. Many of the roadsides around here offer opportunities for red kite spotting and photography.

Best Time of Year/Day

Winter is a good time to photograph kites, they are hungry so will come for food, kites can be attracted with tasty morsels of meat. In late summer the birds are moulting and look scruffy.

Red kite banking. Nikon D4, 300mm, ISO 1000, 1/1600 sec at f/13

The former nuclear weapons base at Greenham Common is now a National Nature Reserve. Composed of heathland with thick gorse patches and edging woodland the Common is home to many species of bird and reptiles.

Adder *(Viperus berus)*

The adder or viper is the UK's only venomous snake. Though bites are rare they are potentially deadly and extreme care is required especially when photographing this protected species.

Adders are a relatively small snake and well camouflaged especially amongst their favoured habitat of gorse and bracken. By far the best time to see these creatures is in February or March when the first warm days of spring bring them out of hibernation. This is good from a photography point of view also as the vegetation will be low making them easier to spot.

Early morning is a good time to look for them as they will be slower in the cooler temperatures and less inclined to disappear at the first hint of a sound. Snakes in theory cannot hear as they do not have ears. They respond instead to vibrations meaning they are in fact very sensitive to sound. The female adder tends to be a brown colouration and the males black and grey. The zigzag pattern on the back is diagnostic and they do not have the yellow collar of the non-venomous grass snake.

In early spring they can be found in groups as males are drawn to the females by scent. Be careful therefore when getting low to the ground to photograph one snake, there may be others in the very close vicinity.

Where to look

This is a big place to look for a small snake. For snakes and slow worms try the south and eastern ends of the Common especially the wooded areas and amongst the gorse thickets.

For birds the central gorse thickets around the old airfield tower are good.

Male stonechat on the lookout. Nikon D4, 300mm + 2 x converter at 600mm, ISO 800, 1/1000 sec at f/13

Stonechat *(Saxicola rubicola)*

Stonechats are easy to find here perching prominently on gorse bushes to mark their territory. Dartford warblers though present here can be difficult to find, listen out for their *churr* alarm call. See also Arne p.210 and Dunwich Heath p.254.

Female adder warming in spring sunlight.
Nikon D800E, 300mm, ISO 160, 1/1000 sec at f/3.2

Technique: Snakes

Walk quietly and look carefully, they are hard to spot but this gets easier once you have seen your first one or two disappear in the undergrowth. If you miss one come back an hour or so later to the same spot.

A low point of view works well for snakes but be careful if kneeling or lying down. Try a long telephoto lens to achieve a narrow depth of field for portraits (facing page), this also allows you to keep a safe distance. If light is good a smaller lens (300mm) will allow better depth of field for the whole snake.

Female stonechat in typical pose. Nikon D4, 300mm + 2 x converter at 600mm, ISO 800, 1/1000 sec at f/13

How To Get Here

Greenham Common is located just to the south east of Newbury in Berkshire. There are many entry points to the common, Greenham Common is signposted from Newbury. There are lots of parking places off Burys Bank Road that runs along the northern edge or if approaching from the east (Thatcham direction) along Crookham Common Road there are places to park off Thornford road.

Main car park Lat/Long: 51.382762, -1.2843548
OS Co-ordinate: SU 499 651
Nearest Postcode: RG19 8BZ

Accessibility

The common is open at all times. The main tracks across the common are level and accessible for those with limited walking ability or wheelchairs.

Best Time of Year/Day

For adders early morning on sunny days from February to March when they awake from hibernation.

Left: Male adder close up. Nikon D4, 300mm + 2 x converter at 600mm, ISO 800, 1/1000 sec at f/5.6

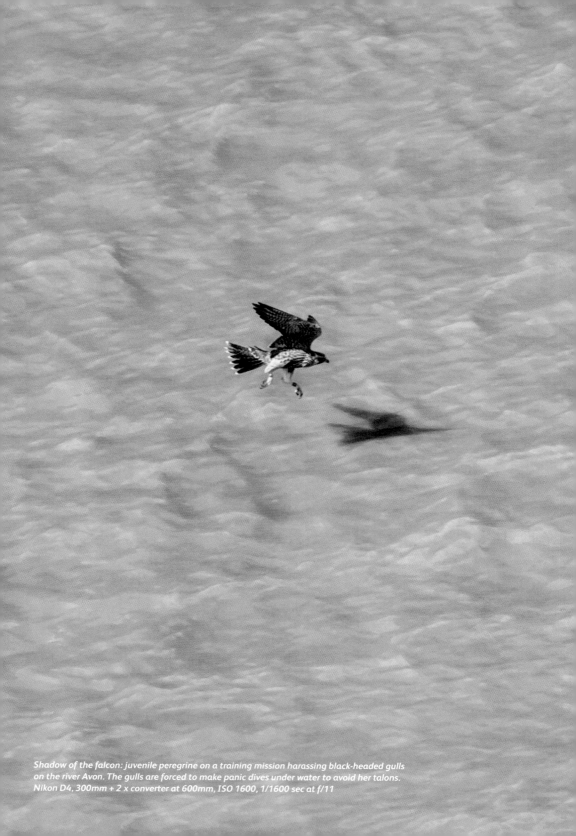

Shadow of the falcon: juvenile peregrine on a training mission harassing black-headed gulls on the river Avon. The gulls are forced to make panic dives under water to avoid her talons. Nikon D4, 300mm + 2 x converter at 600mm, ISO 1600, 1/1600 sec at f/11

Avon Gorge is located on the edge of the city of Bristol with spectacular views of the Clifton Suspension Bridge. The steep cliff faces carved out by the River Avon are home to a nesting pair of peregrine falcons. Keep an eye out also for ravens and kestrels.

The steep cliffs provide only limited opportunities for photographing the peregrines on the cliff face itself where they nest. However the adults coming into and leaving the nest site use the rising air against the cliff to fly almost at eye level to the watchers on the cliff top view point. The best time to visit is in early summer when the young peregrines fledge. The young birds make practice flights and learn to hunt by harrying the local black-backed gulls.

Peregrine falcon *(Falco peregrinus)*

Persecuted and poisoned to the verge of extinction the peregrine is now making a welcome comeback especially in urban areas of the UK. The speed and hunting prowess of the peregrine is legendary. The dramatic markings and striking features make it a top subject for the wildlife photographer.

Juvenile peregrine falcon overhead. Nikon D4, 300mm + 2 x converter at 600mm, ISO 1600, 1/1600 sec at f/14

Above: Adult peregrine on aerial manoeuvres. Nikon D4, 300mm + 1.4 x converter at 420mm, ISO 800, 1/1250 sec at f/11

Juvenile peregrine leaves the cliff face.
Nikon D4, 300mm, ISO 1000, 1/1600 sec at f/16

Where to look

Turning onto the Circular Road in Bristol the road leads along the top of the cliff which forms the bank of the river Avon. There are several viewpoints but the key point nearest the Clifton Suspension Bridge is easily located, not least because photographers and bird watchers are nearly always here keeping a watch on the nesting birds.

Many times the adults can be seen perched far away on the opposite side of the gorge. The 'banana tree' being a favourite perch.

Technique

Binoculars or a spotting scope are useful to locate the birds when they are too far away to photograph. Listen out for the typical falcon calls which indicate activity, perhaps as an adult returns with a kill. Patience is required as through the day either the adults or the fledged youngsters will make sorties across the gorge and come within range.

A 300mm lens is often sufficient as the birds can fly very close and low. A narrow aperture (giving a large depth of field) is preferable especially if capturing action between predator and potential prey.

How To Get Here

Just 3 miles from the centre of Bristol and half a mile west of Bristol Zoo Gardens, the viewpoints are found along the Circular Road, off the A4176 in the Clifton part of Bristol.

Avon Gorge viewpoint Lat/Long: 51.464452, -2.6292434
OS Co-ordinate: ST 563 741
Nearest Postcode: BS8 3HU

Accessibility

The viewpoint is easily accessible but the footpath along the cliff is rough and overlooking a sheer face with a long drop.

Best Time of Year/Day

February through March is a good time to see the male displaying to the female. Eggs hatch in late April and the chicks remain in the nest for 6 weeks. While the young are in the nest adults make frequent hunting sorties. Their return to the nest is often announced by much distinct calling and sometimes a spectacular aerial food pass between the adults. Juveniles start learning to fly from mid June to July which is a good time to photograph them; test flights often result in close landings on the rock ledges near the viewpoints.

The New Forest is a large area of broad leaved woodland and heather heath. The woodland is good for deer and wild New Forest ponies. The heaths are home to stonechat, Dartford warbler, adders and nightjars.

There are five species of deer in the New Forest. You would need to be very lucky to see the sika and muntjak, but fallow, roe and red deer are far less elusive.

Fallow Deer *(Darma darma)*

Fallow deer are common in the UK, typically found in broad leaved woodland and parks. The deer in the New Forest are not difficult to find. As well as possible unexpected meetings in the woodland they are regularly seen at the deer viewing spot at Bolderwood. Here a fence prevents close access but the deer are easy to view and it is a matter of waiting patiently for evening or early morning activity.

This is again a popular spot and likely to be noisy. For a few years some large stags were prominant and easier to photograph at rutting times in fields around the forest however these appear to have been culled and the stags

rutting seem to be largely confined to dense areas of woodland where they cannot be easily photographed. For alternative places to photograph fallow deer try also Richmond Park p.218 and the Forest of Dean p.154.

Technique

The deer in the forest are fairly flighty and good stalking technique will get you closer. At Bolderwood a long lens and tripod would be useful.

New Forest Ponies

Not really a wild animal (you might think.) but get too close and the wild ponies that roam free in the forest can be aggressive. Keep an eye on the tell tale ears, if these go back you are too close. A pony turning to place its rear end towards you may be planning on a kick.

These are attractive photographic subjects and good practice on the way to look for deer. As always look for ways to make the photograph a little bit different; shadows of an overhanging oak created patterns on the tan hide of this pony seeking shade from the midday sun. See photo top right.

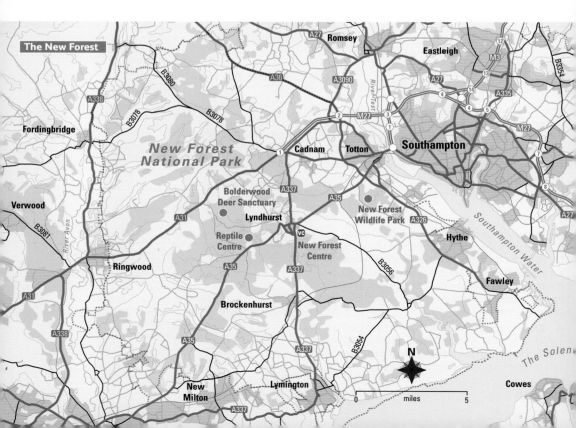

New Forest pony with shade pattern.
Nikon D800E, 300mm, ISO 1250, 1/1000 sec at f/5.6

Fallow deer profile. Nikon D800E, 300mm + 2 x converter at
600mm, ISO 2500, 1/1250 sec at f/5.6

How To Get Here

The New Forest National Park is close to the south coast of England in the county of Hampshire. The Park is bisected by the A31 which meets the M27 motorway in the east at Cadnam (Junction 1). Be aware that the A31 has limited junctions. Cadnam is the biggest gateway into the New Forest from the east and is just a few miles from Lyndhurst which is centrally placed. From the west, the market town of Ringwood marks the National Park boundary on the A31.

Bolderwood Deer Sanctuary is the best place to see deer with a purpose-built platform overlooking a large meadow. Bolderwood is 5 miles west of Lyndhurst

Bolderwood Deer Sanctuary Lat/Long: 50.876746, -1.6569614
OS Co-ordinate: SU242086
Nearest Postcode: SO43 7GE

Accessibility

At Bolderwood there are signposted walks suitable for wheelchair and buggy users. These take you through ancient and ornamental woodland with a good chance of spotting deer.

Elsewhere in the New Forest there are regular car parks. Cycling is a good way to get around on the roads and forest tracks. On foot there is mixed access via woodland tracks or over rough heath trails.

Best Time of Year/Day

Late summer and autumn for stags with full antlers. The rut starts in late September until the latter part of October. Weekdays are better than weekends and holidays and it's best early morning or evening.

Keyhaven Lagoon is part of the Lymington and Keyhaven Nature Reserve managed by Hampshire County Council. This is a great place to photograph coastal wading birds. Inland lagoons provide a feeding and resting place for species such as dunlin and occasional rarer waders such as the curlew sandpiper.

Dunlin *(Calidris alpina)*

These small, beautifully marked waders are common shore birds in the UK. The plumage is delicate and subtle and makes for an interesting subject. Here at Keyhaven they can be approached with care to achieve good close-up images. Look in the lagoons away from the shore line where they feed in the exposed mud probing for lugworms and molluscs.

Curlew sandpiper *(Calidris ferruginea)*

This is a rare species in the UK but can sometimes be found here amongst the flocks of dunlin. The difference in appearance to the curlew is quite subtle for amateur ornithologists. Look closely for the light eye strip above the eye (known as the supercilium) and the longer downwards-curving beak.

Dunlin close up. Nikon D4, 300mm + 2 x converter at 600mm, ISO 500, 1/1250 sec at f/5.6

Opposite top: Dunlin flock settling in the lagoon. Nikon D4, 300mm + 2 x converter at 600mm, ISO 500, 1/1250 sec at f/10

Curlew sandpiper reflected in the still waters. Nikon D4, 300mm + 2 x converter at 600mm, ISO 1600, 1/1250 sec at f/9

How To Get Here

Keyhaven Lagoon is part of the Lymington-Keyhaven Nature Reserve which along with the adjacent Keyhaven and Pennington Marshes Reserve ensure the protection of this extensive area of coastal habitat. Both reserves lie within the New Forest National Park and are located 20 miles east along the coast from Bournemouth. Parking is at Keyhaven Yacht Club.

Keyhaven Lagoon car park Lat/Long: 50.722302, -1.5676036
OS Co-ordinate: SZ 306 914
Nearest Postcode: SO41 0TR

Accessibility

The whole of the 5 mile coastal path from Lymington to Keyhaven is now said to be accessible to people in wheelchairs or with buggies.

Best Time of Year/Day

In winter the flooded lagoons are home to wildfowl such as mallard, shoveler and teal. Black-tailed godwit, curlew and lapwing feed in the flooded pastures alongside wigeon and brent geese. Spring and autumn bring migrant wading birds including whimbrel, curlew sandpiper and little stint.

Brownsea island is the largest island in Poole Harbour. It is famous for being where the scout movement started after an experimental camp in 1907. The island is a Site of Special Scientific Interest owned by the National Trust with its northern part a reserve managed by the Dorset Wildlife Trust.

Elegant avocets overwinter in the lagoon along with greenshank and spoonbill. The surrounding woodland is home to an isolated but very obliging colony of red squirrels offering the best opportunities to see and photograph these fabulous little creatures in the south of England.

Red squirrel *(Sciurus vulgaris)*

On Brownsea the squirrels are habituated to human presence and very easy to get close to. Head for the church and look in the surrounding woodland. If all seems quiet leave a few hazlenuts on appropriate tree stumps and stand quietly back. This is a great place for anyone to learn photography and a good place for children to see wildlife.

See also Lake District p.120 and Formby Point p.138.

Caught red handed. A red squirrel makes off with a hazlenut.
Nikon D4, 300mm, ISO 1600, 1/800 sec at f/8

Above: A great set of ear tufts.
Nikon D4, 500mm, ISO 1600, 1/800 sec at f/8

Crossing swords: a pair of avocets at Brownsea island.
Nikon D4, 500mm, ISO 320, 1/800 sec at f/9

Avocet (*Recurvirostra avosetta*)

The saltwater lagoon has several overlooking hides. The first you get to is large and in an excellent position which can offer close up views of waders especially avocet, godwit and greenshank. The avocets here are essentially overwintering and will be replaced with summer migrants including sandwich terns in the summer.

See also Upton Warren p.166 and Exmouth p.280.

Also at Brownsea island

Diverse habitats here include alder carr woodland, wetland and lagoons. This means this is also a good location for sika deer, water vole, kingfisher and water rail. Time is short on a day trip so this location deserves a second visit.

Avocet taking off.
Nikon D4, 500mm, ISO 500, 1/800 sec at f/11

How To Get Here

Brownsea Island is the largest of the islands in Poole Harbour in the county of Dorset. Access is by boat from Poole Harbour. At Poole there are various pay and display car parks nearby including a large multi-storey car park. At Sandbanks there is free parking subject to availability and beach side pay and display parking.

Poole Quay ferry Lat/Long: 50.712050, -1.9870354
OS Co-ordinate: SZ 010 902
Nearest Postcode: BH15 1HJ

Sandbanks ferry Lat/Long: 50.683217, -1.9486329
OS Co-ordinate: SZ 037 870
Nearest Postcode: BH13 7QN

Boats: Half-hourly boat service (not National Trust) from 10am, departing Poole Quay (01202 631828/01929 462383) and Sandbanks (01929 462383)

The Island is open daily from March to November (10am–5pm) and weekends year round.

Accessibility

Getting here involves a short boat ride. There is good viewing from hides and a system of paths and boardwalks give access to most of the habitats. The National Trust are trialling a new boat from Sept 2015 that is suitable for wheelchairs.

Best Time of Year/Day

Come early in the year for winter bird visitors such as shelduck, black-tailed godwit, redshank, avocet, grey plover, curlew, or in summer for breeding terns amongst others. Red squirrels are present year round but autumn is the best time as they forage for winter feed.

A Greenshank stalks the shallows at Brownsea island.
Nikon D4, 500mm + 1.4 x converter at 700mm, ISO 500, 1/1000 sec at f/8

Overlooking Poole Harbour, Arne is a site of Special Scientific Interest managed by the RSPB. This is an attractive area of heather heath and gorse with Scots pine trees and areas of oak woodland. Key species here are the Dartford warblers and sika deer. In season this is a regular stop off point for migrating osprey.

Dartford warbler *(Sylvia undata)*

This rare and delightful little bird is typical of this type of heathland habitat. See also Dunwich Heath p.254.

From the car park take the track south following the Combe Heath Trail. The lower sections near the woodland are a good place for warblers. Listen carefully for the *churr churr* call especially around the patches of gorse. As elsewhere they are often associated with the more visible stonechats. **Note:** this is a Schedule One endangered bird and should not be disturbed especially at breeding time.

Also at Arne

Sika deer roam freely here, they are most visible at rutting time but evident with youngsters in spring. The hide at the far end of the Coombe Heath Trail overlooks the mud flats and it can be possible to see avocets and spoonbills from here though these are frequently too distant for photography purposes.

Scots pine tree on the heath at Arne.

The ponds on the lower section of Coombe Heath are a good place to look for raft spiders and grass snakes.

The heath is also home to nightjars, adders and lizards.

Story behind the picture

(Running sika deer following double page image).

Whilst photographing the Dartford warblers I noticed a dog walker in the distance with the dog off the lead. I wasnt surprised when a young Sika deer became alarmed. Changing the settings to a higher shutter speed I remained stationary taking several shots as the frightened animal ran close by to escape from the dog.

How To Get Here

RSPB Arne is located on the south west side of Poole Harbour, 4 miles from Wareham in Dorset. From Wareham town centre, head south on the B3075 over the causeway to Stoborough from where Arne is signposted.

RSPB Arne car park Lat/Long: 50.689933, -2.0420778
OS Co-ordinate: SY 971 878
Nearest Postcode: BH20 5BJ
Phone: 01929 553360

Accessibility

There are trails of different length with mostly easily accessible off road paths across heathland, some of which are suitable for wheelchair access. The Shipstal and Coombes trails are open at all times. The car park opens at 8.30 am and is locked at dusk.

Best Time of Year/Day

In spring Dartford warblers and stonechats nest on the heaths and woodpecker activity is at its best. Summer is good for reptiles basking in the sun, at dusk between May and July nightjars dart around catching moths and perform their wing-clapping displays. Autumn sees the return of migrant birds; ospreys linger until mid-October. October sees the sika deer rut. In winter wildfowl and wading birds peak at over 30,000 in the harbour. Morning and evening is best for great light.

Dartford warbler sitting pretty. Nikon D4, 300mm + 2 x converter at 600mm, ISO 1600, 1/1250 sec at f/8

Opposite below: Dartford warbler in the Gorse. Nikon D4, 300mm + 2 x converter at 600mm, ISO 1600, 1/1250 sec at f/9

Below: Sika deer on the alert. Nikon D4, 300mm + 2 x converter at 600mm, ISO 1600, 1/1000 sec at f/8

Running Sika deer at Arne. Nikon D4, 300mm + 2 x converter at 600mm, ISO 1250, 1/1250 sec at f/11

South East and East England – Introduction

On the east side of England lies Norfolk, widely regarded as one of the best wildlife areas in the UK, especially by birders. Here the coastline and low lying marshes have been of little use to mankind either to build on or for agriculture and have remained wild and relatively unvisited. Consequently wildlife has thrived; the coastline is an important overwintering site for waders and wildfowl with Snettisham, Titchwell Marsh and Cley Marshes all world famous reserves.

Norfolk is also famous for barn owls and Sculthorpe Moor and the other reserves just mentioned are great places to see this magical endangered species.

The fens and marshes are the habitat of the once almost extinct marsh harrier. RSPB Minsmere was the site for the resurrection of this spectacular wetland raptor and it is now almost commonplace across most of these reserves.

Suffolk is also home to some of these important wetland reserves and small almost unnoticed Wildlife Trust reserves like Lackford Lakes are absolute gems for close encounters with specialist species like kingfishers.

Further south we hit upon the sprawl of urbanisation that is the capital city, London. Even here we find small islands of peace and tranquility where wildlife survives.

Close and regular contact with humans has led to the wildlife becoming habituated to people allowing close encounters with creatures that otherwise would be difficult to approach. The herons at Regent's Park are a great example of this: try getting close to a heron anywhere else and you will be left with an indignant cronking call as he flaps off to find a quieter fishing ground.

In Richmond park the sights and sounds of the red deer rut are the highlight of many a wildlife photographers' year.

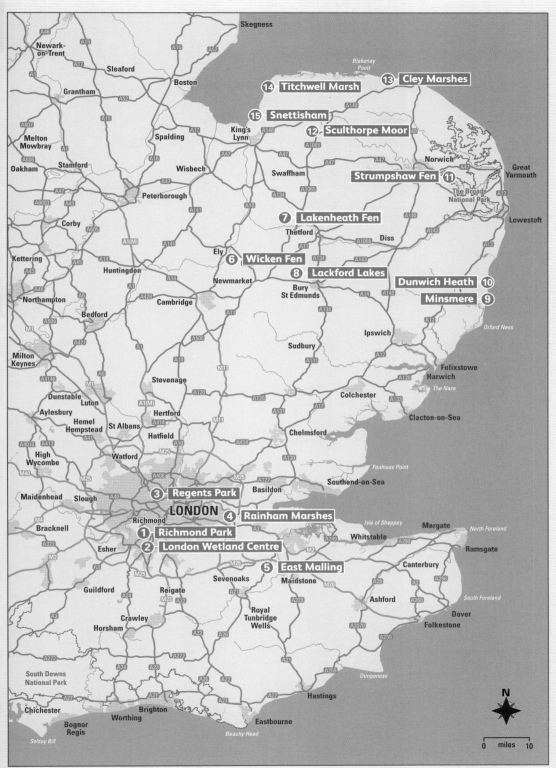

14 Titchwell Marsh

13 Cley Marshes

15 Snettisham

12 Sculthorpe Moor

Strumpshaw Fen 11

7 Lakenheath Fen

6 Wicken Fen

8 Lackford Lakes

Dunwich Heath 10

Minsmere 9

3 Regents Park

4 Rainham Marshes

LONDON

1 Richmond Park

2 London Wetland Centre

5 East Malling

Big old stag silhouetted in the misty morning light at Richmond park.
Nikon D4, 500mm, ISO 250, 1/1000 at f/6.3

Situated in the middle of London, Richmond Park may not seem like the wildest of places to go photographing wildlife. The park's accessibility and popularity means there are a lot of people about, especially at weekends. It is however surprisingly easy to lose yourself in the woodland and be transported back to ancient times when this was a royal hunting forest.

The area is a National Nature Reserve and there is an abundance of wildlife. Apart from the obvious red and fallow deer keep your eyes and ears out for green woodpeckers and increasingly abundant ring-necked parakeets. From late September to mid October is rutting time for the huge red deer stags and this is the time to witness their exciting and impressive displays.

Where to look

Aim for the car park close to Roehampton Gate where you can park for free and there are toilet facilities and a cafe. From the car park head out into the park. Be aware that a small stream crosses the middle of the grassland and you need to cross via one of the road bridges.

If you cannot see any of the herds of red and fallow deer, listen out for the noise of the stags roaring. There are usually several groups of deer in obvious groups on the grassed areas where the dominant stags make their stand bellowing loudly at intervals to warn off their rivals and entice more hinds to join them.

Red deer *(Cervus elaphus)*

The red deer is the largest UK land mammal and not easy to miss. The males or stags have huge and dangerous antlers which they shed and re-grow, incredibly fast, every year. These formidable weapons are used primarily in combat to assert dominance and therefore the right to mate with the females (hinds). In autumn the stags begin to round up hinds and fend off other stags, the loud head thrown back bellowing being the initial sign that the annual rut is underway.

Warning

Red deer are aggressive during the rut and have been known to injure and even kill people. Whilst this is unlikely and the deer here are accustomed to people it is wise to keep a safe distance or photograph from behind a tree. Watch the animal carefully. If he is eyeing you you may be in his line of attack, perhaps a young rival is behind you, be aware and alert and prepared to move quickly.

The clash: two red deer stags engage in combat.
Nikon D800E, 300mm, ISO 6400, 1/640 sec at f/5.6

Red deer stag bellowing in golden sunlight.
Nikon D800E, 300mm, ISO 1000, 1/1000 sec at f/4

A crown of bracken fronds for the forest king.
Nikon D3X, 300mm, ISO 3200, 1/800 sec at f/2.8

Technique

There are estimated to be around 360 red and fallow deer found throughout the park's 2360 acres meaning there are myriad opportunities for the photographer. The time of the year, late September to October, means that early mornings can be misty and light is not always ideal. This can be a good thing too, adding further atmosphere to this medieval forest. The stags are expending massive amounts of energy roaring and chasing off rivals and are frequently steaming with body heat on cold mornings.

Light is as always of key importance and perhaps surprisingly the evening can be more rewarding than early mornings as the sun sets in the west casting low golden light on the woodland edges.

A low angle as always helps to give an idea of size however be aware that these are potentially very dangerous animals and crouching down on the ground in front of a rutting red deer is not to be advised.

The deeper woodland is a better area to capture more natural images and the sight of a red deer stag with his antlers adorned with bracken is a top shot to look out for.

Again be very careful walking around in the tall bracken as the younger sub-dominant males often hide out here waiting for a chance to make a move on unguarded hinds. These stags are likely to be more dangerous with frustration having been beaten back and even possibly injured by the dominant stags.

Larger stags will often walk parallel to each other assessing each other's size before committing to battle. The younger wannabe stags are the ones to watch for, engaged in the classic locked horn sparring.

Equipment-wise either a 300mm f/2.8 or a 500mm on a tripod is ideal for these conditions as this is a large easily approachable subject sometimes in low light conditions.

Ring-necked parakeet checking out a nest hole.
Nikon D4, 500mm, ISO 1600, 1/640 sec at f/6.3

Body heat rising from a testosterone-fuelled stag.
Nikon D3X, 300mm, ISO 3200, 1/800 sec at f/5

How To Get Here

Richmond Park is in south west London, just north of Kingston-upon-Thames, with the A3 to the south of the park and the South Circular Road to the north. Parking is available by several gates. Recommended are the Roehampton Gate (car park) and the Richmond Gate which is walking distance from Richmond Station.

Roehampton Gate Lat/Long: 51.453838, -0.257390
OS map co-ordinate: TQ 211 742
Parking Postcode: SW15 5JP

Richmond Gate Lat/Long: 51.450174, -0.296658
OS map co-ordinate: TQ 184 737
Parking Postcode: TW10 6RR

www.royalparks.org.uk

Accessibility

The park is open 24 hours for pedestrians except for during the deer cull during some evenings in November and February. Vehicle gates close at dusk all year, and open at 7am in the summer and 7:30am in the winter. The park is crossed by several roads and broad paths with easy walking through grassland and woods. Suitable for wheelchair users.

Best Time of Year/Day

Late September through October for the deer rut. Early mornings and evenings being the best times of day.

Stag in golden morning light.
Nikon D800E, 300mm, ISO 160, 1/1250 sec at f/9

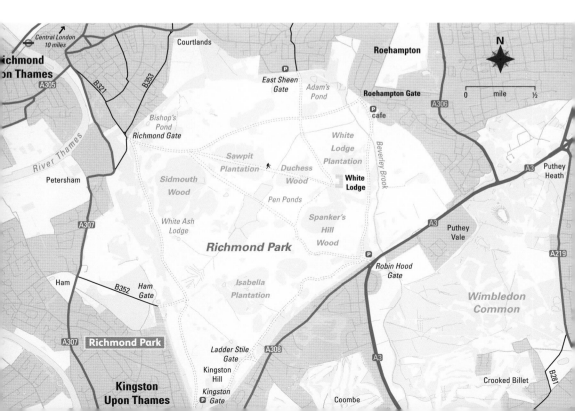

Fallow deer *(Dama dama)*

Present in large numbers and easy to find, the fallow deer here are reasonably tame and easy to approach. This is a very different scenario to places such as the Forest of Dean (p.154) where they are timid and often elusive. The fallow deer is significantly smaller than the red and easily distinguised by its lighter, often spotted hide. Some individuals are almost white. The mature stags have a more palmate structure to the antler which looks less formidable or dangerous. Fallow deer however are nonetheless ready to use their antlers in battle and can still potentially inflict considerable damage.

Technique

With fallow deer there is little danger to life or limb so try and use a low angle to get a more dramatic shot. Take to the woods to find more naturalistic settings, the deer can be more skittish in this environment which also makes it more interesting.

Light in the woods will be either high contrast or low level so be prepared to use a high ISO if necessary. With low light the camera will require a wide aperture and consequently a shallow depth of field so make sure you focus on the eye. (Use a single focus point to make sure).

Grey squirrel munching chestnuts. Nikon D800E, 300mm, ISO 1600, 1/800 sec at f/7.1

Young fallow bucks see the point. Nikon D800E, 300mm + 2 x converter at 600mm, ISO 2000, 1/1000 sec at f/9

Opposite right: Fallow buck portrait. Nikon D800E, 300mm + 2 x converter at 600mm, ISO 2500, 1/1000 sec at f/5.6

The Wildfowl and Wetland Trust have established this popular reserve right in the heart of London. The reserve is home to wintering wildfowl and many wild species that have become habituated to human presence offering easy opportunities for both beginner and experienced wildlife photographers.

Rare species including bitterns turn up in winter and kingfishers are a regular sighting. The endearing little grebes are an easy find in the ditches and, unusually, this is a good place to spot and get close to common lizards.

Where to look

The well-appointed visitor centre and cafe have friendly and informative staff who can point you in the right direction. The Wild Side is a good place to start; look out here for water voles and the bridges over the waterways are a good place to find common lizards basking on a sunny day. Following the South Route will take you past the sheltered lagoon where little grebes can usually be seen, there are lizards here too.

The Wader Scrape Hide is the best bet for kingfishers as there are perches placed around the edge of the scrape.

Common Lizard (*Zootoca vivipara*)

The common lizard is the most widespread of the British reptiles but they are not always easy to find. This is a great place to get close to these elusive animals. Being cold blooded they require the sun's warmth to be active and are therefore dormant during winter months.

Emerging usually in March they are typically seen in sunlit spots basking on stones or wood. Also known as the viviperous lizard they are unusual amongst reptiles in giving birth to live young rather than eggs. They vary in colour widely from yellow to brown but are easily distinguishable from the only other British lizard, the sand lizard, which largely inhabits coastal areas and is far less abundant.

How To Get Here

The London Wetland Centre is located inside a meander of the River Thames in Barnes, close to central London.

By bus: From Hammersmith bus station (stand K) take the number 283 bus direct to the centre.

By rail: Barnes is the nearest railway station and is 25 minutes from Waterloo or 10 minutes from Clapham Junction. It is then a 15 minute walk to the Wetland Centre (or 5 minutes by buses 72 or 33).

By tube: The closest tube station is Hammersmith (on the Piccadilly and District & Circle Lines). From the tube station it's a 10 minute bus ride (see ''By bus'').

By car: The centre is located just off the main A306 which runs from the South Circular at Roehampton (with easy access to the A3) to Hammersmith (just minutes from the A4/M4). Once in Barnes you can follow the brown tourist signs to the centre. The centre is situated outside the London Congestion Charging Zone. There is no charge for car parking.

London Wetland Centre Lat/Long: 51.477206, -0.23592860
OS Co-ordinate: TQ 226 768
Nearest Postcode: SW13 9WT

Phone: 020 8409 4400

Accessibility

'Wetland Centres exist to fulfil founder Peter Scott's vision of connecting people with nature, so it is a principle that our wetlands and wildlife are accessible to everyone.'

There is level access around the site including to the hides, or lifts where required. There are allocated blue badge parking spaces, four manual wheelchairs on loan and one mobility scooter to hire, call ahead to book.

Entry is free to WWT members or £11.59 for adults.

Best Time of Year/Day

Mornings and evenings late September through to November. This is a busy place at most times of the year and the larger hides are probably best avoided at peak times to avoid noise and disturbance.

Summer opening time – from end of March until late October: 9.30am to 6pm (last admission 5pm).
Winter opening time – from late October until end of March: 9.30am to 5pm (last admission 4pm).

A wide angle shot places the tiny lizard in its habitat.
Nikon D800E, 17-35mm at 20mm, ISO 640, 1/400 sec at f/8

Little grebe with reflection in the reeds. Nikon D4, 300mm +
2 x converter at 600mm, ISO 2500, 1/1000 sec at f/8

Common lizard basking. Image from Otmoor. Nikon D4, 300mm + 2 x converter at 600mm, ISO 2000, 1/1000 sec at f/5.6

Technique

The wildlife at the London Wetland Centre is relatively easy to approach and needs no special talents. Keeping all movements slow and quiet will allow you to get much closer. This is a good place to learn photographic skills.

Common lizards are of course not that common and this is a great place to see this British reptile at close quarters. Get down to eye level to get the best perspective.

Depth of field is important. By having a wide aperture (smaller f number, e.g. f/2.8) you will narrow the depth of field meaning only the key focal point (usually the eye) is in focus. If you want the whole lizard in focus reduce the aperture (a higher f number, e.g. f/11).

Tea in the park. Pigeons ate my muffin. Asterix amused in the background.
Regent's park. Nikon D800E, 17-35mm at 20mm, ISO 640, 1/800 sec at f/9

Regent's Park is an island of green space and small lakes in the middle of London's concrete jungle. The park has an annual count of around 114 species of wild bird. The advantages of this as a location are the easy accessibility for many people and the fact the wildlife here is habituated to human presence and consequently easy to get close to. Regent's Park also contains London Zoo if you seek more exotic species.

There are plenty of released exotics that now thrive on the boating lakes including Egyptian geese, black swans and various other waterfowl species that make great subjects.

Heron (Ardea cinerea)

Regent's Park is famous for its heronry. The grey heron nests in small groups building large untidy nests of sticks, in this case in the willows on the islands of the boating lakes. They are easily viewed from the shore and best photographed before the leaves of the willows have fully emerged in April.

This large prehistoric bird is a wonderful subject; the fierce eye, dangerous massive beak and overall large size add up to an impressive subject. Normally a shy bird keen to flap off at the first sign of a human being, here they are casually unafraid and notably are fed by locals. Look out for this as the birds know the score and flock together for the free hand outs often including cat food, bread and cheese. The birds interact in a dramatic dancing movement to fend off rivals for the tastiest food.

See also Leighton Moss p.126.

Nearby

In Central London, the Serpentine and Long Water in Hyde Park, and the Round Pond in Kensington Gardens, are home to a wide variety of birds, including herons, and are very much worth a visit.

How To Get Here

Regent's Park is located on the north side of the River Thames in central London. There is easy acces via tube or bus.

Pay and display parking is available in and around Regent's Park everyday from 9.00am–6.30pm. Use the information below to get you close to the boating lake, Regent's Park covers a large area.

Boating lake Lat/Long: 51.525707, -0.15778095
OS Co-ordinate: TQ 278 823
Nearest Postcode:NW1 4RD

Phone: 0300 061 2300

Disabled badge holders and motor cyclists park free of charge for up to 4 hours maximum stay from Monday to Saturday.

The Tube stations closest to Regent's Park are:
Regent's Park (Bakerloo line)
Great Portland Street (Hammersmith & City, Circle & Metropolitan lines)
Baker Street (Hammersmith & City, Circle, Jubilee, Metropolitan & Bakerloo lines)
St John's Wood (Jubilee line)
Camden Town (Northern line)

Bakers Street or Regent's Park tube stations are the closest to the boating lakes (nearest gate is Hanover Gate).

There are many buses that will take you to Regent's Park.

Accessibility

Easy footpaths and access from nearby tube stations. Suitable for wheelchair users.

The park is open from 5am all year round. Closing times vary depending on the season from 4:30 pm in winter to 9:30 pm in summer.

Best Time of Year/Day

There is something to see and photograph here all year round. At the heronry the best times are mornings and evenings in spring. Migratory birds pass through in spring and autumn using London's green spaces for refuge in bad weather and for feeding.

Regent's Park: plenty of people but wildlife too.
Nikon D4, 17-35mm at 20mm, ISO 640, 1/640 sec at f/9

Group of herons hanging around for food in Regent's Park
Nikon D4, 300mm, ISO 500, 1/1000 sec at f/6.3

Close up heron.
Nikon D4, 300mm, ISO 500, 1/1000 sec at f/9

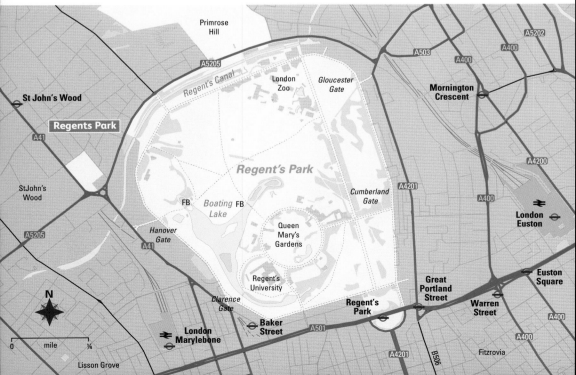

Rainham Marshes is an RSPB reserve situated to the east of London on the banks of the River Thames with fine views across this restored marshland. These medieval marshes were closed to the public for over 100 years and used as a military firing range. The reserve is composed of reed beds and wet meadows and is a great spot for warblers, bearded tits and close encounters with water voles. Access is via a large reception building with cafe and facilities.

Where to look

From the visitor centre the trails lead in a roughly circular route around the reserve. Going anticlockwise with the sun behind you is a good plan to search for bearded tits, reed warblers and sedge warblers in the reeds either side of the board walks.

To the north the Eurostar rail route borders the reserve with the M25 motorway also in view and this make for a noisy and unattractive background. The birds however seem unaffected and in late spring to midsummer the reed beds are alive with bird song and fast-flying dragonflies.

Bearded tits are seen here especially in late summer to autumn as their diet turns from insects to reed seeds.

See also Minsmere p.250.

In the north of the reserve is the large Ken Barrett Hide, a likely place to spot marsh harriers in summer. The hide does face into the sun so is not ideal for photography.

Following the trail back towards the main visitor centre it crosses several small ditches. These points are the best places to look or listen out for water voles. See also East Malling p.234.

The water voles are timid and respond to sound so are unlikely to stay around while people are crossing the bridges. If you can find a quiet time and remain silently on or around the bridge you may be able to hear the voles before you see them. Being rodents water voles are constantly chewing at reed stems especially rushes and this can often be detected as a quiet munching sound.

Frequently a vole will swim across the waterway within feet of the bridge so be ready with a suitable lens (e.g. a 100 to 400mm) for these encounters.

A young water vole tucks into some schoenoplectus stems. Image from private site near Marlborough. Nikon D4, 300mm + 2 x converter at 600mm, ISO 3200, 1/1000 sec at f/5.6

Bearded tit in reed stems. Nikon D4, 300mm + 2 x converter at 600mm, ISO 640, 1/1250 sec at f/9

An industrial backdrop to the reserve at Rainham marshes.
Nikon D800E, 17-35mm at 17mm, ISO 800, 1/640 sec at f/18

How To Get Here

Rainham Marshes is around 19 miles east of London.

By train: The nearest railway station is Purfleet on the C2C line from Fenchurch Street. The reserve is a 15 minute walk from the station following the brown pedestrian signs along the riverside path.

By bus: The Ensignbus 44 bus route runs between Lakeside and Grays and stops near the reserve entrance on New Tank Hill Road. This bus runs every hour and is operated by Ensignbus (01708 865656)

By road: The reserve is located off New Tank Hill Road (A1090) in Purfleet which is just off the A1306 between Rainham and Lakeside. This is accessible from the Aveley, Wennington and Purfleet junction off the A13 and J30/31 of the M25.

Car park Lat/Long: 51.486912, 0.22776514
OS Co-ordinate: TQ 547 787
Nearest Postcode: RM19 1SZ

Accessibility

Trails and boardwalks are level and suitable for wheelchairs. Hides are level entry or have a lift for wheelchair access.

From 1 November to 31 January, open from 9.30 am to 4.30 pm. From 1 February to 31 October, it's 9.30 am to 5 pm.

Best Time of Year/Day

Spring for warblers, late summer / autumn for bearded tits and water vole. Note the limited opening hours which makes catching early morning and late evening light in the summer months not possible.

Hidden away in a small village in Kent a small clear stream running through an old mill pond is the location for some of the best opportunities to photograph the endangered and charming water vole. This is a private location and access needs to be booked and paid for in advance.

Water vole *(Arvicola amphibious)*

The water vole is a charismatic and attractive animal to photograph, it is also an endangered species in the UK. Their numbers were decimated due to pollution of waterways, habitat loss and the release of the non-native American mink which unfortunately is an efficient hunter of this species.

Water voles are smaller and have a shorter tail than the brown rat for which they may sometimes be mistaken. Their diet includes a wide variety of aquatic marginal plants, fruits and berries. Commonly they are known to be attracted to apple and this is often used as a food to draw them closer for photography.

What to expect

This location has been monitored and photographed for some time and you will be met on site and pointed in the right direction. Though the water voles are likely to appear this can never be guaranteed.

Expect to wait for a few hours in waders sat on a chair in very cold water up to your knees. There may be little other wildlife around to distract you other than passers-by with dogs and children asking you what you are trying to photograph. These drawbacks aside, when the little furry fellows make an appearance it's a great location with a backdrop of liverworts, stone walling and the calm water likely to offer great reflection possibilities.

There are two main sections to the millpond and the smaller upper section offers closer encounters with opportunities to use a smaller lens.

Technique

Great patience is required. Though habituated to photographers, the voles are by nature nervous, flighty and may appear only briefly. Remaining still and quiet will produce better opportunities. Working close to and in the water requires great care with equipment. The pond floor is unstable so be careful when mounting the tripod and siting a chair in the water. Most camera equipment will not survive immersion.

Top tip

Short bursts of activity can be interspersed with long periods of nothing happening. After getting some shots head for a local pub and warm up while downloading the morning's work and look for ways to improve what you have taken already for an afternoon session.

For other water vole opportunities see Minsmere p.250 and Rainham Marshes p.232.

Vole in the hole.
Nikon D4, 500mm, ISO 2500, 1/640 sec at f/4.5

Below opposite: emerging for a snack of rowan berries.
Nikon D4, 500mm, ISO 2500, 1/640 sec at f/5.6

Below: The tiny paws are part of the character.
Nikon D800E, 300mm, ISO 2500, 1/500 sec at f/4.5

How To Get Here

East Malling is 5 miles west of Maidstone in Kent. The water voles are photographed in a private location in the stream that runs through the village. You will need to be guided and it's necessary to book through Terry Whittaker Photography.

www.terrywhittaker.com

Phone: 01303 258322 / 07971 194115

Accessibility

Some shots could be taken from land but by far the best angles require wading in the stream, use of waders is highly recommended.

Best Time of Year/Day

Voles are present year round but autumn is good when the young voles are fattening up for winter.

Hen harrier in flight taken during a rare winter encounter at Otmoor. Nikon D4, 300mm + 2 x converter at 600mm, ISO 640, 1/1250 sec at f/13

Wicken Fen is one of Britain's oldest nature reserves and was the first reserve cared for by the National Trust starting in 1899. This is one of only four wild areas that survive in the enormous Giant Fen Basin of East Anglia where 99.9% of the area has been drained and cultivated. It is considered one of the most important wetland reserves in Europe.

With more than 8500 recorded species this beautiful fenland landscape is host to some rare and wonderful wildlife including barn owls, short-eared owls and hen harriers. The area is large and for the sake of this guide includes an adjoining area known as Burwell Fen.

Hen harrier *(Circus cyanaera)*

One of the UK's most endangered birds of prey, the hen harrier remains a rare sight due unbelievably to its continued persecution.

The male and female have distinctly different plumage; the female being brown with the marked ring tail, the male is pale grey and a sight to behold, known sometimes as 'the ghost'. From a distance the size and colouration of the ringtail may be mistaken for a buzzard however the low owl like flight often with dangling legs and the distinctive white patch at the rump are key to identification. Juveniles and 'first winter' birds may appear similar in plumage to the female.

Hen harriers breed mainly in Scotland but often overwinter further south on fenland and marsh reserves such as Wicken Fen and Burwell Fen.

Where to Look

From the Lode Lane car park you can cross via the visitor centre onto Sedge Fen where the Ten Metre Tower Hide is sometimes a roost for barn owls. Hen harriers also roost on Sedge Fen in winter.

Continue past the visitor centre to follow the Adventurers' Trails around several different hides overlooking open water frequented by waterfowl, hobbies (in summer) and occasionally great white egrets.

The main trail also links up with Burwell Fen by crossing over the Cock Up Bridge. This is a fair walk from the Lodes Lane car park and there is an alternative car park for Burwell Fen nearer the bridge, see panel opposite.

Burwell Fen has for several years been a good spot for short-eared owls. Locate yourself around the central barn to see them emerge to hunt from around 3pm on a calm winter afternoon. The shorties are frequently joined by barn owls.

Hen harrier (ringtail) at Burwelll Fen. Nikon D4, 500mm + 1.4 x converter at 700mm, ISO 160, 1/1000 sec at f/8

Roe deer family in golden evening light. Nikon D4, 500mm + 1.4 x converter at 700mm, ISO 1600, 1/1600 sec at f/9

Windmill at Wicken Fen near the visitors centre on Lode Lane. Nikon D800E, 17-35mm at 32mm, ISO 800, 1/800 sec at f/16

How To Get Here

Wicken Fen is located 17 miles north east of Cambridge. Take the A10 north from Cambridge for 12 miles then turn right along the A1123 for 4.8 miles to Lode Lane and the reserve.

Wicken Fen Car park Lat/Long: 52.311347, 0.29372469
OS Co-ordinate: TL 564 706
Nearest Postcode: CB75XP

Burwell Fen Car parking Lat/Long: 52.297463, 0.29203355
OS Co-ordinate: TL 563 690
Nearest Postcode: CB25 0BN

Bicycle: Cycle hire is available from Wicken Fen and is one option for accessing Burwell Fen if you don't fancy the walk.

Accessibility

Access to the reserve is from dawn till dusk. Most of the trails away from the vicinity of the visitor centre are grassy and rough and can get muddy when wet. Waterproof boots are recommended. There is 3/4 of a mile of all-weather plastic boardwalk suitable for wheelchairs including access to the two hides and the hide at Tubney Fen.

Best Time of Year/Day

In winter there are large flocks of wigeon, teal and shoveler, various swans and geese as well as barn, short-eared, little & tawny owls. Spring sees the arrival of summer migrants, swallows, sand martins, swifts, warblers and cuckoos. Summer is great for wild flowers, butterflies, dragonflies and marsh harriers. In autumn lots of birds fly in either on migration or to start their overwinter residence. Murmurations of starlings over the reedbeds at dusk, continuing throughout the winter.

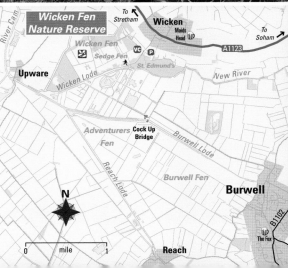

Barn owl with Lakenheath poplars backdrop. Nikon D4, 500mm + 1.4 x converter at 700mm, ISO 1600, 1/1250 sec at f/5.6

Lakenheath is a fabulous RSPB reserve with almost everything you could hope for. Sometimes the wait and watching can be long and fruitless and at other times encounters can be frequent and spectacular. Visit here for the marsh harrier roost in winter sometimes accompanied by male and female hen harriers. Kingfishers are frequent visitors and bearded tits and bittern may be options on a lucky day.

Where to look

At Lakenheath it's more a question of where not to look, there are possibilities everywhere. From the car park and before the entrance to the RSPB visitor centre is a short track through to the washland viewpoint. This area can be a good place for barn owls at dawn and dusk.

The walk from the visitor centre past the tall poplar trees is quite long and hard on a cold winter's day but this is a good place to spot stoats and the poplars can be perches for hobbies.

The first real viewpoint is at New Fen which is a great location for kingfishers. Harriers and hobbies both hunt low over the reeds here.

Past New Fen is a track on the left through to Mere Hide which was built in 2014. Perches situated close to the hide attract kingfishers. Bittern and bearded tits can also be seen from here.

Further still lies Joist Fen viewpoint from where distant harriers can occasionally come in close. Cranes may be seen flying overhead and bitterns do occasionally skulk out of the reeds and stalk the pool's edge.

Top tips

Running to one side of the reserve is the river Little Ouse. Save some time and energy to go a little further from the madding crowd and walk the raised river bank in search of common cranes.

The sun always seems to be a factor at Lakenheath as from Joist Fen you are looking directly west into the afternoon sun. Use this to your advantage for backlit harriers hunting the reed beds in evening light.

Barn owl in golden light over Lakenheath Fen. Nikon D800E, 500mm + 1.4 x converter at 700mm, ISO 1600, 1/1250 sec at f/5.6

How To Get Here

RSPB Lakenheath Fen is located 30 miles north east of Cambridge and around 13 miles west of Thetford. From Lakenheath village, go north on B1112 for about 2 miles. Go over the level crossing and after 200 m, turn left into the reserve entrance.

Lakenheath car park Lat/Long: 52.447807, 0.53064018
OS Co-ordinate: TL 720 863
Nearest Postcode: IP27 9AD
Phone: 01842 863400

Rail: At weekends a number of trains on the Norwich-Ely-Cambridge service call at Lakenheath. Check connections on National Rail Enquiries website: **www.nationalrail.co.uk**

Accessibility

Trails range from hard-packed gravel to wet grassland. A full circuit of the reserve is 8 km/ 5 miles but there are shorter walks including a 1.1km 3/4 mile circuit. Some of the trails are wheelchair accessible. Open dawn till dusk.

Best Time of Year/Day

This is good all year round. Booming bitterns can be heard in spring and hobbies are most numerous in May – with up to 40 in the air at any one time. Marsh harriers are present all year and roost in large numbers through the winter.

Above: Marsh Harrier coming in low over New Fen. Nikon D800E, 300mm + 2 x converter at 600mm, ISO 800, 1/1250 sec at f/11

Below: Kingfisher close up at the new Mere Hide. Nikon D800E, 500mm + 1.4 x converter at 700mm, ISO 1000, 1/1600 sec at f/5.6

Bittern *(Botaurus stellaris)*

This secretive and extremely well-camouflaged member of the heron family has a limited in range in the UK. They are mostly found in wetland habitats in southern and eastern England and also at Leighton Moss p.126 in Lancashire. The bird's cryptic colouration and slow silent motion makes it one of the most difficult subjects to locate and photograph. Even at close quarters a motionless bittern is difficult to spot in a reed stand. The bittern has a beautifully evolved habit of standing motionless and sky pointing to increase its camouflage.

Lakenheath is an exceptional location having been developed by the RSPB with bitterns in mind. Your chances of seeing one are much greater here than anywhere in the UK possibly with the exception of Minsmere p.250.

To increase your chances arrive early and stay late. Choose a weekday in the winter, set up with tripod at the Joist Fen viewpoint and stay still and quiet. Distant harrier activity over the reed bed will keep you entertained while you wait.

It is well worth visiting in spring just to hear the bittern's extraordinary booming noise, akin to the sound made by blowing over an empty bottle.

Low evening light catches the eye of the bittern. Nikon D800E, 300mm + 2 x converter at 600mm, ISO 1600, 1/1250 sec at f/9

Bittern stalking the shallows. Nikon D800E, 300mm + 2 x converter at 600mm, ISO 1600, 1/1250 sec at f/9

Wren (Troglodytes troglodytes): a tiny bird with a big voice. Nikon D4, 300mm + 2 x conv at 600mm, ISO 800, 1/1600 sec at f/6.3

Pair of common cranes, possibly 'Little and Large,' one of the resident pairs at Lakenheath. Nikon D4, 300mm + 2 x converter at 600mm, ISO 1250, 1/1250 sec at f/7.1

Right: Male stonechat from Mere Hide. Nikon D800E, 300mm + 2 x converter at 600mm, ISO 1600, 1/1000 sec at f/8

Male kingfisher at Lackford Lakes.
Nikon D4, ISO1600, 600mm, f/9, 1/2000

Lackford Lakes is a wonderful little reserve managed by the Suffolk Wildlife Trust. Best known for its kingfishers, the lakes also attract summer hobbies, early morning stoats and occasional daylight glimpses of barn owls.

Kingfisher (*Alcedo atthis*)

The irridescent kingfisher is a huge draw for the wildlife photographer and this is one of the best places in the country to have a high chance of a sighting. The hides have some well placed perches at fairly close range but, as with all wildlife, there are no guarantees. Great patience may be required as the bird's visits to the fishing perches can be infrequent. You are also unlikely to be alone in your quest here. This is a popular reserve and the hides are likely to be busy at key times of the year.

As elsewhere photographers and other visitors do not always have the same agenda and it can occasionally be frustratingly noisy. It's best to go early or late midweek and avoid weekends when this location may be busy.

See also Upton Warren p.166, Lakenheath Fen p.242 and Strumpshaw Fen p.256.

Anywhere will do to fish from. Nikon D4, 300mm + 2 x converter at 600mm, ISO 1600, 1/2000 sec at f/8

Tortoiseshell butterfly on vipers bugloss. Nikon D4, 300mm + 2 x converter at 600mm, ISO 800, 1/800 sec at f/9

Female kingfisher at Lackford Lakes.
Nikon D800E, ISO1000, 600mm, f/11, 1/1600

Below: Flash of blue, juvenile kingfisher diving. Nikon D4, 300mm +
2 x converter at 600mm, ISO 2000, 1/2000 sec at f/5.6

How To Get Here

The Suffolk Wildlife Trust reserve at Lackford Lakes is located 6 miles
north west of Bury St. Edmonds. Take the A1101 north out of town
to find the reserve signposted after 6 miles on the right hand side.

Lackford Lakes car park Lat/Long: 52.304090, 0.63894260
OS Co-ordinate: TL 800 706
Nearest Postcode: IP28 6HX
Phone: 01284 728706

Accessibility

Hides located around the lakes are accessible from all-weather gravel
tracks suitable for wheelchair access.

Best Time of Year/Day

Kingfishers are present all year round though summer is best when
the young are newly fledged. This is a great reserve for dragonflies
and butterflies in summer, and stoats are frequently spotted especially
early mornings. Hobbies visit only in summer and in winter the reserve
is popular for waterfowl including shoveler, goldeneye and goosander.

Opposite: Long shot. Insert 'no fishing' sign here. Nikon D4, 300mm
+ 2 x converter at 600mm, ISO 1000, 1/1250 sec at f/5.6

Minsmere is the flagship RSPB reserve on the east coast of Suffolk. It's a place that almost has it all for the wildlife photographer. Habitats here include reedbeds, both freshwater and saltwater lagoons, a strip of beach as well as foreshore, heath and woodland. This has been the base for the BBC's 'Springwatch,' boasting species as diverse as red deer, adders, stoats, bitterns, marsh harriers and bearded tit.

Where to look

There is a large visitor centre with staff on hand to inform you of recent sightings. There are many different options here so have an aim in mind and prioritise your route. If time is short head straight for the Bittern Hide and beyond that the Island Mere Hide.

Otherwise, to explore the whole area leave the reception building and walk around to the rear and down towards the North Wall. This track leads over a small pond which does have water vole. This can be a difficult place to photograph as the path is busy and anyone crossing the bridge will usually scare off any voles that may appear. The path leads across heathland offering potential encounters with red deer and heath birds such as stonechat, before passing through reed beds on either side. This can be a great place for bearded tits and marsh harriers passing overhead. Once at the beach the path turns south where you should look out for strikingly marked wasp spiders in the grass.

Water rail stalking amongst the fresh cut reeds. Nikon D4, 300mm + 2 x converter at 600mm, ISO 5000, 1/1250 sec at f/5.6

The East Hide

The East Hide overlooks the scrape which is the best place to photograph waders such as avocets especially in the morning when the sun is behind you.

Following the beach path further south to the sluice, swallows can be found nesting here.

The South Hide

This hide also overlooks the scrape and can be a better option in the afternoon when the sun has moved round.

The walk from here back towards the visitor centre has reed beds down one side and Cetti's warblers can usually be heard singing if not seen on this route.

Once back in the woodland keep an eye out for woodpeckers, muntjac deer and stoats.

The Bittern Hide

This large elevated hide has plenty of space and great views across the reed beds and pools. It may be a good place to see bittern but sightings here tend to be distant, not least because you are quite a height off the ground.

The main path continues through woodland and past fields full of rabbits and occasionally red deer towards the large modern and excellent Island Mere Hide.

Island Mere Hide

This hide has huge easy-to-open windows and a great panoramic view. From here you will likely see marsh harriers hunting, possibly great white egrets at a distance, hear if not see squealing water rails and if you are lucky catch a view of an otter or a fly by, by a bittern.

Female marsh harrier in good light showing off her rich chocolate plumage. From the Island Mere Hide. Nikon D4, 300mm + 2 x converter at 600mm, ISO 800, 1/1600 sec at f/8

Male bearded tit shows off his excellent moustache. A misty morning hence the very high ISO. Nikon D4, 300mm + 2 x converter at 600mm, ISO 5000, 1/1250 sec at f/9

How To Get Here

RSPB Minsmere is located on the Suffolk coast 30 miles north of Ipswich and 22 miles south of Lowestoft. Access is via the A12 turning off at Saxmundham if coming from the south and Blythburgh from the north.

RSPB Minsmere car park Lat/Long: 52.247438, 1.6188902
OS Co-ordinate: TM 471 672
Nearest Postcode: IP17 3BY
Phone: 01728 648281

A bus picks up from the rail station at Darsham and Saxmundham, phone: 01728 833526 to book.

Admission: Free to RSPB members or £8 for adults.

Accessibility

Open dawn till dusk. The reserve has a mix of different paths, both flat and undulating where walks can be enjoyed. Some nature trails and hides are more accessible than others. As with most RSPB sites the tracks are reasonably good for access. Allow for muddy conditions and possibly flooding depending on weather and time of year.

Best Time of Year/Day

Early mornings and late evenings are better for having fewer people and more wildlife. Spring is good for emerging adders and activity from breeding birds like the avocets and bearded tits. Summer is best for harriers hunting the reed beds and juvenile birds increasing the numbers of subjects. Rutting red deer are evident in autumn and bearded tits can become more visible then. Winter is best for bitterns and water rail becoming more visible on the ice. Winter is also the time for murmurations of starlings.

Marsh Harrier (*Circus aeruginosa*)

This large and dramatic bird of prey is now a fairly common and obvious sight around the Fens and Broads and locals nowadays are unlikely to be excited by their appearance. The marsh harrier was once an extremely rare bird in the UK and its welcome return is largely thanks to conservation projects especially by the RSPB to conserve and rebuild wetland reserves such as Minsmere.

The female bird is dark, almost chocolate in plumage with a light coloured head whereas the males are more colourful with tan, silver and grey plumage. Juveniles of both sexes can look similar to the female of the species.

Marsh harriers have a distinctive flight with legs dangling low to snatch unwary prey. At Minsmere they can be seen harrying water birds especially coots which can be panicked and drowned. More frequently they take fledgling birds, snakes and rats.

Watch for mating ritual flights known as skydancing in spring. In nesting season males fly over the nest site causing the females to fly up to meet them for a spectacular food pass in mid air.

See also Lakenheath Fen p.242 and Cley Marshes p.260.

Rainbow from Island Mere Hide. Nikon D800E, 70-200mm at 77mm, ISO 400, 1/250 sec at f/8

Backlit marsh harrier over the reed beds. Nikon D4, 300mm + 2 x converter at 600mm, ISO 800, 1/1250 sec at f/9

Muntjac in the woods. Nikon D4, 300mm + 2 x converter at 600mm, ISO 2500, 1/1250 sec at f/5.6

Spot the Snipe: very well camouflagesd in the sedge. Nikon D4, 300mm + 2 x converter at 600mm, ISO 800, 1/1250 sec at f/7.1

Bittern *(Botaurus stallar)*

This is one of the best places in the country to look for bitterns. The species is well established here and is present all year round. Winter is an excellent time to look for them as when the ground is frozen they can be seen venturing out on the ice. In spring they are often heard and seen in flight as they travel to and from the nest sites.

See also Lakenheath Fen p.242.

The Bittern Hide and Island Mere Hide are the best places to look. Scan the far side of the lagoon for the incredibly well-camouflaged birds hunting on the water's edge, though this will be too distant for anything other than a landscape shot.

In the mornings bitterns seem to fly in from the south eastern end of the reserve.

Top tip

Early morings especially in autumn can be very misty, use a high ISO to allow a faster shutter speed and shoot in RAW to allow for exposure adjustments to reduce the effects of the mist.

Bittern in the mist: ghosts of silver birch trees in the background. Nikon D4, 300mm + 2 x converter at 600mm, ISO 5000, 1/1600 sec at f/5.6

Dunwich Heath is a stone's throw from RSPB Minsmere, just walking distance in fact. Well worth a visit, this area of heathland and pine wood is managed by the National Trust. The heathland is home to the endangered and protected Dartford warbler. Red deer roam here all year round and in winter short-eared owls hunt over the heather.

Dartford warbler *(Sylvia undata)*

Smartly dressed in metallic grey head plumage and rusty red on the chest, this characterful little bird is rare and can be tricky to photograph. Whilst classic photographs portray the male bird perched outstanding on gorse bushes, the bird is flighty and fast moving and prefers to remain unobserved in thick undergrowth. In early spring (February onwards) the males start to proclaim their territory and this can be the best opportunity to photograph them. Be aware however that as a schedule one bird it is illegal to disturb them especially during the breeding season.

Technique

First familiarise yourself with the Dartford warbler's call; the soft *churr churr* sound is the easiest way to find them. Territorial males will be in full song in spring.

From the car park go down past the toilet blocks and walk in a big loop listening carefully. There is a dilemma here as the birds are elusive and wary of people; either pick a spot you know is good territory and stay very still and quiet with tripod mounted camera and wait for the birds to come to you or keep walking with hand held set up and hope for random encounters.

The birds do turn up unexpectedly at the path side but you need to be fast on the draw to get a decent image. Keep the shutter speed fast, up to around 1/1250 second, to avoid motion blur when hand holding the camera.

Weekdays and early mornings are best to avoid dog walkers and family outings.

Red deer on the lookout. Nikon D4, 300mm + 2 x converter at 600mm, ISO 800, 1/1250 sec at f/11

Dunwich Heath in February sunshine.
Nikon D800E, 70-200mm at 145mm, ISO 640, 1/640 sec at f/11

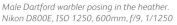

Male Dartford warbler posing in the heather.
Nikon D800E, ISO 1250, 600mm, f/9, 1/1250

Dartford warbler perched on bracken stalks. Nikon D4, 300mm +
2 x converter at 600mm, ISO 1600, 1/1250 sec at f/8

How To Get Here

Dunwich Heath is only a mile and a half walking from Minsmere but 4.6 miles by car.

Dunwich Heath car park Lat/Long: 52.252364, 1.6265586
OS Co-ordinate: TM 476 677
Nearest Postcode: IP17 3DJ
Phone: 01728 648501

Accessibility

Open dawn till dusk. Trails are varied with some accessible routes but with slopes, undulating terrain and uneven paths with some soft sand and off-road footpaths across heathland.

Best Time of Year/Day

Visit in early spring (February onwards) to see Dartford warblers singing. The red deer rut occurs in autumn from October until early November. In summer the heath is a beautiful location with purple heather and yellow gorse in flower. As usual early morning is good for light and less disturbance from other visitors.

Strumpshaw Fen is a wonderful RSPB fenland reserve which in summer is buzzing with insects especially dragonflies and butterflies. These include the rare and exotic swallowtail butterfly. The reed beds are hunted over by marsh harriers and hobbies and home to the secretive Chinese water deer. The friendly staff are happy to let you know the latest sightings and point you in the right direction.

Swallowtail butterfly *(Papilionidae)*

This really is a spectacular native species. Larger than you might expect and beautifully marked and coloured, they may not be easy to find however. Choose a warm sunny day in June and try the Meadow Trail or walk right around the reserve to the cottage at the top of Tinker's Lane where the owners sometimes allow photography of the butterflies in their garden. Please ask first.

Kingfisher *(Alcedo atthis)*

See also Upton Warren p.166 and Lackford Lakes p.248.

Here the kngfishers are a regular sighting from the Fen Hide. The perches are rather distant for full frame shots but good for 'small in the frame' type shots.

Chinese water deer *(Hydropotes inermis)*

These are a non-native species. This peculiar looking deer loves marshland habitat and is now resident in the Fens and Broads. Tusk like canine teeth are characteristic as is a fluffy coat giving its face a teddy bear like appearance. Chinese water deer are secretive and shy but regularly seen at dusk and dawn.

Where to look

On arrival at the reserve the main viewpoint next to the reception building is a good spot to start. Kingfishers, marsh harriers and hobbies are all likely here.

Folllow the orange trail to access the meadow which is full of orchids in June. Keep an eye out for the rare Norfolk hawker dragonfies which are brown with green eyes and 'hawk' the ditches.

Further round follow the purple route markers for the Fen Hide (first turn on the right). This is a great hide for kingfishers, marsh harriers and possibly otter and bittern. The sun is behind you for much of the day which is ideal for spotting and photography.

The Tower Hide further on offers more distant views but can be good for hobbies rushing by in pursuit of dragonflies.

Hobby hunting out of a blue sky, image from Otmoor. Nikon D4, 300mm + 2 x converter at 600mm, ISO 2000, 1/3200 sec at f/13

Fenland reeds and water lillies. Nikon D800E, 17-35mm at 35mm, ISO250, 1/320 sec at f/11

The shy and elusive Chinese water deer. Nikon D4, 300mm + 2 x converter at 600mm, ISO 1600, 1/1000 sec at f/10

Above: Swallowtail butterfly. Nikon D4, 300mm + 2 x converter at 600mm, ISO 1000, 1/1250 sec at f/5.6

Below: Sedge warbler are common at Strumpshaw, pictured here with damselflies at Otmoor. Nikon D4, 300mm + 2 x converter at 600mm, ISO 1600, 1/1600 sec at f/91/1600

How To Get Here

RSPB Strumpshaw Fen is located near the village of Brundall, 10 miles east of Norwich on the banks of the River Yare.

Dunwich Heath car park Lat/Long: 52.607091, 1.4567305
OS Co-ordinate: TG 341 066
Nearest Postcode: NR134HS
Phone: 01603 715191

Accessibility

Entry to the reserve involves crossing an active railway line. If you have mobility difficulties, poor vision, or will take time to cross, please use the phone at the crossing gate to check for trains. There are numerous trails around the reserve, most paths are uneven and some are prone to flooding in winter. Reception Hide has a wheelchair-accessible viewing area, the other two hides have steps.

Best Time of Year/Day

Any day is a good day to be at Strumpshaw Fen. In spring courting pairs of marsh harriers can be seen performing their spectacular 'sky-dancing' displays. The reserve comes alive with the songs of spring migrants including sedge and reed warblers, cuckoos, grasshopper warblers and whitethroats. In summer hobbies can be spotted hunting dragonflies and marsh harriers bringing food to their young. Spectacular swallowtail butterflies can be seen late May to early July and again in mid-August. In autumn ospreys stop off to fish on their southward migration. This is also a good time for kingfishers and bearded tits.

Sculthorpe Moor is a great little reserve located in the north of Norfolk. It is recognised both nationally and internationally as important for its wildlife. Located in the beautiful Wensum Valley, it is managed by the Hawk and Owl Trust. The reserve is home to a rich variety of wildlife in its woodland, fen and reed bed habitats including marsh harriers, kingfishers, water vole and barn owl amongst many other species.

Where to look

As usual the helpful friendly staff at the information office will have the latest information on what is happening on the reserve. My advice would be to head for the outermost parts of the reserve, this takes you away from most of the other visitors and it is possible to find some peace and quiet in the furthest hides overlooking the scrape. In late summer this is a great place to see kingfishers (see also Upton Warren p.166 and Lackford Lakes p.248) and is also very close to a regular nesting spot for marsh harriers.

See also Lakenheath Fen p.242 and Cley Marshes p.260.

Kingfisher hovering. Nikon D800E, 300mm +
2 x converter at 600mm, ISO 1250, 1/1250 sec at f/9

Technique

This is one of those places where you never know exactly what you might see so its worth taking a range of lenses and equipment. The hides are all good but there is not always room for tripods so a bean bag is more practical for bigger lenses. The kingfishers and barn owls especially are likely to be reasonably distant so a good telephoto lens is best.

From the deck walkways there are also great opportunities to spot water vole in the ditches below. Go quietly especially at evening time to look for these feeding on water plants. Look for chewed plants and listen carefully for munching sounds as they are often easier to hear than see. See also East Malling p.234 and Rainham Marshes p.232. The barn owl typically hunts the far section of the reserve and can be seen at dusk and dawn. See also Titchwell Marsh p.262.

How To Get Here

Sculthorpe Moor is located 21 miles east of King's Lynn and just off the A148 2 miles west of Fakenham in North Norfolk.

Sculthorpe Moor car park Lat/Long: 52.838712, 0.81940820
OS Co-ordinate: TF 899 305
Nearest Postcode: NR21 9GN
Phone: 01328 856788

Accessibility

'The entire reserve has been designed with a step free philosophy in mind. All raised areas and hides are accessible by ramps and boardwalks. Viewing platforms provide areas where visitors can view the river wildlife, hides have windows designed at a lower height with areas where people can place their wheelchair.'

Further afield some paths across fen banks are a little rough.

Reserve opening times: April to Mid October 8 am – 6 pm, November to March 8 am – 4 pm

Best Time of Year/Day

Spring sees the return of the marsh harriers, water rails calling, barn owls hunting and woodpeckers drumming. In summer look out for fledgelings including barn owls, hobbies hunting over the reed beds, butterflies, moths and dragonflies, young marsh harriers and sparrowhawks. The harriers leave in the autumn but siskin and redpoll return, also look out for fieldfares and redwings. Winter is good to catch some action at the feeders and roosting long-eared owls.

Barn owl hovering over the reed bed. Nikon D800E, 300mm + 2 x converter at 600mm, ISO 640, 1/1000 sec at f/5.6

Kingfisher on the scrape from the Paul Johnson Hide. Nikon D800E, 300mm + 2 x converter at 600mm, ISO 800, 1/1250 sec at f/5.6

Situated on the north Norfolk coast and a short drive along the coast from the next location at Titchwell Marsh is the Norfolk Willdlife Trust Reserve at Cley. An impressive new eco-friendly visitor centre houses a large cafe and shop and sells tickets to access the reserve. The cafe is a good place from which, with binoculars or scope, to look for signs of life out on the lagoons whilst enjoying tea and chocolate cake.

Where to look

From the car park cross the road and turn right (east) to follow the track down to Bishop's Hide. This overlooks a wetland area favoured by godwits and other waders.

Alternatively having crossed the road follow the track to the left (west) and down to the group of hides there.

Marsh Harrier *(Circus aeruginosa)*

Along the West Bank path can be a great spot to catch a hunting marsh harrier passing high overhead The female pictured right known as Goldie is a common sight around the centre of the marsh and is typical of the harrier sightings here in Norfolk where locals are so used to this once extremely endangered bird that they seldom give it a second glance. See also Lakenheath p.242 and Minsmere p.250 for more on marsh harriers.

Black-tailed Godwit *(Limosa limosa)*

This is a very photogenic wader with large bill and attractive plumage. The adult has orange-brown on the head and chest in breeding season, they are especially attractive in flight.

Male marsh harrier out of the blue. Nikon D4, 300mm + 2 x converter at 600mm, ISO 500, 1/1250 sec at f/8

Female marsh harrier known as 'Goldie.' Nikon D4, 500mm + 1.4 converter at 700mm, ISO 1250, 1/1250 at f/13

Waders in low light at Cley. Nikon D800E, 300mm + 2 x converter at 600mm, ISO 2500, 1/1250 sec at f/9

Male marsh harrier winging it over the reed beds. Nikon D4, 300mm + 2 x converter at 600mm, ISO 500, 1/1250 sec at f/8

Below: Black tailed godwit stretching at Farmoor Reservoir, Oxfordshire. Nikon D800E, 300mm + 2 x converter at 600mm, ISO 640, 1/1250 sec at f/9

How To Get Here

NWT Cley Marshes is Norfolk Wildlife Trust's oldest and best known nature reserve. Located on the north Norfolk coast on the A149 coast road, 4 miles north of Holt. The visitor centre and car park are located directly across the A149 coast road from the car park.

Cley Marshes car park Lat/Long: 52.954304, 1.0548620
OS Grid Reference: TG 053 440
Nearest Postcode: NR25 7SA
Phone: 01263 740008

The Coast Hopper bus service stops just outside the nature reserve:
www.coasthopper.co.uk

Accessibility

Reserve open dawn till dusk. To get to the trails and hides you initially need to cross a major road. Once across, the trails are well surfaced to the hides with access for wheelchairs. Away from the main trails the going is soft, wet and can be muddy.

Best Time of Year/Day

In spring look out for sky dancing marsh harriers and bearded tit nesting activity. Autumn is good to catch the bearded tits as the families move from feeding on insects to the reed seeds at the top of the reed stems. In winter, waders and waterfowl gather on the lagoons. Short-eared and barn owls can be seen out on the marshes in late autumn and winter.

Titchwell Marsh is located a short distance down the coast from Snettisham (next location). This is an extremely popular flagship RSPB reserve and is a mixed marshland reserve. The facilities here are very good including cafe and shop. There is an area of beach well worth visiting for shore birds. The huge well-designed Parrinder Hides overlook the freshwater and salt marshes. Large windows can be opened easily allowing wide views of the lagoons. This is a great place to photograph waders such as spotted redshank and snipe and waterfowl such as the common but vividly coloured teal.

Where to look

Close up opportunities for birds such as snipe, little egret and godwit are easy enough from the well travelled West Bank footpath that leads past the main lagoons to the sea wall. Although views can be at close quarters this is a raised walkway and creates difficult angles for photography as you find yourself looking down on top of the subject rather than being at a more desirable eye level. Try to get as low as possible and use a longer focal length on birds some distance away.

The Parrinder Hide overlooking the salt marsh lagoon. Nikon D4, 70-200mm at 105mm, ISO 250, 1/200 sec at f/14

Whilst the first main lagoon is known as the Freshwater Marsh, with high tidal surges this can be flooded with seawater changing the environment drastically. Normally this area is home to flocks of teal, lapwing and avocets.

Beyond the dividing Parrinder Wall (on which the huge Parrinder Hide sits) an area of saltwater marsh offers a different environment attractive to birds such as shelduck and spotted redshank.

Drake teal dabbling. Nikon D800E, 300mm + 2 x converter at 600mm, ISO 1000, 1/1000 sec at f/7.1

The big advantage of the West Bank path (the raised footpath that leads to the sea) is that you are given excellent views over the reedbeds.

In winter these are hunted over by barn owl and short-eared owl. Both hen and marsh harriers can be seen from here especially in winter evenings and mornings as they move to and from their roost sites.

Bearded tits are sometimes seen in the reeds especially in the autumn so keep an ear out for the pinging contact call. Look out for the Island Hide which is a smaller wooden hide overlooking the lagoon which benefits from a much lower viewpoint. This can allow very close views of waders including ruff and godwit as well as a different angle if the sun is too direct on the Parrinder Hide.

Snipe probing the soft mud in the freshwater marsh. Nikon D800E, 300mm + 2 x conv at 600mm, ISO 1000, 1/1000 sec at f/7.1

Below right: Ruff feeding in the shallows.Nikon D800E, 300mm + 2 x converter at 600mm, ISO 400, 1/1250 sec at f/6.3

How To Get Here

Titchwell Marsh is located on the north Norfolk coast 22 miles north of King's Lynn and 6 miles east of Hunstanton, just off the A419.

Titchwell Marsh car park Lat/Long: 52.963008, 0.60413926
OS Grid Reference: TF 750 438
Nearest Postcode: PE31 8ED
Phone: 01485 210779

The Coast Hopper bus runs between King's Lynn and Cromer once every hour, 7 days a week. **www.coasthopper.co.uk**

Accessibility

All major paths are level and made of compacted aggregate or boardwalk suitable for wheelchairs. The short boardwalk to the beach however is often sandy and access may not be possible for visitors with limited mobility.

Best Time of Year/Day

Something is usually happening here all year round. Sunlight direction, as with many hides, can be an issue and from afternoon to late evening the freshwater side of the hide is looking directly towards the sun making photography difficult.

Space can be at a premium at busy times and there's not always room to squeeze a tripod in.

Barn owl *(Tyto alba)*

Alongside marsh harriers, the county of Norfolk is widely regarded as the best place in the country to see and photograph the beautifully photogenic and endangered barn owl. Titchwell is a good place to hope for a sighting.

Walking along the main West Bank path at dusk especially in the autumn and winter is the best place to spot these wonderful birds as they quarter the reed beds and fields.

This whole part of Norfolk is good for barn owls and it is worth following the roads around Titchwell at dusk to try and locate suitable fields.

See also Sculthorpe Moor p.258 for barn owls.

Little egret *(Egretta garzetta)*

Once an unusual sight in the UK these are now a fairly common species at many wetland reserves. This small and elegant white heron is an interesting subject especially when hunting its prey of small fish and insects.

Technique

Exposure can be difficult with these all white birds. Check the histograms to make sure the plumage is not overexposed and be prepared to compensate.

Consider bracketing exposures and always shoot in RAW to allow you the greatest latitude in post-processing.

Above: Little egret snacking on small fish. Nikon D800E, 300mm + 2 x converter at 600mm, ISO 500, 1/1600 sec at f/10

Another post-processing tip for birds or animals in or near water is to clean up the water surface using the spot removal to take out floating debris. This leaves a background that is free of distractions.

Barn owl quartering the salt marsh at Titchwell. Nikon D800E, 300mm + 2 x converter at 600mm, ISO 3200, 1/1000 sec at f/5.6

Above: Little egret stalking the freshwater lagoon. Nikon D800E, 300mm + 2 x converter at 600mm, ISO 500, 1/1600 sec at f/8

Below: Along the shore: oystercatchers on the wing. Nikon D800E, 300mm + 2 x converter at 600mm, ISO 800, 1/1600 sec at f/9

Where to look

A third ecosystem of pebble beach and mud flats is located further towards the sea and is home to waders such as sanderling, turnstone and oystercatchers.

Technique

Shore birds such as egrets are easy to approach slowly and quietly on foot to a certain point when they will take flight and move further along the coast. The shore line can be muddy with deep pools and to avoid disturbance these are best photographed from a distance with a tripod and large focal length lens. Be aware of tide times, it's better to set up at a distance and wait for the incoming tide to bring the birds towards you.

Top tip

High key and black and white images work well to depict the wildness of the shoreline. This effect can be applied post production using software such as Lightroom or Photoshop.

Below: Down on the beach: Turnstone in black and white. Nikon D800E, 300mm + 2 x converter at 600mm, ISO 800, 1/1600 sec at f/8

A deceit of golden plover at Snettisham:
Nikon D4, 300mm + 2 x converter at 600mm, ISO 1600, 1/1000 sec at f/16

Snettisham is home to two of the UK's great wildlife spectacles. On high tides tens of thousands of wading birds are displaced off their feeding grounds by the rising tide and onto the banks and islands in front of the RSPB hides. At dawn and dusk in midwinter thousands of pink-footed geese fly in V-formation between their inland feeding grounds and their night time roost on the mud flats.

What to expect

Large flocks of golden plover and knot gather to feed on the exposed mud flats of the estuary. At high tide the flocks are sometimes forced up over the shingle beach to small lagoons where they roost and await the retreat of the tide. The hides here overlook the roost site and are a great place to photograph roosting waders close up.

Be aware that not every high tide will push the waders into the lagoon. Don't be disappointed if this does not happen since the waders can still be viewed out on the mudflats where they make for spectacular images as they fly in fascinatingly large swirling flocks.

Technique

Time your visit for a high tide but take heed of storm warnings, the area can flood. The incoming tide approaches extremely rapidly across the mudflats, be aware of this. Arrive under cover of darkness to witness the spectacle of thousands of waders at close quarters.

Below: Lone oystercatcher with a storm of knot.
Nikon D800E, 500mm + 1.4 x converter at 700mm, ISO 1600, 1/2000 at f/6.3

How To Get Here

RSPB Snettisham is located on the north Norfolk coastline 5 miles south of Hunstanton. The reserve is clearly signposted down Beach Road from the A149 Snettisham and Dersingham bypass. Continue down Beach Road for about 1.5 miles, and the reserve car park is signposted on your left.

Snettisham car park Lat/Long: 52.963008, 0.45208097
OS Grid Reference: TF651329
Nearest Postcode: PE31 7PS

Accessibility

There are no facilities here and following storm surge damage in 2014 some of the former hides were damaged. These are now being replaced with the key viewpoint at the far end of Pit 4 reinstated, check the RSPB website for updates.

Two hides and part of the Loop trail have been adapted for wheelchair use. Some narrow paths can be difficult. There is a danger of flooding with high tides.

Best Time of Year/Day

For the wader spectacle it's best to be here 30-90 minutes before high tide between August and January. Pink-footed geese fly over an hour or so after dawn from mid-November to late January. See the RSPB website for tide timess and best viewing times.

Dawn at Snettisham, mixed waders in the foreground, plover in the air with pink-footed geese incoming in the distance. Nikon D4, 300mm + 2 x converter at 600mm, ISO 6400, 1/1000 sec at f/8

Below: Golden plover in March changing from winter to summer plumage. Nikon D4, 300mm + 2 x converter at 600mm, ISO 6400, 1/1000 sec at f/14

South West England – Introduction

The South West of England is a relatively small area of land with a lot of coastline. The central land mass rises up to the north coast to form the Exmoor National Park, an area of windswept moorland with steep-sided river and stream valleys or combes. Pockets of deciduous woodland are found here where redstarts and flycatchers nest in summer, and dippers and grey wagtails hunt in the fast flowing streams. The higher moors are the rutting ground of the spectacular red deer which can be elusive and a challenge to photograph, especially compared to the relatively relaxed specimens found in Richmond Park.

The coastline is hugely varied as are the species found there. From rugged cliff outcrops like Baggy Point where ravens fly over to gorse heaths where stonechats and meadow pipits hunt to the muddy estuaries and their large populations of waders and wildfowl.

At Exmouth the River Exe issues out into the sea depositing its suspended sediment to form mud banks. These are an important feeding point for flocks of waders including the striking black and white avocet with its amazing upturned bill and black tailed godwits which are spectacular in flight.

Further out to sea around Lundy Island grey seals bob amongst the waves and the comical puffins that were once far more common are struggling to make a comeback.

A patchwork of arable farmland from Croydon Hill, Somerset.
Nikon D800E, 70-200mm at 140mm, ISO 1600, 1/640 sec at f/13

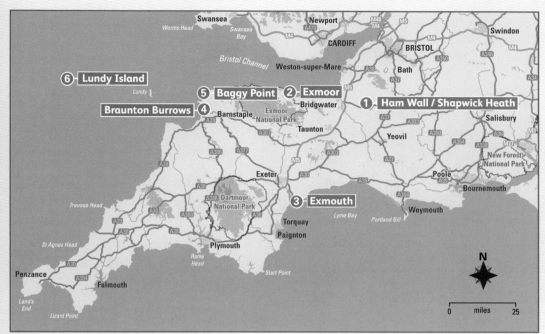

Map; Contains Ordnance Survey data © Crown Copyright and database right (2016)

SOUTH WEST ENGLAND

Glastonbury Tor from Ham Wall

Located on the Somerset Levels in sight of Glastonbury Tor, the National Nature Reserve of Shapwick Heath is immediately opposite the RSPB reserve of Ham Wall. Both are large places and the wide track, especially through Shapwick Heath, makes it a good option to use a bicycle to access the different hides.

The reserves are home to bitterns, marsh harriers, kingfishers and otters. As subjects these are fairly elusive and sometimes distant subjects for the photographer so whilst keeping an eye open for them it is an opportunity to work closely with some of the more common species.

Great Crested Grebe *(Podiceps cristatus)*

The great crested grebe is one of the country's most elegant water birds with the bonus of a unique and interesting courtship display. The courtship involves mimicry and complex head shaking, sky pointing, preening and sometimes the male will delicately offer pond weed or feathers to the female.Courtship typically takes place in early spring, especially prior to and during nest building. In early summer the stripey youngsters take piggy back rides on the parent's backs backs making for some great photo opportunities.

Great crested grebe courtship ritual. Image from Farmoor Reservoir Oxfordshire. Canon EOS 1 Ds Mark ii , 300mm + 2 x converter at 600mm, ISO 400, 1/500 sec at f/14f14, 1/500

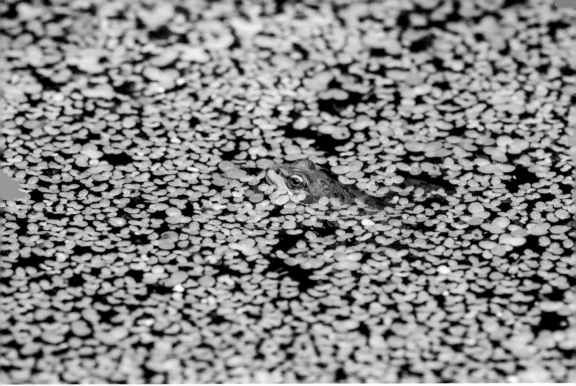

Marsh frog in the duck weed. Nikon D4, 300mm + 2 x converter at 600mm, ISO 3200, 1/1250 sec at f/11

Where to look

Park at the car park which effectively serves both reserves, this is within walking distance of the Railway Inn. Note there are no other facilities here and the pub is not always open. If visiting Shapwick Heath first follow the main track along the waterway to the first bridge. Keep an eye out for marsh harriers overhead on this stretch and waders on the scrape though these will be distant for photography.

At the bridge you can turn left through woodland to Noah's Hide which is best for views of water birds, especially great white egrets and, with lots of luck, you may see otters too. This hide faces towards the sun in the afternoon.

From the car park if heading for Ham Wall, cross the road and the track again follows a waterway to the first platform viewpoint which is theoretically good for sightings of bittern and harriers. Following the footpath further and taking a right turn leads down to the Loxtons Screen. This is a great place for grebes, kingfishers and occasionally bittern.

Ham wall is also famous for the autumn/winter starling murmuration, the location of which can change on a daily basis. For more information on locating this there is a starling murmuration hotline: see grey box information. For more murmuration locations see Gretna Green p.92.

Above: Great white egret photographed at Otmoor RSPB. Nikon D4, 300mm + 2 x conv at 600mm, ISO 640, 1/1250 sec at f/5.6

How To Get Here

RSPB Ham Wall and Shapwick Heath are located 5 miles west of Glastonbury and 10 miles east of Junction 23 on the M5.

Ham Wall car park Lat/Long: 51.153548, -2.789624
OS Co-ordinate: ST 448 396
Nearest Postcode: BA6 9SX
The Avalon Marshes Starling Hotline: 07786 554142

Accessibility

Both locations have wide easy access with flat trails and some boardwalks. Some trails are suitable for cycling. Some hides have steps but also some flat viewing platforms for disabled access.

Best Time of Year/Day

Spring is best for courtship displays and November to February is best for starling murmurations.

Trapped between the Atlantic coast to the north and the rolling Devonshire farmland to the south, the high moorland of Exmoor is a truly wild and wonderful upland. Creating its own weather it is frequently windy and wet or clad in thick mist. Exmoor's wildlife has been hunted for centuries and has adapted to survive conditions here by being wild, rugged and untamed.

Red deer *(Cervus elaphus)*

Having already talked about the red deer at Richmond Park in London (p.218) it may seem unnecessary to cover them again here. The red deer on Exmoor are however a different kettle of fish. They have been hunted for centuries and even now with the recent banning of hunting mammals with hounds, the deer on this moor are not only wild but timid and extremely difficult to approach closely. Photographing deer here requires either good luck or extreme patience and good field skills.

It's all a bit of a laugh for the Exmoor ponies.
Nikon D800E, 300mm, ISO 1000, 1/800 sec at f/2.8

Technique

As elsewhere a good time to look for red deer is during the annual autumn rut. Essential equipment are a map and a pair of binoculars. The deer here are highly mobile and roam across a vast area including private farmland which you cannot access. The deer also roam down to the sea on steep inaccessible sea cliffs.

First scope out the area with binoculars either early morning or late evening. Stags are territorial so once they have set up a territory they will try to defend that area and the hinds within it. Though an impressive size the deer are beautifully camouflaged here and can be easily missed. Sound is your friend and you may well hear a stag roaring before you pick out either him or his hinds.

The next step is check the wind. Basic stalking techniques, as a ghillie would use to hunt a stag, are essential to get close. There is no point approaching with the wind behind you, you will disturb the herd and they will disappear. Keep a low profile, stick to gullies and low points and be prepared to walk a long way in a circular track to come in from the right direction with the wind in your face. Note, on Exmoor the wind usually blows in from the sea, though this is not always the case.

Camouflage clothing is good but pointless if you stand out on a skyline or approach with the wind behind you.

How To Get Here

Use an OS map to locate suitable streams for dippers and research footpaths for access. Red deer roam over huge areas so pinpointing locations is always going to be a problem. Good bases to start from include Simonsbath and Porlock. Suggested places to look:

Exford Common Lat/Long: 51.152291, -3.6394948
OS Co-ordinate: SS 854 405
Nearest Postcode: TA24 7NU (800m)

Dunkery Beacon car park Lat/Long: 51.166078, -3.5692424
OS Co-ordinate: SS 903 419
Nearest Postcode: TA24 7EE

Map: Ordnance Survey Explorer OL9 (1:25000): Map of Exmoor.

Numerous local operators do red deer safaris, check the internet for information. The Porlock Visitor Centre organise 'Rutting Weekends' in autumn, booking is essential. **Phone:** 01643 865150.

Accessibility

Exmoor is typically rough heath and moorland often with stream crossings and bogs. Good outdoor clothing including waterproof boots are recommended.

Best Time of Year/Day

Red deer are present all year round with the rut starting in late September, or later if it remains mild, and continuing until early November. October is the best time to witness the rut. Dippers are present all year round.

Opposite: Close encounter of the herd kind. Nikon D800E, 500mm + 1.4 x converter at 700mm, ISO 1000, 1/1250 sec at f/9

Above: A good-sized herd with two stags and several hinds beautifully camouflaged on the moor. Nikon D800E, 500mm + 1.4 x converter at 700mm, ISO 1600, 1/1250 sec at f13

Below: A quiet approach with the wind in your face can get you really close to a hidden stag. Nikon D800E, 500mm + 1.4 x converter at 700mm, ISO 640, 1/1250 sec at f/5.6

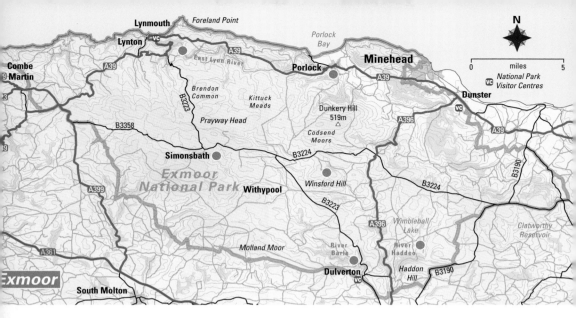

The story behind the picture

It took a few scouting trips to work out where the deer were gathering. It was a little early in the season for the rut and the stags were not yet roaring. Spotting a distant group of deer laid up in the bracken we trekked over the moor down into a combe, across a stream and approached amongst some thick gorse and bracken. An outlying hind was lying closer than I thought and spotted us, as we took the first shots she spooked and led the herd down into thicker cover.

Staying up high and remaining quiet we were able to get some good shots from across the combe as they emerged and resumed grazing on the far bank.

The following day returning to the same spot we again struggled to find the deer even with binoculars. Eventually finding some distant hinds on the horizon we took a circuitous route with the wind in our faces, following the low ground to come up below the hinds.

Suddenly close by I spotted the two prongs of antlers sticking out of the bracken, (image below left). Remaining quiet I stayed still with camera mounted on the tripod. After around twenty minutes I saw a dog walker approaching and signalled to her to please stay away and walk around the spot where the stag lay. The stag however scented the dog and arose from his bed of bracken (see image previous page).

Giving the dog and then this photographer a disdainful glare he rose higher from the bracken showing his impressive size then moved off taking his hinds who had been totally hidden with him.

Game over, the herd scents people and heads off. Nikon D800E, 500mm + 1.4 x converter at 700mm, ISO 1600, 1/1250 sec at f/5.6

The fast running streams that pour down from the moors towards the sea are picturesque and rewarding locations to photograph. The waters run rapidly and noisily through narrow cuts in the steep sided wooded valleys or combes. The deciduous woodland is home to pied flycatchers and redstarts in summer and the streams are the haunt of dippers and grey wagtails.

Where to look

Most of the fast flowing streams flowing off Exmoor are good dipper territory; The Haddeo and East Lynn Rivers around Dulverton and the River Barle are all known dipper hotspots.

Technique

The wooded river valleys are difficult for lighting so use as high an ISO as necessary to get the required shutter speed to prevent camera shake but hopefully without compromising image quality. A low angle is good and this may involve getting wet. Do not chase the birds up and down river, they have favourite territories and if you stay still and quiet in a good place they will come to you.

*Above: Two rivers come together at Watersmeet.
Nikon D800E, 17-35mm at 19mm, ISO 1000, 1/400 sec at f/8*

Ruffled feathers: dippers need to preen regularly to preserve their water repellant plumage. Nikon D4, 300mm + 2 x converter at 600mm, ISO 1600, 1/1000 sec at f/5.6

Right: Dipper in the stream at dawn. Nikon D4, 300mm + 2 x converter at 600mm, ISO 4000, 1/1000 sec at f/5.6

The river Exe flows out into the sea at Topsham near Exeter. Heavy with mud and silt from the Devon countryside the river runs wide and sluggish into the salt water and deposits its sediments on vast mud flats. These provide rich pickings for waders such as avocet and black-tailed godwit which flock here especially in winter.

The RSPB runs boat trips down the tidal river to view the birds at closer quarters and one current option is a specialised photography trip. This has limited departures and needs booking well in advance. Alternatively by knowing the tides and the birds' habits you can often get fairly good views as they come closer to land on rising tides.

What to expect

An early start is required for the photography trips which start under cover of darkness to allow photographers to be in-situ for the rising sun. Tripods now appear to be not permitted but would be awkward and limited in the small open boat and a handheld setup is more flexible. Allow for fast shutter speeds to compensate for the instability.

After the boat trip it is worth taking a walk along the estuary as there may be opportunities for viewing the avocets from the shore. Keep an eye on the tide coming in however.

Avocet *(Recurvirostra avosetta)*

A beautifully marked black and white wading bird with the distinctive upcurved bill. The avocet features as the emblem for the RSPB and is regarded as an example of a great conservation success. As with other black and white subjects images can look really striking if desaturated as a monochrome photograph.

Avocets at rest. Nikon D4, 300mm + 2 x converter at 600mm, ISO 1600, 1/1000 sec at f/8

Godwits in silhouette at sunrise. Nikon D800E, 70-200mm at 135mm, ISO 5000, 1/320 sec at f/13

How To Get Here

Leave the M5 at J30 and follow the A376 to Topsham. There are two pay and display car parks: Holman Way car park and the Quay car park, these car parks can fill up very quickly.

Topsham Quay car park Lat/Long: 50.680828, -3.4648106
OS Co-ordinate: SX 966 878
Nearest Postcode: EX3 0JH

Accessibility

The RSPB boat trips leave from Topsham harbour aboard the Sea Dream boat which takes 40 passengers. Access from the jetty to/ from the boat can present difficulties, a degree of mobility (assisted if necessary) is required for boarding the boat. Wheelchair users should contact the skipper prior to booking. **Phone:** 01392 432691

Best Time of Year/Day

The RSPB boat trips run from early November to late February coinciding with the arrival of the avocets and other species.

Cormorant on the river Exe. Nikon D4, 300mm + 2 x converter at 600mm, ISO 1600, 1/2000 sec at f/5.6

The distinctive upturned bill of the avocet, taken at the Flashes, Upton Warren. Nikon D4, 500mm, ISO 320, 1/1600 sec at f/9

Black-tailed godwits in flight. Nikon D4, 300mm + 2 x converter at 600mm, ISO 1600, 1/1000 sec at f/9

An unexpected bonus; A pair of red-breasted mergansers. Nikon D4, 300mm + 2 x conv at 600mm, ISO 1600, 1/1000 sec at f/10

On the north coast of Devon close to the town of Barnstaple and the village of Braunton lies this wild and exposed strip of sand dunes, the largest dune system in the UK. Part of the North Devon UNESCO Biosphere Reserve, an SAC (Special Area of Conservation), SSSI (Site of Special Scientific Interest) and an army training ground, it is also a fantastic place for a wildlife photographer.

What To Expect

From the car park in Sandy Lane a maze of tracks lead out through scrubby woodland into the dunes and towards the sea.

The scrubland is a good place for birds like whitethroat, stonechats and linnet. The scrub gives way to an area of marsh with small freshwater pools or slacks and beyond this rising high towards the coast are the impressive sand dunes covered in marram grass and bramble thickets. The dunes are pockmarked with rabbit burrows which give the area its name.

In spring the close-cropped grass areas browsed by the rabbits become spotted with colour from a wide array of rare and beautiful wildflowers: viper's bugloss, hemp agrimony, valerian and fleabane all burst into flower.

The early flowers draw in a cloud of butterflies and moths, with common blue and fritillaries mixing with the exotic hummingbird hawk moth. In early spring sunshine adders can be seen basking on the dunes.

The sand dunes of Braunton Burrows in the foreground looking out across the Taw Estuary to Appledore.

Whitethroat singing on a blue sky day. Nikon D4, 300mm + 2 x converter at 600mm, ISO 800, 1/1600 sec at f/10

A big male adder basking in the dunes. Nikon D800E, 300mm + 2 x converter at 600mm, ISO 640, 1/1250 sec at f/6.3

How To Get Here

Braunton is located 6 miles west of Barnstaple in the north west of Devon. Sandy Lane car park is a further 2.5 miles to the south west. Take the B3231 west out of Braunton for 0.8 miles then turn left on Moor Lane then left again after a further 0.8 miles onto Sandy Lane to find the car park after 0.8 miles.

Sandy Lane car park Lat/Long: 51.094474, -4.199793
OS Co-ordinate: SS 463 350
Nearest Postcode: EX33 2NU

Accessibility

Sandy footpaths access most of the dunes. The dunes themselves are hard work to cross. It is easy to get lost here as there are few landmarks. As you leave the car park take a bearing point on the low Devon hills behind you to help orientate your return.

Best Time of Year/Day

Warm February mornings are good for adders. The dunes have a huge variety of flowering plants and these are best from late spring right through the summer. Low carpets of aromatic purple thyme mingle with pink-flowered restharrow, the delicate lemon yellow of mouse-ear hawkweed, striking blue spikes of viper's bugloss and amazing numbers of pyramidal orchids.

On a sunny day, butterflies such as marbled whites, graylings, ringlets and skippers are plentiful.

Adder *(Vipera berus)*

See also Greenham Common p.196.

The adders here are difficult to find and some field skills are required. As always with wildlife a chance encounter on the sandy tracks is a possibility, but if not expect to do some legwork and spend time to get a decent shot.

Timing is crucial; the first warm days in spring are best, a warm sunny February day is ideal. Aim for the remoter dunes, often those with bramble thickets nearby, and check sunny slopes. Vipers emerging from their winter dormancy will need to heat up in the weak sunshine.

The adders here are difficult to approach so in the event of a missed opportunity where you see only a disappearing tail, mark the spot and return several hours later or ideally earlier the next day. A silent approach is essential, snakes do not technically have ears but treat them as if they do. They sense vibration and will disappear at the slightest sound. Once you have spotted an adder move very slowly indeed to get close enough. Grass and brambles are often obscuring the view so position yourself carefully to get the best image.

Top tip

Braunton Burrows cover a arge area and even on a spring day you can find yourself a long way from the car park, hot and tired. Make sure you have a big bottle of water with you and plenty of time to spare. Carrying heavy kit with you through the sand dunes can be hard work so consider leaving the tripod at home and using for example a 300mm lens with 2 x converter rather than a heavy 500mm lens.

The small things in life are worth looking out for here: butterflies, beetles and wildflowers all make it worthwhile to carry a close focussing or macro lens.

Also at Braunton Burrows

Keep an eye out for quick moving sand lizards in the dunes nearer the coast.

It is possible to sometimes spot ospreys here passing through on their migratory route north in spring time.

Kestrels often hover in the breeze above the dunes.

Kestrels hunt the sand dunes looking for lizards and voles. Nikon D4, 300mm + 2 x converter at 600mm, ISO 1600, 1/1600 sec at f/9

A buzzard (buteo buteo) wheels in a blue sky. Nikon D800E, 300mm + 2 x converter at 600mm, ISO 640, 1/1250 sec at f/6.3

Hummingbird hawk moth taking nectar from valerian flowers. Nikon D4, 300mm + 2 x conv at 600mm, ISO 2500, 1/1600 sec at f/6.3

Hawthorn shrubs at the foot of the dunes are regular perches for beautifully marked Stonechats. Nikon D4, 300mm + 2 x converter at 600mm, ISO 1250, 1/1250 sec at f/8

A little further north along the coast from Braunton Burrows, (previous pages), lies the beautiful promontory of Baggy Point. This is a National Trust site with spectacular views from a rugged coastal path. The cliffs are home to nesting fulmars and gulls, and the low growing gorse heathland is a great place to photograph linnets, stonechat, meadow pipits and swallows. Kestrels and ravens also ride the updraught from the sea cliffs.

Where to look

From the car park a tarmac road leads uphill to the start of the sea cliff footpath. The gorse bushes here are good for flocks of linnet and stonechats. Keep an eye out to sea for fulmars riding the air currents above the waves. Parts of the footpath are close to the cliff so if you are not comfortable with steep drops follow the higher footpath which passes through the gorse and heathland up to the top of the cliffs. A narrow footpath leads out to the point itself with steep cliffs either side.

From the tip of the point fulmars can be seen nesting on the cliff face though these are not easy to frame unless you have a head for heights. (See also Shetland Isles).

The cliff face has a fence line in places protecting it and this is a great place to look for migratory birds such as swallows as they return from Africa in the spring. Stonechats, meadow pipits and kestrels also perch here.

The path continues and it is possible to walk in a loop via the beautiful bay at Putsborough then back down the road to Croyde. The section from the point to Putsborough has thick gorse bushes on steep-sided cliffs and this area is frequented by ravens.

The classic Devonshire stone walls that follow the footpath here are good for wheatear.

Raven (*Corvus corax*)

See also Shetlands: Noss p.82 and Lundy Island p.290.

This incredibly dramatic large black crow is a difficult subject to photograph. A black bird with a dark eye it requires good light and careful exposure to make it work. Against a bright sky ravens are likely to come out dark and underexposed. Use exposure compensation to bring out feather detail.

Ravens are very intelligent birds and a good subject for behavioural shots. Watch for them harassing other sea birds for food and for dramatic aerial acrobatics as they roll and tumble in courtship displays.

View from Baggy Point: dramatic in late spring sunlight.
Nikon D800E, 17-35mm at 17mm, ISO 100, 1/160 sec at f/11

Below left: Male kestrel perched on fence line on the cliff edge.
Nikon D3X, 300mm + 2 x converter at 600mm, ISO 800, 1/1000 sec at f/8

Raven fly past. Nikon D4, 300mm + 2 x converter at 600mm, ISO 1600, 1/1600 sec at f/11

How To Get Here

Take the A361 from Barnstaple to Braunton. At Braunton take the B3231 to Croyde, then follow National Trust brown signs to Baggy Point. Exit the NT car park on foot and turn right along the road, turn left after 130m. Follow for a further 200m to the start of the coastal footpath on the left.

Baggy Point NT car park Lat/Long: 51.134984, -4.2423226
OS Co-ordinate: SS 432 396
Nearest Postcode: EX33 1PA

Accessibility

An easy access path follows a well-surfaced path to close to the end of Baggy Point and back. It is suitable for wheelchairs and all-terrain mobility scooters part of the way to the end of the headland. The path can be rough and may be eroded in places and if following the coastal route there are steep sides falling away to the sea below. The final 100m out to the point itself is rough and not suitable for those without a head for heights.

Best Time of Year/Day

Early morning is the best time to have the place to yourself. This area can get busy during holidays, at weekends and sunny days.

Lying 12 miles off the north coast of Devon this granite outcrop is only three miles long and half a mile wide. The name 'Lundy' derives from the Norse word for puffin but this is not necessarily the best spot in the UK to see these photogenic sea birds. Puffin numbers are now drastically reduced though making a comeback in recent years. See the Shetland Isles (p.66) and Skomer island (p.320) for better puffin photography opportunities.

Lundy Island does however offer a wide range of other wildlife and is in itself a delight to visit. Day trips offer limited time to explore properly so it is recommended you stay over for at least a night, camping is available in addition to other accommodation but it needs booking well in advance.

What to expect

The boat trip to the island takes around two hours each way but this can be time well spent. Many seabirds can be spotted en route including gannets, guillemots, shearwater and petrels. Capturing a decent photograph of birds at sea is quite a challenge. The boat is moving even on the calmest days and the vibration from the engines means you need a really fast shutter speed to get a sharp image. Fast moving shearwaters dipping behind the crests of the waves make for a tricky target.

The boat docks at a small harbour at the foot of a steep climb. It's worth checking the beach around the harbour for grey seals before starting the climb up the cliff.

How To Get Here

The island of Lundy lies 12 miles off the coast of Devon and is accessed by boat from Bideford and Ilfracombe. The MS Oldenburg leaves from the harbour at Ilfracombe. Book in advance, Lundy is very popular during the summer holidays. The Lundy Booking Office is located at the pier in Ilfracombe, EX34 9EQ.

Phone: 01271 863636. It is advisable to phone after 8pm the evening before sailing to get up to date sailing conditions and times.

Long stay car parks are available on the opposite side of the harbour to the booking office.

Marine Drive car park Lat/Long: 51.209065, -4.1121939
OS Co-ordinate: SS 525 476
Nearest Postcode: EX34 9NU

Accessibility

Lundy is a steep-sided island with no roads. It is a steep hike up from the harbour to the top of the island. Rough footpaths lead the full length of the island and are well worth exploring.

Best Time of Year/Day

It's best to avoid the busiest times if possible so try to choose times away from peak holidays. The mid summer is however the best time to see puffins, that is from May to the end of July.

North West Point
North East Point
Long Ruse
Gannets' Bay
St Jame's Stone
Threequarter Wall
Tibbett's Hill 136m
Tibbett's Point
Lundy
Jenny's Cove
Halfway Wall
Halfway Wall Bay
Lundy Marine National Nature Reserve
Lundy Roads
Quarter Wall
Beacon Hill 143m
Inner Anchorage
Old Lighthouse
Marisco Tavern
Landing Bay Jetties
Ferry to Ilfracombe, Bideford, Clovelly
Pilot's Quay
Goat Island
Surf Point
Shutter Point
The Rattles
The Race
Rattles Anchorage
Black Rock

N
0   mile   ½

Puffin portrait. Taken on Skomer island. Nikon D4, 300mm + 2 x converter at 600mm, ISO 400, 1/1250 sec at f/8

Big old grey seal hauled out on the beach. Nikon D4, 300mm + 2 x converter at 600mm, ISO 1600, 1/1250 sec at f/5.6

Sika deer in evening sunlight. Nikon D4, 300mm + 2 x converter at 600mm, ISO 1000, 1/1000 sec at f/9

Take your time up the steep climb, not necessarily to catch your breath but to watch for fulmars and gulls riding the updraughts. Lundy is a stop off place for rare and migrant birds and the shrubs here are often mist netted for ringing migrants such as wrynecks.

At the top of the climb there is a Tourist Information office, shop and – thank goodness – a great pub; the Marisco Tavern.

Make sure you pick up a map of the island, some of the footpaths are poorly marked and fade into goat trails leading out to the cliffs. Mist and fog can be an issue and distance is difficult to keep a track of unless you pay attention to the significant and appropriately named walls which run crossways at convenient intervals: Quarter, Halfway and Threequarter Wall divide the island fairly evenly. The only other significant landmarks are the main lighthouses.

Walking out along the exposed heather moorland look for wheatear, stonechat and linnets, especially along the stone walls.

If you are here to see puffins head for Jenny's Cove. Note: the steep cliffs are unguarded and potentially dangerous. Puffins will only be here during the breeding season from late March to mid-August before leaving for their life on the ocean waves.

If time allows – probably not feasible during a day trip – the walk to the lighthouse at the north end of the island is welll worth it. Here ravens play on the updraughts and peregrines are a fairly common sight; watch for the crossbow-shaped silhouette and listen out for the typical call especially between St. John's Stone and Long Roost.

Feral goats on the island also make an interesting photographic subject, they are easy to approach and often found beyond the Threequarter Wall. They are a good practise subject for photographing the Sika deer.

Sika deer, *(Cervus nippon)*

Sika deer are native to Asia but now roam wild on the windswept moors, coming closer in to graze on the farmed fields at dusk. They emerge from the bracken as if by magic and leap over the fences with ease.

The wildlife generally is aware of the rush of visitors between morning and 4pm so schedules its activities outside of these hours, another reason to make sure you stay overnight rather than try to cram a visit into a day.

The low evening light on Lundy can be amazing, finishing off a great trip here followed, of course, by a quick pint in the Marisco Tavern.

Right: Pergrine falcons hunt the sea cliffs. Nikon D4, 500mm, ISO 800, 1/1250 at f/11

Wheatears perch on stone walls and granite boulders. Nikon D4, 300mm + 2 x converter at 600mm, ISO 1000, 1/1250 sec at f/8

Linnets on a barbed wire fence. Nikon D4, 300mm + 2 x converter at 600mm, ISO 2500, 1/1000 sec at f/9

Above: Feral goats roam wild towards the north of the island. Nikon D4, 300mm + 2 x converter at 600mm, ISO 1000, 1/1000 sec at f/8

WALES: Introduction

Wales is a wonderful location for wildlife; the wild interior holds wooded valleys and mountain regions that are remote and retain much of their natural habitat. The woodlands are managed for forestry and the uplands for sheep farming, both of which have positive aspects for many forms of wildlife.

In the centre of Wales near the town of Rhayader there are three locations worth visiting within a few miles of each other. The red kite centre at Gigrin Farm puts out food each day making this one of the best places to see and photograph this once incredibly rare bird of prey. Nearby the quiet and beautiful Gilfach Farm nestles on the wooded hillside above a river valley. This is a special place to find summer migrant birds like flycatchers, redstart and wood warbler with the added possibility of catching an otter moving through. Further up the Elan Valley the wooded slopes are a good spot to catch wood warblers and many different deciduous woodland species from woodpeckers and nuthatches to sparrowhawks.

Further west the coast of Pembrokeshire is an incredibly beautiful, little visted and wild coastline inhabited by that charismatic and rare member of the crow family, the chough. Peregrine falcons are seen regularly along the cliff walks, and offshore lie the superb reserves of Skomer and Skokholm. Skomer is an absolute must-see for the wildlife photographer offering close encounters with many different sea birds but especially the puffin.

Ruabon Moor in North Wales during the spring is an excellent spot to witness the fascinating spectacle of a black grouse lek.

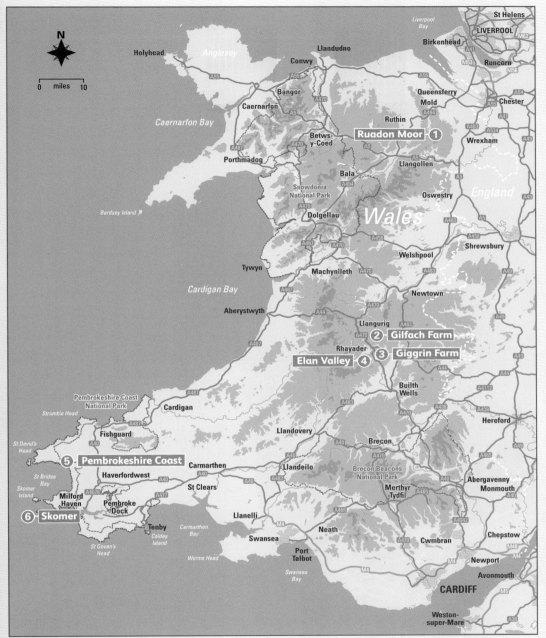

N

miles
0 — 10

St Helens
LIVERPOOL
Birkenhead
Runcorn
Holyhead
Anglesey
Llandudno
Conwy
Queensferry
Mold
Chester
Bangor
Caernarfon
Ruthin
Wrexham
Caernarfon Bay
Betws-y-Coed
Ruadon Moor — ①
Bala
Llangollen
Oswestry
England
Bardsey Island
Snowdonia National Park
Dolgellau
Wales
Shrewsbury
Porthmadog
Welshpool
Tywyn
Machynlleth
Newtown
Cardigan Bay
Aberystwyth
Llangurig
② Gilfach Farm
Rhayader
③ Giggrin Farm
Elan Valley ④
Builth Wells
Pembrokeshire Coast National Park
Strumble Head
Cardigan
Hereford
St David's Head
Fishguard
Llandovery
Brecon
⑤ Pembrokeshire Coast
Carmarthen
Llandeilo
Brecon Beacons National Park
Abergavenny
Monmouth
St Brides Bay
Skomer Island
Haverfordwest
St Clears
Merthyr Tydfil
Milford Haven
Pembroke Dock
Llanelli
Llandeilo
⑥ Skomer
Tenby
Caldey Island
Carmarthen Bay
Neath
Cwmbran
Chepstow
St Govan's Head
Worms Head
Swansea
Port Talbot
Newport
Avonmouth
Swansea Bay
CARDIFF
Weston-super-Mare

Contains Ordnance Survey data © Crown Copyright and database right (2016)

Two rivals argue the point: black grouse at World's End.
Nikon D800E, 500mm, ISO 4000, 1/800 sec at f/4.5

Ruabon Moor is a wild and wonderful area of moorland renowned in the past as the grouse shooting capital of North Wales. Overshooting and moorland being lost to agriculture in the 20th century lead to a huge reduction in the grouse population.

Today Ruabon is a black grouse stronghold where the birds flourish due to new management strategies. The moor is also known for upland birds such as skylark, curlew, snipe and meadow pipits.

Black grouse *(Tetrao tetrix)*

This large and dramatic game bird is a red list endangered species in the UK. Black grouse are found here on the high moors of Northern Wales. In spring the males gather at traditional sites known as leks to compete for dominance and to mate with the shy and reclusive females known as grey hens.

A black grouse lek is a sight and a sound to behold. Beginning just before dawn, the rivals gather to call, strut and leap vertically in the air in an attempt to draw the attentions of females and to fend off the territory from rival males.

Above: The road to Minerva , World's End.

Technique

At leks seen close to the roadside it's best to stay in the car to use as a hide. Leaving the car may well flush the birds and it could be argued is disturbing a red list species at a critical time in its breeding cycle.

Light conditions are likely to be poor at least initially and this means using high ISO and wide apertures to get fast enough shutter speeds. Using a prime lens without a converter is the best option if available.

Watch for interaction between two males, commonly this begins with a low run towards each other with calling and bowing of heads. Actual combat is flurried and fast so a high shutter speed is needed.

Above: claiming the high ground. Black grouse males at the lek.
Nikon D800E, 500mm, ISO 4000, 1/800 sec at f/5

Below opposite: Struttting his stuff, a black grouse on patrol.
Nikon D800E, 500mm, ISO 4000, 1/800 sec at f/5

Below: Black grouse calling "Goaway."
Nikon D800E, 500mm, ISO 4000, 1/800 sec at f/4.5

How To Get Here

Ruabon Moor is an area of upland moorland situated to the west of Wrexham. A small road crosses the moor between Minera in the north to World's End in the south.

Follow the A525 west from Wrexham for 4 miles then turn left on the B5426 to Minera after 0.4 miles. Continue on the B5426 for 0.7 miles to crossroads. Turn sharply right and follow this road up onto Ruabon Moor, it's around 4.5 miles across the moor to World's End.

Ruabon Moor north Lat/Long: 53.053274, -3.092938
OS Co-ordinate: SJ 264 513
Nearest Postcode: LL11 3DR

Accessibility

Many leks are viewable from the roadside where you should stay in the vehicle to avoid flushing the birds. Park safely and considerately off the road, if there is no room to park try elsewhere.

There is a black grouse walking route to a viewing hide in Llandegla Forest nearby. The RSPB conduct guided walks that require booking in advance. Tel: 02920 353 008

Best Time of Year/Day

Black grouse are active from mid-March to mid-May in the very early morning before daybreak. The action is often all over at around 8 am.

Where Else to See

Glenlivet Wildlife Black Grouse Hide p.42, Cairngorm Mountain p.52 and North Pennines p.116.

Male redstart in late summer plumage.
Nikon D4, 300mm + 2 x converter at 600mm, ISO 1600, 1/1250 sec at f/8

Gilfach is a hill farm of open moorland, flower-rich grasslands and oak woodland, situated at the confluence of the Marteg River and the River Wye in the Cambrian Mountains of Mid-Wales. The farm and its land is now a beautiful nature reserve run by the Radnorshire Wildlife Trust. This is one of the best places to photograph small summer visitors such as pied flycatcher, redstart and whinchat.

Pied flycatcher *(Ficedula hypoleuca)*

A beautiful and rare bird, the migrant pied flycatcher is exactly what it says on the tin. The male at least is dramatically marked in black and white which stands out a mile in the oak woodland where it is resident in the UK in summer only. The birds feed, as their name suggests on flies but also on insect grubs.

Timing is critical for these little beauties; go too early in the year and they will not have returned from Africa, visit in mid-June and photographing them becomes difficult as the leaf canopy obscures your views and creates too much shade for a good photograph. By August the fledglings have left the nest and the birds are widely distributed and/or beginning their migration south again. The best time to visit is therefore the beginning of May, early in the morning.

Where to look

The reserve has a multitude of nest boxes. The pied flycatcher uses either ones with small round entry holes or triangles in the top corner. The Otter Hide overlooks the stream next to the small bridge you will have crossed to get here. This is a great place to get really close views in early spring as the male birds sing from lower branches at eye level from the hide windows. Dippers and grey wagtails are common along the stream though this is often dark and shady and it is a difficult angle to get a good shot.

Opposite top: Male pied flycatcher singing for a mate. Nikon D800E, 500mm + 1.4 x converter at 700mm, ISO 1000, 1/800 sec at f/9

Below: Sitting pretty. Male pied flycatcher. Nikon D800E, 500mm + 1.4 x converter at 700mm, ISO 1600, 1/800 sec at f/9

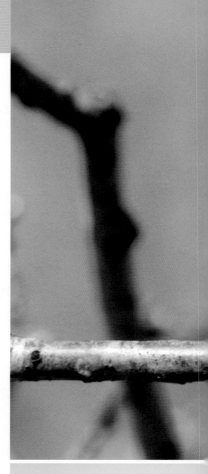

How To Get Here

Gilfach Nature Reserve and Visitor Centre is located in Mid-Wales around 50 miles east of Aberystwyth and 4 miles north of Rhayader in the Marteg River Valley, a tributary of the Upper River Wye.

Radnorshire Wildlife Trust – Gilfach Nature Reserve
Address: St. Harmon, Rhayader/Rhaeadr Gwy, Powys
Phone: 01597 870301

Lat/Long: 52.339245, -3.522977
OS Co-ordinate: SN 963 723
Nearest Postcode: LD6 5LF

Accessibility

Expect narrow roads with a steep hill climb, be considerate and park within the limited designated spaces. The Otter Hide is roadside but downhill from the parking. The rest of the farm is open moorland and hillsides.

Best Time of Year/Day

For pied flycatchers, redstarts and woodwarblers the beginning to mid-May is best for visibility as the deciduous trees will just be starting to leaf. By August the young should be fledged then leave by the end of the month.

Close up: cropped in portrait of pied flycatcher. Nikon D800E, 500mm + 1.4 x converter at 700mm, ISO 1000, 1/800 sec at f/10

Male redstart at Gilfach. The lichens growing on the branches here are due to the unpolluted air and make an attractive backdrop. Nikon D800E, 500mm + 1.4 x conv at 700mm, ISO 800, 1/1250 sec at f/8

Redstart *(Phoenicurus phoenicurus)*

As small UK birds go the redstart or 'fireflirt' is one of the most attractive. The orange breast and grey head of the male with the distinctive orange red tail which gives it its name makes this an easy bird to identify. Often seen perching on fence posts they also have a liking for hawthorn bushes from which they make regular short flights to the ground in search of grubs and insects. Like the pied flycatcher this is an oak woodland specialist and a summer visitor to the UK.

Technique

Timing again is crucial, arriving in early May could be too soon to find the males courting the duller brown females. Wait until mid-May at least, when territories have been established, to stand a better chance of a close encounter. By September redstarts start to migrate back to warmer climates.

Where to look

The farm courtyard was for several years the best place to get a good photograph, the birds were lured in with mealworms to close proximity to allow great images. Unfortunately the large numbers of photographers attracted here has meant the local wildlife trust has decided to now ban tripods and the use of mealworms

as bait in the courtyard area. This is not the end of the world though as the birds can be photographed elsewhere on the reserve. Check the surrounding small enclosed fields, especially those with low shrubs and trees. Familiarise yourself with the song and watch for quick movements as the birds fly down to feed. Redstarts tend to have a routine based around a number of favourite perches so anticipate their movements and remain still and camouflaged for best results.

Also at Gilfach

This is a truly beautiful and enchanting reserve. If time allows take a walk along the stream to look for dippers and grey wagtails. The meadows are managed for wildlife and redstarts are often seen along the fencelines here as well.

The steeply sloped hillside above the farm is worth exploring in search of whinchat. This jaunty little bird, with the distinctive white supercilium (eye stripe), may be found perching on the bracken and foxgloves often together with the elusive willow warbler.

See also Elan valley p.312.

Male redstart in full breeding plumage. Nikon D800E, 500mm + 1.4 x converter at 700mm, ISO 800, 1/1250 sec at f/8

Whinchat perched on bracken stalks at Gilfach. Nikon D4, 300mm + 2 x converter at 600mm, ISO 1000, 1/1250 sec at f/6.3

Red Kites wheeling in the sky over Giggrin, no cutting and pasting required.
Nikon D4, 70-200mm at 86mm, ISO 800, 1/1250 sec at f/13

Gigrin Farm is located in the heart of Mid Wales close to the attractive village of Rhayader. The 200 acre family-run working farm overlooks the Wye and Elan Valleys and has gained a reputation for being one of the best places in Europe to see and photograph red kites.

The kites here are fed on a daily basis and the spectacle of huge numbers of this once very rare bird of prey wheeling and swooping overhead is an experience not to be missed.

What To Expect

Feeding time is what everyone is here for. The birds are fed at regular times and it can get busy, especially at weekends and school holidays. Get here in plenty of time before feeding commences. There is an option to pay extra and use a photography platform hide. This gives a better vantage point and more space to set up a tripod.

Kites and sometimes buzzards will begin to gather before the feeding starts so it makes sense to get set up and in position early.

A tractor delivers raw meat and this is spread on the field in front of you resulting in a sudden rush of activity as the birds circle before falling from the sky to snatch the scraps of meat from the ground. Visiting kite numbers range between 300 and 600 birds depending on season and weather with more kites visiting during periods of bad weather.

Red Kite *(Milvus milvus)*

Wales was for many years the last stronghold of the red kite in the UK. From an incredibly small breeding population the birds were gradually brought back from close to extinction to become the locally common raptor we see here today. The genetic pool from which the population recovered was very limited and a large percentage of the current population is descended from one female. Consequently there is a large amount of variation in colour of plumage; some birds are almost black and others have very pale colouration. The darker birds naturally stand out more dramatically against a light sky. See also the Chilterns p.194.

Top tip

The feeding frenzy is spectacular and very fast, the flurry of activity which occurs initially may die off suddenly and unexpectedly. Be prepared to wait patiently for the birds to regain confidence as, after a rest in the surrounding trees, the activity is likely to restart several times.

Red Kite dropping in for a feed at Gigrin. Nikon D4, 300mm + 2 x converter at 600mm, ISO 1000, 1/1000 sec at f/8

How To Get Here

Gigrin Farm is located in mid-Wales less than a mile to the east of Rhayader, just off the A470 and 13 miles north of Builth Wells.

Address: Gigrin Farm, South Street, Rhayader, Powys.

Lat/Long: 52.297307, -3.499793
OS Co-ordinate: SN 978 676
Nearest Postcode: LD6 5BL
www.gigrin.co.uk   Phone: 01597 810 243

Accessibility

Easily accessible off-road tracks into wooden hides. Four of the regular hides as well as the photographic hide (£12) are suitable for wheelchairs. Parking is available immediately outside the hides for disabled use, please call to pre-book this however.

Best Time of Year/Day

Jan to start of Nov: open from 12:30pm to 5pm daily with feeding at 2pm in winter and 3pm after the clocks change for British Summer Time. November open daily 12:30 to 4pm but closed on Mondays. December: weekends only, closed for Christmas. Check website for latest opening times.

Above: Red kite falls out of a white sky.
Nikon D4, 300mm, ISO 1600, 1/1000 sec at f/11

Below: Close fly by at eye level from the photography hide. Nikon D4,
300mm + 2 x converter at 600mm, ISO 1000, 1/1250 sec at f/5.6

Red kite in free fall.
Nikon D4, 300mm, ISO 1600, 1/1000 sec at f/11

Technique and tips

These are relatively slow moving birds normally but break into a sudden fast swoop when going in for their food. For photographing, good manoueverability is essential so consider a smaller lens rather than a large heavy telephoto. A zoom lens here is a good option. A wider angle lens is useful for the large group shots.

This scenario offers a bewildering array of targets to photograph and it can be tricky to pick your subject from the crowd. Immature birds are often more hesitant and may circle several times before swooping. Spot a subject and follow it round before shooting on the swoop to get the best action shots.

Exposure is complicated as the birds move quickly from a bright sky to the darker background, flying in front of woodland or dropping in to the field.

It is worth keeping the shot you are after in mind and setting the camera according to whether you want to shoot against the sky or the much darker vegetation.

Use a high ISO to ensure sufficient speed and a narrow enough aperture to keep most of the bird in focus.

Shoot in RAW so you can fine-adjust exposure afterwards. Photographing against a bright blank sky will usually lead to underexposed birds – use exposure compensation and check your LCD. Shooting in RAW will give you the best chance to adjust exposure later.

Opposite: On the edge, kite lining up for a descent.
Nikon D4, 300mm, ISO 1600, 1/1250 sec at f/11

Elan Valley is a beautiful landscape carved out by the Elan river, its slopes clad with broadleaved woodland. It is an important area for birds and is well-known for the oak woodland trio: pied flycatchers and wood warblers, along with willow warblers, nuthatches, and the great and lesser spotted woodpeckers.

It is located close to Gilfach and Gigrin Farms, see previous pages.

Wood warbler (Phylloscopus sibilatrix)

Very similar in appearance to the willow warbler the wood warbler can be distinguished by its chunkier body shape and usually by a much whiter chest than the frequently greener willow warbler. Both are secretive, flighty and a tricky target to spot and photograph amongst the trees.

Nuthatch *(Sitta europaea)*

This is an enigmatic little bird, basically a very small woodpecker in habit. Nuthatches are denizens of broadleaved woodland such as the wooded slopes found at this location. Look for the slate-blue coloured bird moving up and down trunks of trees. They can be drawn in to bird feeders especially for peanuts and sunflower seeds. See also Dumfries and Galloway sparrowhawk hide p.96.

Where to look

Cross the river via the metal bridge at the entrance to the large and convenient Elan Valley Visitor Centre. From here a winding narrow track zigzags up to the top of the woods with beautiful views as well as great opportunities to spot wildlife in the tree canopies as you climb higher up the hill.

The wooded slopes of the Elan valley rise steeply from the river. Nikon D800E, 17-35mm at 17mm, ISO 320, 1/160 sec at f/13

How To Get Here

The Elan Valley is located in Mid Wales 3.7 miles south west from Rhayader along the B4518. Head for the visitor centre, signposted after 3 miles on the left, set in spectacular surroundings next to a Victorian dam. There is a cafe and parking here.

Lat/Long: 52.271970, -3.565667
OS Co-ordinate: SN 928 646
Nearest Postcode: LD6 5HP

www.elanvalley.org.uk   **Phone:** 01597 810880

Accessibility

A steep track up the hill requires some level of physical fitness especially if carrying a heavy lens and tripod on a hot spring day. There are good disabled facilities at the visitor centre and the first part of the 8 mile Elan Valley Trail is wheelchair accessible.

Best Time of Year/Day

The best time to spot woodland birds is in early spring before the leaves open. Pied flycatchers are best from the beginning of May. Redstarts and wood warblers from around mid-May. By August most of the young will have fledged and the adults move up to the high tree canopies.

Left: Pied flycatcher photographed at Gilfach Farm. Nikon D800E, 500mm + 1.4 x converter at 700mm, ISO 1000, 1/800 sec at f/9

Above: Wood warbler in an ash tree before the leaves open in May. Nikon D800E, 500mm + 1.4 x converter at 700mm, ISO 1600, 1/1250 sec at f/11

Nuthatch posing in dappled sunlight. Nikon D800E, 500mm + 1.4 x converter at 700mm, ISO 1250, 1/800 sec at f/7.1

This stunning area of South West Wales is both beautiful and dramatic. Even at peak times the coastline here is remarkably unpopulated with visitors and a fabulous place to look for wildlife. This is effectively the same location from which the boat leaves for Skomer (following pages), so ideal to combine on the same trip. Much of the coastline of Pembroke is worth exploring if you are on an extended stay.

This makes an ideal diversion if the Skomer boat does not sail. The nearby cliff tops are home to rare and enigmatic choughs, peregrines hunt the skies and seals bob around in the ocean swell.

Male linnet in the gorse. Nikon D4, 300mm + 2 x converter at 600mm, ISO 250, 1/1250 sec at f/5.6

Chough *(Pyrrhocorax pyrrhocorax)*

Whilst the common name chough is usually pronounced chuff I have no idea how to pronounce the latin name. The call of this member of the crow family is actually *chow* and some say this is how its name should be pronounced. Either way this is a rare and charismatic bird which is a delight to photograph.

Where to look

From the Skomer ticket office cross the road and go through the picket gate and across the cliff top towards the sea. Use binoculars to scan the cliff tops and skyline and listen out for the *chow chow* call.

Footpaths lead along the cliff tops and if you have no immediate luck its's worth asking other walkers if they have seen the birds. June is a good time to visit when the youngsters (with yellow rather than red beaks) are fledged and requiring their parents' attention.

Choughs tend to gather in family groups and small flocks on the cliff tops feeding on grubs and insects. They take flight if disturbed, but can be relaxed in human presence.

Also keep an eye out for small birds like linnets and stonechats amongst the gorse on the cliff tops.

Chough on the lookout against a turquoise sea. Nikon D4, 300mm + 2 x converter at 600mm, ISO 800, 1/1250 sec at f/9

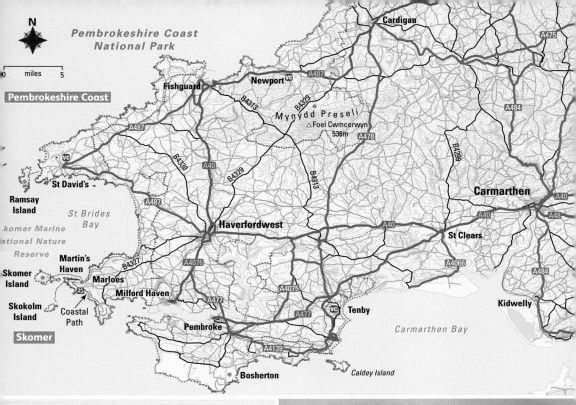

N

Pembrokeshire Coast
National Park

miles

Pembrokeshire Coast

Fishguard

Newport

Mynydd Preseli
△ Foel Cwmcerwyn
536m

Cardigan

St David's

Ramsay
Island

St Brides
Bay

komer Marine
ational Nature
Reserve

Skomer
Island

Martin's
Haven

Marloes

Skokolm
Island

Coastal
Path

Milford Haven

Haverfordwest

Carmarthen

St Clears

Kidwelly

Skomer

Pembroke

Tenby

Carmarthen Bay

Bosherton

Caldey Island

How To Get Here

Lockley Lodge is the visitor centre at Martin's Haven, near Marloes in Pembrokeshire. From Haverfordwest take the B4327, signposted Dale, and follow until you pick up signs for Marloes. Drive through Marloes and continue for 2 miles to the NT car park

Lockley Lodge is where all tickets are bought for Skomer Island trips.

Lat/Long: 51.734923, -5.244603
OS Co-ordinate: SM 760 089
Parking Postcode: SA62 3BJ

The Lodge is open from either the 1st April or Good Friday (whichever comes first) to the middle of September, Tues – Sun 8.30am untill the last boat comes back.

Accessibility

The trails here are off-road and cliff top tracks are uneven and rough in places. Good outdoor clothing and walking boots are recommended.

Best Time of Year/Day

June and July in good weather is the best time, when the birds have finished nesting. Early mornings and late evenings, the 'Golden Hours' are best for good light.

Curious chough always alert and interested. Nikon D4, 300mm + 2 x converter at 600mm, ISO 1000, 1/1000 sec at f/9

315

Peregrine fly by.
Nikon D4, 500mm, ISO 800, 1/1250 sec at f/13

The stunningly beautiful and rugged pembrokeshire coast. This view is a short stroll from the Skomer boat ticket office.
Nikon D800E, 17-35mm at 17mm, ISO 400, 1/320 sec at f/14

Peregrine falcon *(Falco peregrinus)*

Peregrines haunt the cliffs and can be seeen at any time of day. A sudden flurry of noise and activity from a flock of choughs is a good sign to scan the skies. This is a difficult bird to predict but frequently seen from the queue whilst waiting for the Skomer boat tickets so have your camera on standby with a fast shutter speed, (1/1250 upwards) and a narrow aperture (f/8 upwards).

See also Avon Gorge p.200.

Swallow *(Hirundo rustica)*

The dark, glossy-blue backs, red throats, pale underparts and long tail streamers make this bird easy enough to identify when close. In flight they are often confused with house martins (black and white with a shorter tail), or swifts (with long scythe shaped wings). Swallows nearly always nest inside buildings, especially barns.

Swallows happily nest in the toilet block next to the Skomer boat ticket office so again another potential diversion while your friend or partner waits patiently in the queue for boat tickets.

Catching these fast moving birds on the wing as they flit in and out of the building is a challenge. Hanging around a public convenience with a large telephoto lens is ill advised, however most of the would-be users of the facilities are likely to understand your intentions are purely ornithological. Swallows are migratory and only present for the brief summer months, coinciding with the puffins visiting Skomer.

Grey seal *(Halichoerus grypus)*

Seals live all along the coastline here, most frequently spotted as a bobbing head in the water watching you from afar. Seals are curious and it is quite easy to get close simply by lying down and motionless on the shore.

For easy views of grey seals try the boat trip round Ramsay Island which leaves from St. Davids. Taking photos from the small RIB power boat is difficult but the close quarters mean heavy equipment is not required. Remember to check your exposure and perhaps use some positive exposure compensation for a grey seal in light water. You will need a faster shutter speed to compensate for the movement of a boat.

See also Shetland Isles p.66 and Donna Nook p.146 for more on seals.

Silhouetted against a blue sky the distinctive outline of a chough. Nikon D4, 300mm + 2 x converter at 600mm, ISO 400, 1/1250 sec at f/11

Swallow lit by morning light. Nikon D4, 300mm + 2 x converter at 600mm, ISO 1000, 1/1250 sec at f/5.6

Grey seal wondering what's going on. Nikon D4, 300mm + 2 x converter at 600mm, ISO 800, 1/1250 sec at f/9

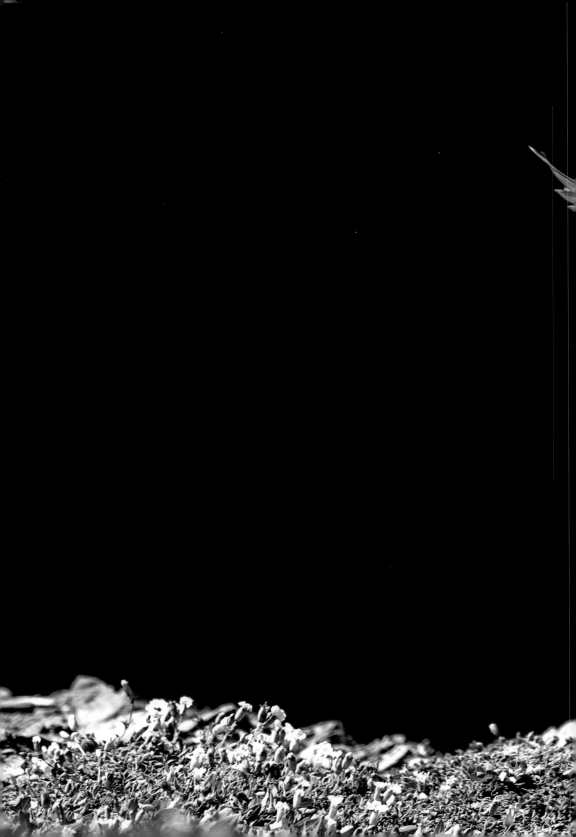

Coming into land, puffin landing at the Wick.
Nikon D4, 300mm, ISO 1000, 1/1250 sec at f/4.5

This beautiful little island lying off the Pembrokeshire coast is a superb location for extremely close encounters with some fabulous wildlife especially puffins, guillemots and razorbills. A jewel in the crown of the Wildlife Trust of South and West Wales, it can be a tricky place to get to but is well worth the trouble. This is a great place to bring the family or friends as the wildlife here is accustomed to the limited human presence.

What to expect

The queue for the boat tickets is a nervous wait to find out if you have a ticket and if the boat will even sail that day. With ticket in hand the short boat trip takes about fifteen minutes.

Approaching land expect the rafts of sea birds bobbing on the ocean to take off as you approach. The steps up the cliff are steep so take your time and the opportunity to photograph the guillemots and razorbills at this point. A brief and interesting talk is given by the warden on the island before you are free to wander.

Where to look

You will see puffins almost immediately and this first section at the top of the steps is a good place to see them flying out to sea. A great spot to head for if puffins are your priority is 'The Wick'. Here puffins fly in from the sea, hopefully with beaks full of sand eels. The path passes close by to nest burrows and some puffins cross the path to take food to their burrows.

The boat returns to take you back to the mainland.
Nikon D800E, 17-35mm at 35mm, ISO 500, 1/1250 sec at f/8

How To Get Here

The trip – or failed trip! – to Skomer is the stuff of legend. For many the journey to this remote part of Wales will be lengthy and requires some planning. Head for the small boat landing at Martin's Haven, see directions for Pembroke Coast, previous pages. Suggested accommodation overnight would be at the nearby campsite with superb sea views.

Important: the 15-minute boat ride cannot be booked in advance, consequently a very early start is needed to join a queue and ensure a ticket to sail on a first come first served basis. Boats are not guaranteed to sail and it is not uncommon for all sailings to be cancelled for the day if weather (including strong breezes) make landings problematic.

Departs from Martin's Haven daily at 10am, 11am and 12 noon (1st April–30th September). There are no sailings on Mondays except bank holidays.

Web site: www.pembrokeshire-islands.co.uk
Lat/Long: 51.734923, -5.244603
OS Co-ordinate: SM 760 089
Parking Postcode: SA62 3BJ

Accessibility

This requires some physical fitness to get around the island on a day trip although good views of many seabirds are available immediately on setting foot on Skomer. Facilities are limited on the island. There are toilets but bring a packed lunch, including drink and adequate clothing

Best Time of Year/Day

For the must-see puffins visit from May to the end of July. For evening light book to stay on the island well in advance.

Right: Gathering nesting material. Nikon D800E, 300mm +
2 x converter at 600mm, ISO 640, 1/1250 sec at f/8

Razorbill love: A pair of razorbills display by the Skomer landing. Nikon D800E, 300mm + 2 x converter at 600mm, ISO 500, 1/1250 sec at f/9

Guillemot posing for a portrait. Nikon D800E, 300mm + 2 x converter at 600mm, ISO 500, 1/1250 sec at f/9

Bringing back the supper, puffin with sand eels. Nikon D800E,
300mm + 2 x converter at 600mm, ISO 800, 1/1250 sec at f/8

Guillemots *(Uria aalge)* and Razorbills *(Alca torda)*

These seabirds are usually best seen at close proximity near the steps at the landing point. Guillemots, razorbills and the puffins spend most of their time at sea and are on the island to pair up and breed. By the end of July the young will have fledged and the birds will return to life on the ocean wave where they feed mainly on fish and crustaceans.

The guillemot has a finer, sharper beak and is browner on the upper parts than a razorbill. The razorbill is very black on the upper parts and head; consequently exposing correctly for the black eye can be tricky. The blunt broad bill of a razorbill has beautifully marked fine white lines and, when opened, it exposes vivid yellow inner mouthparts.

Both species tend to nest in large mixed colonies on cliff faces, guillemots being the more numerous of the two.

Puffin *(Fratercula arctica)*

This is an easy subject here on Skomer where puffins can literally be running around your feet. If the light is strong look for high contrast opportunities where, by correctly exposing for the bird, the background is underexposed creating a dramatic image on a dark background. See double page spread 2 pages back.

See also Shetland Isles p.66 and Lundy p.290.

Top tip

Plan your route round the island to get back in time to enjoy the guillemots and razorbills by the steps. You can also see puffins in the water from here while you wait for the boat back.

It is roughly 4 miles right round the island but if time is pressing you can cut back across the centre and save some time. On arrival on the island you are provided with a map with marked trails.

Puffin calling, Skomer. Nikon D4, 300mm + 2 x converter at 600mm, ISO 800, 1/1250 sec at f/8

Guillemot floating on calm seas. Nikon D4, 300mm + 2 x converter at 600mm, ISO 500, 1/1000 sec at f/8

A male black redstart in winter sunshine. Nikon D800E, 500mm + 1.4 x converter at 700mm, ISO 800, 1/1000 sec at f/8

Rare and Migratory Birds

Some wildlife does not have a regular location but turns up seemingly at random and in the unlikeliest of places. Rare and migratory species are best located by joining a group such as Bird Guides or Rare Bird Alerts and paying attention to the species you are particularly keen to see or the areas you are able to visit. Most counties have a local bird group who post local sightings and these are well worth joining. It's amazing the knowledge you can pick up from local experts in the field.

Wryneck *(Jynx torquilla)*

The wryneck is one of the most sought after and amazing looking migrant birds. Wrynecks are a rare but regular visitor to the UK. They are usually seen in spring as they move north to breeding sites in Scandinavia and Northern Europe and in autumn as they move south to escape the cold northern winter.

Very much like a woodpecker in appearance it spends much of its time on the ground foraging for ants. Be prepared to get down low on the ground to get a good perspective.

Wryneck moving into the light. Nikon D4, 300mm + 2 x converter at 600mm, ISO 1000, 1/1000 sec at f/6.3

Where to look

There are numerous resources on the internet that provide up-to-date information on the latest migratory bird sightings. Most of these rely on individuals to report their personal sightings. It's easy to get involved via the British Trust for Ornithology website:

www.bto.org/volunteer-surveys/birdtrack/bird-recording

'**BirdTrack** is an exciting project, through a partnership between the BTO, the RSPB, Birdwatch Ireland, the Scottish Ornithologists' Club and the Welsh Ornithological Society, that looks at migration movements and distributions of birds throughout Britain and Ireland. BirdTrack provides facilities for observers to store and manage their own personal records as well as using these to support species conservation at local, regional, national and international scales.'

Other useful websites and organisations:

www.birdguides.com – Sign up for up-to-the minute information

Rare Bird Network on Facebook and Twitter – for latest sightings

www.rarebirdalert.co.uk – longest running UK birdnews service
iwww.birdnet.co.uk – an optics sales website with list of sightings

www.birdinformation.co.uk – for serious birders, a pay-for website, twitter and Birdnet pager news service.

Best Time of Year/Day

Spring and autumn are when the main migrants arrive and leave.

Wryneck laying low amongst grasses. Nikon D800E, 300mm + 2 x converter at 600mm, ISO 1000, 1/1000 sec at f/5.6

Below: Wryneck on the sea wall. Nikon D4, 300mm + 2 x converter at 600mm, ISO 800, 1/1000 sec at f/8

Hoopoe *(Upupa epops)*

More usually a bird of Southern Europe hoopoes often get swept off course en route back to Africa. They are rare in the UK and at the time of photographing this individual was probably the only one in the country at the time.

Hoopoes are a fabulously exotic looking bird with the curved bill and the amazing crest which it erects if alarmed, but also when preening. They hunt for grubs and insects on the ground with surprising efficiency and have a wonderful habit of tossing the captured food up in the air before swallowing.

Technique

A largely ground-dwelling bird so get down low to be at eye level. To capture the bird swallowing prey it's a matter of getting used to the birds habits and using the fastest burst rate on your camera to hopefully catch the moment the insect is tossed in the air.

Hoopoe portrait with raised crest. Nikon D4, 500mm + 1.4 x converter at 700mm, ISO 800, 1/1250 sec at f/8

Below: Backlit hoopoe on a fence, Bedfordshire 2015. Nikon D4, 500mm + 1.4 x converter at 700mm, ISO 500, 1/1250 sec at f/5.6

Hoopoe catching a bite to eat. Nikon D4, 500mm + 1.4 x converter at 700mm, ISO 640, 1/1600 sec at f/8

Hoopoe stretching. Nikon D4, 500mm + 1.4 x converter at 700mm, ISO 640, 1/1000 sec at f/8

Short-eared owl in flight, a relatively slow-flying large bird in good golden hour light. Nikon D4, 500mm + 1.4 x converter at 700mm, ISO 1000, 1/1000 sec at f/9.

The eyes have it. Short-eared owl on the hunt.
Nikon D800E, 500mm, ISO 1600, 1/1250 sec at f/6.3

Short-eared owl *(Asio flammeus)*

The short-eared owl is perhaps the number one bird subject in the UK for wildlife photographers. This wonderful owl with the stunning yellow eyes and beautifully camouflaged plumage breeds in the north of Europe, including northern Scotland, returning south in winter. The number of birds that arrive in central and southern UK in winter fluctuates depending largely on climatic influences but also on available food i.e. vole populations.

Where to look

Favoured sites in the UK vary year on year. Otmoor RSPB p.176, Burwell Fen and also Aust Warth and Blueberry Farm, Maidwell are all favourite spots but these can and do change every year. As with other migratory birds check the Bird Guides website and Rare Bird alerts for good locations for the year. See box section 'Where to Look' on p.328.

Technique

Short-eared owls are perhaps one of the more complicated species to photograph. They are active in low light and typically hunt among thorn scrub or long grass, all of which is likely to trick autofocus away from the subject.

A large lens and tripod are beneficial for sharpness but a hand held set up works well most of the time for these highly mobile birds. Generally but not always a high ISO is necessary as they are usually active from around 2:30 in the afternoon on a winter's evening (bearing in mind it can be dark by 4:30 in winter). Although a blue sky is great for sharp detail a misty low light day can be better for activity from the birds and less contrasty for photography.

Down to earth. A shortie lands with a vole and sits low, mantling the prey with his wings. Nikon D4, 500mm + 1.4 x converter at 700mm, ISO 1250, 1/1600 sec at f/7.1

The eyes are all part of the subject with shorties, so position yourself with the light in the right direction. If you can get a day when the breeze and sun are on your back then that's perfect as the birds tend to hunt into the wind.

Although these owls are slow fliers it's worth maintaining a high shutter speed as they can suddenly stall and drop like a stone into the grass. Also interaction between other birds, especially other owls but also kestrels is common; arguing over territory or prey. Get used to the difference between slow hunting flight and the sudden rapid wing beats as they build up for an argument.

On the wall, a short-eared owl perched up in bright winter sunshine.
Nikon D4, 500mm, ISO 500, 1/1000 sec at f/8

Short-eared owl in golden evening light. Nikon D4, 500mm + 1.4 x converter at 700mm, ISO 1000, 1/1000 sec at f/9

The snatch. A kestrel steals a vole from the talons of a surprised short-eared owl. Nikon D4, 500mm + 1.4 x converter at 700mm, ISO 800, 1/800 sec at f/10

Capercaillie (Tetrao urogallus)

The capercaillie is a rare and iconic bird of the Caledonian pine forests. Controversy surrounds this species as a photographic subject due to the fact it is a red-listed species and must not be disturbed during the breeding season. The males are however a large and dominant bird and make themselves very evident to the point of being aggressive at certain times of the year.

Individuals can become well known and notorious for 'attacking' dog walkers and cyclists whereupon they have been referred to as rogue capercaillies. Sadly this notoriety has made them even more sought after as a photographic subject to the point where concern has been raised for the protection of these birds, especially from photographers who it is often wrongly asssumed are more interested in the pictures than the bird's wellbeing.

A good wildlife photographer needs to have an empathy for and a responsibility towards the wildlife.

Above: Capercaillie feeding on soft pine shoots.
Nikon D800E, 300mm, ISO 3200, 1/320 sec at f/5

Technique

Number one is to keep the bird's wellbeing foremost: maintain a discreet distance, this may mean backing off if the bird is approaching you. Stick to footpaths and trails and avoid lekking sites where birds gather during the breeding season to perform courtship displays, especially between the months of April and July.

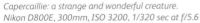

Capercaillie: a strange and wonderful creature.
Nikon D800E, 300mm, ISO 3200, 1/320 sec at f/5.6

Strutting his stuff: capercaillie displaying.
Nikon D800E, 300mm, ISO 3200, 1/320 sec at f/5.6

Below: Capercaillie in the dark pines.
Nikon D800E, 300mm, ISO 3200, 1/320 sec at f/2.8

Where to look

Finding a Capercaillie is a big thrill and an exciting experience and is not impossible given time and patience exploring suitable habitat. The places to look are in Caledonian pine forests, for example the Abernethy Forest and the Rothiemurchus Forest near Aviemore and also Glen Tanar Estate near Aboyne, Aberdeenshire:

Estate Phone: 013398 86451
Countryside Ranger Phone: 013398 86072

Glen Tanar Lat/Long: 57.048510, -2.8658438
OS Co-ordinate: NO 475 956
Parking Postcode: AB34 5EU

The RSPB run a Caper watch from Loch Garten Reserve near Aviemore though sightings are usually distant.
Phone: 01479 831476

Best Time of Year/Day

Early mornings are best. Avoid lekking time from April through to July to keep disturbance to a minimum. The RSPB caper watch is safely distant and only available in spring.

Common frogs, an easy find if you have a pond in the garden. Nikon D800E, 300mm, ISO 800, 1/320 sec at f/4.5

Whether you live in the UK or abroad, some of the locations in this book will be distant and require time and money to reach. Many people however will have a garden of their own or know someone whose garden they can use to photograph widlife. This is the best place to start as a beginner and even the best travelled of us can sometimes be surprised by what you can find living so close to home.

If your garden is seemingly bereft of wildlife there are some simple tips you can use to encourage birds, animals and insects. For the best results redesign your garden for wildlife: for help with this contact a garden design company such as:

www.gowildlandscapes.co.uk

(Other garden designers are available).

Goldfinch *(Carduelis carduelis)*

The goldfinch is a small finch with the most beautifully coloured markings. They are easily drawn to gardens especially those close to arable farmland. These birds are specialist seed eaters and are particularly keen on nyjer seed. This can be bought from pet shops and supermarkets but needs the right feeder (with tiny holes) to work properly. Alternatively plant the correct plants (lavender and teasel) and the birds will be drawn to this more natural food source.

Rarer birds such as brambling, siskin and redpoll are also drawn to these feeeders in cold winters. Feeding sunflower seeds will also draw in larger beaked finches such as the greenfinch and house sparrow.

Robin in a hedgerow. Nikon D4, 300mm + 2 x converter at 600mm, ISO 800, 1/1250 sec at f/5.6

Hedgehog *(Erinaceus europaeus)*

What used to be a common garden species has been declining terribly in numbers over recent years and needs every bit of help to prevent it becoming extinct in the UK. Yes really.

Populations are now becoming so isolated and small that the genetic viability is in question. Hedgehogs often keep themselves well hidden so you may have one in your garden without knowing it. Go out with a torch around midnight on a still and calm summer evening and listen for a rustle in the hedgerow. Hedgehogs are attracted to bird feeders, eating both fallen food and the slugs and snails that feed there too.

Hedgehog hiding in the flower border. Nikon D4, 70-200mm at 185mm, ISO 6400, 1/250 sec at f/2.8, Nikon flash

A good rotten log pile, an unkempt compost heap and cutting small holes at ground level in your fence are the best ways to help a hedgehog.

For technique see night photography p.362.

Wood mouse peeking out of a log pile.
Nikon D4, 500mm, ISO 10000, 1/640 sec at f/7.1

Common frog *(Rana temporaria)*

Frogs are common throughout the UK although they have been in decline due to the removal of ponds, drainage for house building and viral infection. A pond is a simple and easy way to attract frogs and may also bring in newts and toads at breeding time.

Many insects including dragonflies can be attracted to the smallest garden pond and other wildlife including birds will use the water to bathe and drink. Again, having log piles and compost heaps are all important as these provide a place to shelter but also a source of insects and molluscs which are food for amphibians.

Wood mouse *(Apodemus sylvaticus)*

Mice are reasonably common in the UK but often go unnoticed, typically hiding out under sheds and in log piles. The wood mouse is a wonderful though tricky subject being shy and very fast. Try tempting them out with sunflower seeds, peanuts or berries and do your best to keep cats away.

Goldfinch dropping a seed. Nikon D4, 500mm + 1.4 x converter at 700mm, ISO 10000, 1/1000 sec at f/5.6

Wherever you live in the UK there is wildlife around you. If you are lucky you may have one of the reserves or public places in this book on your doorstep. The most exciting and interesting subjects for photography however are those that hardly anyone else knows about, on a local patch near you. Finding wildlife locations close to your home enables you to get to know these places and their species intimately. This will increase your chances of getting great photographs of behaviour, special individuals and different habitat.

Wildlife such as foxes, hares, badgers and owls are common throughout the UK and not necessarily in public places.

This all requires time to investigate, to look for clues, learn where the wildlife is and in the case of private land find the owner and build up a relationship where you can get permission to photograph on their land. The best method is through friends and contacts but alternatively don't be afraid to write letters or knock on doors and explain what you want to do, most landowners are pleased to see images of their wildlife. Just ask first.

Red fox (*Vulpes vulpes*)

Ubiquitous throughout the UK the fox is a fabulous animal to get close to. Whether you are in the city or the country the chances are there will be a fox population not too far away.

Go out very early in the morning for the best chances to locate them. Autumn is good as the vixens are noisy and will be meeting up with dog foxes to mate. Alternatively look for their dens in spring, just before the bluebells emerge is a good time. Dens can be shared with rabbit warrens and/or badgers setts so don't assume if there are signs of one species the other is not present.

Foxes tend to leave signs of their meals lying around outside; rabbit skin or pheasant feathers are a pretty good sign a den is occupied.

The town fox and the country fox are almost different species in that the two are very different to approach. Rural foxes have been and in many areas are still hunted making them more nervous of humans. Be careful who you tell about the location of a fox den, not all land owners will be happy to know they have a family of foxes on their land.

Still no luck finding foxes? Try the outskirts of big cities like Oxford or Bristol at dawn. Alternatively there are pay-for red fox photography hides, see:

www.naturephotographyhides.co.uk

Fox cub amongst the bluebells. Nikon D800E, 300mm + 2 x converter at 600mm, ISO 1600, 1/640 sec at f/5.6

Country fox on the alert. Nikon D4, 300mm + 2 x converter at 600mm, ISO 1600, 1/640 sec at f/5.6

Technique

Rural foxes require good field craft to get close to. Approach upwind, i.e. with the wind in your face. Wear dull or camouflaged clothes and move slowly and quietly. If appropriate use a pop-up hide. Foxes are active at dusk and dawn which means low light so a lens with a wide aperture (f/2.8) is best. Unless you can set up a hide at a feeding spot or den then a hand held set up may be more versatile than a tripod.

Curious fox cub. Nikon D4, 300mm + 2 x converter at 600mm, ISO 1600, 1/1000 sec at f/5.6

Badger *(Meles meles)*

Like foxes, badgers are fairly widespread in the UK though are most numerous in southern counties such as Gloucestershire and Devon. When you find a badger sett it is relatively obvious what it is due to their huge earthworks. These are typically found in broad leaved deciduous woodland where the badgers dig very large tunnels with large mounds of earth immediately around the entrance and often with grass or hay lying around outside.

Badger toilets are another obvious sign of an active sett. Badgers dig small pits in which they deposit their scat, these are usually some distance from the sett but a good indication if they are being used.

Sadly the most common sign of a large badger population are the roadkill bodies seen on the roadside. Being largely nocturnal badgers are normally difficult to see in daylight hours, however during the summer, as the daylight hours are longer and the cubs are more active, they can be seen leaving the setts before dusk and returning after dawn.

Right: the huge earthworks of an active badger sett. Nikon D4, 17-35mm at 17mm, ISO 500, 1/320 sec at f/13

Peeking through the fallen logs, eye of a badger. Nikon D4, 300mm + 2 x converter at 600mm, ISO 4000, 1/1000 sec at f/5.6

Technique

Badgers are largely nocturnal so they are best seen at the ends of the day when the light levels are low. This means either using high ISOs or a flash. By staying still and silent it is possible to have badgers come very close indeed. Badgers have poor eyesight but great hearing and sense of smell so remain quietly downwind. It is quite an experience to have a badger walk up and sniff your boots. No luck on your own patch? Try Aigas Field Centre p.36 and Sibford Gower p.168.

Badger rooting around in the woods.
Nikon D4, 300mm, ISO 1250, 1/800 sec at f/2.8

It can be surprisingly easy to get close to a badger.
Nikon D4, 300mm, ISO 1600, 1/800 sec at f/5.6

Little owl *(Athene noctua)*

This is a widespread but elusive little owl. They are common in farmyards and parks especially across the south of England. The best way to photograph them is to find a suitable location and talk to the landowner so you can establish your own hide.

Little owls are an introduced species but seem to have found an unused niche amongst British wildlife and have therefore been allowed to flourish. Feeding on a wide diet including earthworms, beetles, moths and small rodents they are largely nocturnal but often seen before dusk and after dawn, especially in summer when feeding their young. Usually located by their calls, especially at dusk when their cries can sound like a mewing cat.

Technique

These owls are largely active at dusk and dawn so a high ISO and a wide aperture are likely to be the norm. Although this is frequently a perching bird when a slow shutter speed will suffice, their flight can be extremely rapid requiring a fast shutter speed to capture them in the air. Photographing from a pop-up camouflage hide works well especially when you have a site where the birds are feeding young.

If you have no luck finding little owls on your local patch try Richmond Park p.218 or a pay-for photography hide such as that run by Natureshots in Worcestershire.

Adult little owl taking flight.
Nikon D4, 500mm, ISO 1600, 1/1600 sec at f/10

Family group (adult on the right).
Nikon D4, 500mm, ISO 3200, 1/320 sec at f/4

Adult little owl sitting pretty on a strategically placed perch. Nikon D4, 500mm + 1.4 x conv at 700mm, ISO 1600, 1/800 sec at f/5.6

Three's a crowd.
Nikon D4, 500mm, ISO 1600, 1/1600 sec at f/10

Technique
Section

Camera choice

Most of the photographs in this book were taken with high-end expensive equipment. After starting out with very modest equipment and getting reasonable results I have gradually upgraded my kit to allow me to try and get the best results possible.

IMPORTANT: It must be stressed that camera equipment is only part of the story with getting good wildlife images. More important is being in the right place at the right time and that takes practice and learned field skills.

All the locations in this book can be enjoyed with any camera. There are however cameras capable of doing much more than others and producing better results albeit at a price.

Consider therefore why you are taking photographs and what you intend to do with them. If you are shooting only for you and your friend's pleasure, you are likely to be showing your pictures perhaps on Flickr or Facebook, then you do not necessarily need a very high resolution camera and you are probably better off with a cropped sensor than a more expensive full frame camera.

All singing all dancing

Digital cameras have lots of functions and features and when searching for a new camera it's worth making a list of what is important to you. Online comparison sites where you can directly compare models are an excellent resource. One of the better sites is:

www.dpreview.com

New or secondhand?

Consider buying secondhand if budget is an issue. It's better to have a quality camera that takes really good images than have a brand new body that doesn't really do what you need. Technology is changing so quickly now that you can get an incredibly good camera for a fraction of the price it cost new. If in doubt set off with a cheaper model secondhand and see how you get on, you are likely to be able to trade it back in with less financial loss than having bought a brand new camera which didn't work out for you.

One current advance in new cameras is the incredible improvement in noise reduction at high ISO's so consider this if you intend to do a lot of low light photography.

Lens versus camera body

Arguably it is the lens that makes the real difference when it comes to quality of image so consider buying a cheaper camera with a better lens. (See next pages).

Below: One of my first wildlife images, a red kite in a cloudy sky. Taken with a Canon EOS 40D and a 100 to 400mm lens: a great set up to start off wildlife photography with. Canon EOS 40D, 100-400mm at 400mm, ISO 400, 1/2000 sec at f/7.1

Above: Short-eared owl: taken on an old high resolution full frame camera with 100 to 400mm lens and heavily cropped. Canon EOS 1DS mark ii, 100-400mm at 340mm, ISO 400, 1/2500 sec at f/13

Below: Short-eared owl on a new Nikon D4, full frame camera with 500mm lens and converter, cropped slightly. Nikon D4, 500mm + 1.4 x converter at 700mm, ISO 800, 1/1250 sec at f/13

*'When people ask what equipment I use –
I tell them my eyes'* – Anon

Lenses

There are a multitude of different lenses available on the market all of which have pros and cons. In wildlife photography especially it's nearly always assumed that getting close is the aim of the game. This is not necessarily so and some of the best photographs are those that include wildlife within its habitat and not just a close up of every detail in sharp focus.

Zoom lenses

Zooms are a great compromise and a really good choice for anyone starting out. These give you huge flexibility and allow much more room to compose especially when creating landscape shots. They allow good close up ability and reduce the possibility of being caught out with wildlife too close to the frame (see image opposite top). A good starter lens for a DSLR is a zoom around the range 100 to 400mm.

Prime lenses

These are lenses with a fixed focal length, i.e. no zoom. They are expensive but absolutely top quality; the ultimate tool of the wildlife photographer. For most people they are impractical and too costly. Anything above a 300mm prime lens is also likely to be too heavy for most people to hand hold succesfully and will rely on the use of a tripod.

Think about the subjects you are wanting to capture: a 300mm lens (with converter) is great for fast moving birds and can also be used without a converter for larger mammals like seals, badgers and red deer. If you are mainly shooting small birds at a distance you are likely to require a 500mm or even the huge 600mm prime lens for ultimate quality.

Consider buying secondhand initially to save money. Whilst the reduction in price from new is not as significant as with camera bodies there is likely to be no reduction in the quality of the images they take as long as the lens has been looked after properly.

Teleconverters

These are a relatively cheap way of increasing the focal length and therefore the magnification of your image. There are as always pros and cons. Converters are generally available in 1.4 x, 1.7 x and 2 x magnifications. The main advantage of magnification can be negated by a loss in quality of image. For most purposes this may not be significant but image quality may not hold up if being enlarged or under close scrutiny by image editors.

Converters also reduce the light entering a lens. For example a 500mm f/4 lens will be reduced to f/5.6 using a 1.4 converter. For anybody owning a 300mm prime lens, a 2 x converter is a good way to convert to a huge 600mm focal length without much loss in quality. This is a combination used for many of the images in this book.

This combination works really well for example on a bright day photographing fast moving highly mobile subjects like hobbies. Here you need the magnification but also the advantage of hand holding the kit so you can quickly track or take overhead shots, something very difficult to do with a large prime lens on a tripod.

Depending on available light, a 2x converter does not always work well with a larger lens such as a 500mm prime lens. The furthest you can sensibly boost a 500mm lens is with a 1.4 x converter to give you a 700mm focal length as in many of the images in this book. A further downside of using a converter is that some cameras require adjustments to the fine focusing when a converter is applied, make sure you check this when you fit the converter for the first time.

Tripods

The best tip in this book for sharp photographs is to use a tripod. Even a 300mm lens will benefit, cumbersome and adding extra weight they are worth the effort if sharpness is important to you. But don't be restricted by your tripod, be prepared to hand hold when needed, and a bean bag is often better than a tripod if in a hide or lying on the floor.

*Boxing backlit hares in low evening light.
Nikon D4, 500mm, ISO 4000, 1/1000 sec at f/8*

There is such a thing as too close. An unexpected encounter with an otter on Mull whilst carrying a 500mm lens with a 1.4 x converter. I had to lean backwards to get this in focus. Nikon D4, 500mm + 1.4 x converter at 700mm, ISO 1600, 1/1600 sec at f/5.6

Kingfisher in the rain using. Canon EOS 1DS mark ii, 100-400mm at 400mm, ISO 1600, 1/160 sec at f/5.6

Field Craft

We all have different reasons for wanting to photograph wildlife. For many it's part of a wider enjoyment which involves being outside in a natural environment and enjoying that experience as much as the encounters with the wild creatures themselves. We all come from different walks of life and not everyone is familiar with wildlife and wild places.

Respect

Respect for the subject and its environment is paramount. Keep a sensible distance from the subject at all times but especially at breeding times. Avoid noise or actions that may frighten the subject. This applies to all wildlife and it should be obvious that if you want to get close to a wild animal to take its photograph you need to be quiet, move slowly and ideally be hidden from view.

If you can't be hidden completely then keep a low profile, stay stationary when the animal is looking in your direction and where possible use shade or the cover of trees and rocks to break up your outline.

Some species are protected by law and require special licenses to be photographed especially at breeding time. For example barn owls and kingfishers are Schedule One birds and cannot be disturbed by photography at or near the nest.

Some things just drive me nuts. Nikon D3X, 300mm + 2 x converter at 600mm, ISO 2500, 1/250 sec at f/6.3

Be prepared

Being out of doors means you can potentially get wet and cold or too hot and dehydrated. Many of the areas listed in this book are remote and most have no facilities or require a good deal of walking away from any facilities. Carry waterproofs, a snack, a bottle of water and a hat in a backpack just in case. A mobile phone is

Full camouflage is a good idea for stalking wild red deer. Photo credit: Anna Riddle.

useful for emergencies, make sure it's either turned off or switched to vibrate only when looking for wildlife.

It is interesting to see how many people turn up to bird reserves wearing bright red jackets or pink hats. Some wildlife cannot see the same colours as humans but birds and animals generally respond strongly to colour. Many female birds are naturally camouflaged to avoid being noticed by predators. Many male birds have bright coloured plumage to attract attention at breeding time. Do not therefore be surprised if you don't see much wildlife when out with a red rucksack on your back.

Some photographers go the whole hog using full military sniper camouflage to get close to their subject. Whilst it may be a bit extreme to turn up at the Island Mere Hide at RSPB Minsmere in a full snipers ghillie suit, a compromise is sensible. Birds flying above you will have an aerial view of whatever colour hat you are wearing so a camouflage cap or my favourite, a wide brimmed brown leather hat works well at hiding your face and also acts as a good shade for the viewfinder in bright sun.

Shut up

Being quiet is equally if not more important than your visual appearance. Soft clothing which doesn't rustle will help you move quietly and go unnoticed. Many waterproof jackets and leggings can be quite noisy so choose the fabric carefully.

Learn to walk quietly through woodland; walking on the edge of your feet reduces the chances of snapping a twig as you creep up to a group of timid roe deer.

In a public hide try and be as quiet as possible and encourage everyone else to do the same. If your camera has beeping focus sounds, switch that off. If your shutter has a quiet mode, use that. Being as quiet as possible will maximise your chances of sightings.

Billy no mates

Going alone in search of wildlife is often more productive than taking friends or family. Choose your visit time if you possibly can; you will see more wildlife during a quiet midweek morning at a nature reserve than at midday on a bank holiday weekend. There are however some great locations to visit where wildlife does not shy away so easily, try Brownsea Island p. 206 or the London parks.

Hides

Having established that being quiet and camouflaged are all good things the next consideration is the use of hides. Many of the locations in this book have purpose-built wooden hides. In many cases it is not necessary or appropriate but if you are able to access (with permission) private land then setting up your own hide perhaps using a portable pop-up hide may be a perfect solution. This system works best when located next to a regular feeding or drinking spot.

Know your subject

Having turned up at the right place at the right time of year and day you also need to know a little about the subject you are looking for. With birds especially it is a huge bonus to know their call. Kingfishers are a good example of this. Although strikingly vivid when sitting right in front of you this is also a very small bird and surprisingly hard to spot when in the shade and with its orange breast facing towards you. Hearing the piping call at a distance will indicate you are in the right spot. You can then be alert for its fast low flight over the waterway and be ready as it alights on the perch in front of you. Sometimes this may be a fleeting moment and being ready can make all the difference. If you have awoken really early and driven a long way to be in a hide somewhere you may well be dozing off slightly but recognising that piping call will bring you back into focus.

Let sleeping foxes lie. Go quietly and with the wind in your face. Nikon D4, 300mm + 2 x at 600mm, ISO 2500, 1/1000 sec at f/9

Show me a sign

With mammals especially it is worth learning some basic tracking skills in order to recognize the signs that can tell you the animal is living in the area. Badgers, foxes and rabbits all have distinctive setts, dens and burrows. Experience will tell you the difference between the three though perhaps surprisingly all three may live in the same spot.

Badgers will have their toilet pits not too far away and tend to have much larger earthworks with big fresh mounds of earth at the entrance, often with signs of bedding (old hay and bracken) being dragged about.

Foxes tend to be messy and will leave telltale pheasant feathers and bits of rabbit skin outside. Urban foxes may have brought back rubbish in the form of wrappers, etc from discarded takeaway meals.

It's worth checking used sites regularly, maybe you think it's just used by rabbits but you never know who you might meet checking out the burrows as well.

What's that smell?

When approaching mammals, especially those with a keen sense of smell such as deer, badgers and foxes, it is always important to move forward with the wind in your face. It's pointless being fully camouflaged and quiet as a mouse if you approach from the wrong direction. Wild animals rely on their sense of smell and your underarm deodorant or lack of it will alert a vixen and her cubs to your presence over several hundred metres away.

Red fox checking out the rabbit warrens, early morning. Nikon D4, 300mm + 2 x converter at 600mm, ISO 1600, 1/800 sec at f/5.6

Basic camera technique

Read your camera's manual and understand the basic modes. Learn the difference between shutter priority (S or Tv) and aperture priority (A or Av) and make sure you know how to change the ISO and switch from multi-point to single point focus.

When starting out as a wildlife photographer the priority is to be able to achieve a good sharp in-focus picture of the subject. To this end there are some basic simple steps that make the whole process easier.

Keeping the image sharp depends on several things: lens focus, shutter speed, movement of the subject and any movement of the camera.

Most digital cameras have a 'Sport 'setting. This is the easiest and quickest way to get good images of wildlife as a beginner. With the 'Sport' mode selected the camera will automatically use multi-point focusing to pick out the subject in the centre of the frame and will also use a fast shutter speed to freeze the moving target. As a beginner this will work well to capture flying birds in a clear sky and large animals in open landscapes.

The main drawback of this technique is that it allows no room for artistic impression, and may create problems with wildlife in a woodland or grassland habitat where the autofocus will pick out foreground grasses and branches instead of the creature you want to portray.

To advance beyond the sports setting learn how to switch between single-point and multi-points quickly without thinking so you can change from the overhead kestrel in a clear sky to picking out the reed warbler in the reeds.

Shutter Speed

When photographing wildlife the subject is usually some distance away and often moving. High magnification lenses allow us to get close but require fast shutter speeds to prevent blur caused by subject movement. If you are hand holding the equipment rather than using a tripod you require even faster speeds to allow for camera shake and movement of your body.

A basic rule of thumb for any lens is that the shutter speed in seconds should be at least the reciprocal of the focal length. For example a 500mm lens needs a shutter speed of at least 1/500th of a second to avoid camera shake. Fast moving subjects such as peregrines, kingfishers and hobbies need shutter speeds in excess of 1/2000th to freeze the motion.

For creative reasons it can be good to slow the shutter speed down so you can give an impression of motion. This can require a bit of trial and error. One technique is to pan around with the moving subject, for example a bird in flight, hopefully leading to a blurred background and wings but a sharp head and eye.

Aperture

The aperture of the camera controls how much light enters the sensor. In low light a wider aperture (smaller f number) is required so for example if shooting badgers at dawn or dusk a wide aperture (f/2.8) lens would be ideal.

Aperture also affects depth of field (DOF). This is effectively the amount of the image that is in sharp focus. For example if you take a picture of a field of wildflowers you will need a narrow aperture (f/11) to get most of the wildflowers in focus. If you shoot the same image at f/2.8 only a small section of the flowers will be in focus, with flowers in front and behind the focus point blurred.

In wildlife photography using a wide aperture and consequent narrow depth of field you will not get all the animal in focus. Here it is of prime importance to have the eye sharp – focus on the eye.

ISO

If you need a fast shutter speed to freeze movement and prevent blur and the aperture is as wide open (smallest f/ number) as it will go you need to increase the ISO.

ISO is an indication of the camera sensor's sensitivity to light. ISO numbers are carried over from film days (100, 200, 400, etc) and double or halve the sensitivity of the sensor with each step. Higher ISO values allow shooting in lower light conditions at a cost of increased 'grain' or noise on the image. Continued improvements in camera sensor sensitivity allow us to use higher and higher ISOs with much reduced noise.

It's good to be aware of your individual camera's ISO capability and know how far you are comfortable pushing the ISO before you get too much noise. As a beginner you can set your camera to adjust the ISO automatically however it is worth getting used to selecting your ISO according to the light conditions.

Mode

DSLRs, most bridge cameras and some compact cameras offer three user defined modes: Shutter Priority, Aperture Priority or Manual. Which of these you use depends on what you are photographing. Personally I prefer shutter priority as this allows you to rapidly change the speed according to what subject you meet and what that subject is doing like moving from a perch to flight. If you know you are shooting only flying birds you might prefer to use Aperture Priority so you can set it at f/8 for example. Whichever mode you choose stick to it so changing settings quickly becomes second nature.

Weasel in the bluebells. A fast and remarkably small creature, it is tricky to see an animal like this in the undergrowth. This is a good example where a single focal point is necessary to focus on the animal. Nikon D800E, 500mm + 1.4 x converter at 700mm, ISO 2000, 1/640 sec at f/9

Even at very fast shutter speeds you can still get some motion blur at the wing tips as the sedge warbler takes off. Nikon D4, 300mm + 2 x converter at 600mm, ISO 1600, 1/2500 sec at f/9

Metering

Most cameras have different ways of measuring the amount of light in a scene to control exposure. Most commonly these are spot, partial, centre-weighted and evaluative or matrix metering.

Evaluative or matrix metering

This is the default metering mode on most DSLRs and the only mode on most compacts. This takes a reading from the whole scene and then gives priority to an area around the point of focus.

Centre-weighted average metering

This meters from the whole scene but prioritises a small portion in the centre, the amount of which can sometimes be changed. The importance of this central portion is weighted to 60 to 80 % of the whole reading making it a good option for portraits.

Spot metering

This takes a reading off only a small part of the view, typically 2 to 5 %. The spot is usually in the middle of the viewfinder but in some cameras you can move it around to save you metering then re-framing. This is particularly useful in tricky lighting conditions, for example a backlit subject. This is the easiest metering to get wrong by not correctly pointing at a mid tone.

Partial metering

Quite similar to a spot meter but measuring an area of 8 to 13 %, also useful for a backlit subject.

Exposure Compensation

The camera light meter works automatically and will give you a suggested exposure shown on a meter usually to one side of the viewfinder. The camera does not know what it is looking at so cannot allow for a light coloured bird on a dark background or a dark bird in a light sky. The most common example of this is birds flying against a bright sky. The camera will without any adjustment produce a very dark looking subject on a nicely exposed sky. In this case be prepared and for a start shoot in RAW files so you can adjust the exposure later if you get it wrong. Next try exposure compensation of plus 1.0 as a starter. This tells the camera to over-expose the shot but hopefully with the result that the bird is correctly exposed and the sky is brighter than it would have been.

The next scenario is a light bird on a dark background, for example a barn owl in a field at dusk. Here the camera will typically overexpose thus blowing the whites out on the bird's plumage. Here use negative exposure compensation to underexpose the background and keep the plumage of the bird correctly exposed.

Focus Points

Modern digital cameras have a number of active focus points in the centre of the viewfinder. These can be set so that either one point or a group are active. One of the main differences between an entry level and a pro level DSLR is the complexity of the autofocus system. A top end camera will have many more focus points that are highly configurable.

There are also two types of focus points: vertical and cross type. Cross type focus points detect contrast in both the vertical and horizontal planes making them much more accurate than vertical. The more cross type sensors your camera has, the more accurate the focus system.

With a configurable focus system you can chose which focus points are active. The advantage of having several points active is that the camera can pick up and focus on anything moving into these points, for example a flying bird in an empty sky.

A problem arises when other objects clutter the frame, for example with a bird in a tree the focal points may trip out on the branches or foliage and not focus on the bird. In this case it's best to use a single focus point. Typically the central focus point is the most accurate (cross type) so is good as a quick 'go to' option. Learning how to move the active focus point is a useful technique if you want your subject positioned to one side of the frame or you need to focus specifically on one area, for example the eye.

Tracking and Continuous Focus

Nikon and Canon as well as other manufacturers have continuous focus modes on their DSLRs (AF-C on a Nikon and AI Servo on a Canon). These allow the camera to continually re-focus on the subject so long as it is within the reach of the autofocus point selected. This is the best mode to use for any moving creature.

Parakeet party at Richmond Park. Nikon D4, 500mm, ISO 800, 1/800 sec at f/8, EV plus 2

Little owl fledgling calling for food: The brightly lit perch allowed me to check the exposure, underexposing to allow for the sunlit bird. Nikon D800E, 500mm, ISO 1000, 1/800 sec at f/6.3, EV minus 1.0

Birds in Flight

This is one of the most favoured subjects in wildlife photography and one of the trickiest to accomplish. Many different factors conspire to create problems for the photographer. A moving bird requires a fast shutter speed. Allowance can be made for wing blur but ideally you need to be around 1/1600th or higher for fast birds.

Aperture: A good fallback aperture for bird in flight is f/8. Generally this means most of the bird will be in focus. If it is a large bird like an osprey or eagle it is worth going narrower if possible. Some people prefer to shoot with a single focal point which works well if you are fast enough to follow the eye of the bird in flight. It is easier to have a cluster of points active and these will pick up on the bird as it moves.

Puffin in flight on the Isle of Noss, Shetland. Nikon D4, 300mm, ISO 500, 1/1000 sec at f/9

The Advantage of RAW Files

Always shoot in RAW format, this allows you to make better adjustments to the exposure of the image later. Bracketing shots (taking photographs at different exposures) is not so useful in wildlife photography where the subject will usually have moved by the time you take the second or third image but can help with stationary subjects in difficult light.

Check your histogram and LCD display every few shots to see what your image is looking like.

Composition

Focal points: The eyes are dead centre with equal space around the wings giving the bird room to fly. Nikon D4, 500mm + 1.4 x converter at 700mm, ISO 1000, 1/1000 sec at f/10

Negative space. This is a habitat shot: roughly adhering to the rule of thirds the owl needs plenty of open space to look out into. Nikon D4, 500mm, ISO 2500, 1/1000 sec at f/7.1

Leading lines. Here the cotswold stone wall leads the eye to the main subject but is a key part of the image. Nikon D4, 500mm + 1.4 x converter at 700mm, ISO 2000, 1/800 sec at f/5.6

'There are no rules for good photographs, there are only good photographs' – A. Adams

Composition is about arranging the various elements of a scene to produce a pleasing image. An effective composition is one that is interesting to the viewer and clearly conveys the message the photographer intended.

Digital photography gives us the luxury of being able to review on the spot, make changes and experiment. When a composition doesn't work, curb the instinct to immediately delete. Study the image and try to work out what's wrong, we can learn a lot through our mistakes. Indeed, sometimes our mistakes inspire the best photographs.

Light

The quality of the light is what will make a photograph. An ordinarily dull subject can make a fantastic photograph in the right light. There is always an element of luck involved but learning to recognise favourable conditions for photography is an art that comes with practice.

The Rule of Thirds

This is a simple compositional technique based on ancient aesthetic principles that is remarkably effective most of the time. The principle is to divide your image into thirds both horizontally and vertically and align your subject along imaginary lines or the intercepts of those lines. Many camera viewfinders have the grid already to aid composition. Use this as a rough guideline and for most situations it will give a balanced feel to your photographs. The thirds rule reminds us to avoid placing the main subject in the middle of the frame. There are many exceptions to this rule. A good example is reflections where dividing the frame in half enhances symmetry.

Focal Points

In wildlife photography the focal point is nearly always the eye of the subject. Make sure this is in focus and position it at a key point in the frame. Dead centre can be good for dramatic portraits, but unless looking directly at you it's best to offset the subject leaving some negative space for the animal to look into.

Portrait of a pair of shags. Getting down at eye level makes for a more dramatic point of view.
Nikon D800E, 420mm, ISO 800, 1/800 sec at f/4.5

Leading Lines

Look for natural lines in the landscape that lead your eye into the frame. Obvious examples are footpaths, dry stone walls, streams or the edge of a lake.

Viewpoint and Perspective

Exactly where you take your photo from significantly affects the composition and the impact of a photograph. If the subject is comfortable with your presence get down low, being at eye level with wildlife is always effective.

The eyes are the focal point on this little owl.
Nikon D800E, 500mm, ISO 3200, 1/400 sec at f/4

Light

'You only get one sunrise and one sunset a day, and you only get so many days on the planet. A good photographer does the math and doesn't waste either.' **– Galen Rowell**

As a wildlife photographer you need to be able to get up early and stay out late. Making the effort of photographing during the Golden Hour around sunrise and sunset will make a major difference to the quality of your photographs.

Good light is a crucial ingredient for good photographs and the golden hour is the time to get wonderful light. Happily this coincides with the best time to see many of the crepuscular species, those that are active at dusk and dawn.

Timing

The position of sunrise and sunset changes with the seasons from NE and NW in the summer and SE and SW in the winter. Winter is a far more civilised time of year for sunrise photography, you certainly get more time in bed. Ideally arrive well before dawn to be in a good position for the rising sun and don't pack up until it's really over; the best colours often occur 15 to 30 minutes before actual sunrise and a similar time after sunset.

Golden sunlight highlights a backlit barn owl. Nikon D4, 500mm + 1.4 x converter at 700mm, ISO 1600, 1/800 sec at f/11

The Golden Hour

The golden hour is that period of around an hour after sunrise and before sunset when the low sun is filtered by the atmosphere leading to softer, less harsh or contrasting light with warmer tones. Almost any image is enhanced by this magical light. The duration of this 'golden' period varies with the seasons and conditions. In the middle of winter the low sun gives you a longer 'hour' of favourable light conditions.

One of the biggest barriers to shooting in the Golden Hour is making the effort to get out at ridiculous o'clock, especially in mid-summer when the sun rises before 5am. Make a plan based on the forecast and the time of year.

Exposure and metering

Pointing a camera towards the sun will produce an underexposed and dark picture. Sometimes this is the desired effect to achieve a silhouette image. Experiment with under and over-exposure to get the most pleasing result. Use the exposure lock on compact cameras then move the camera to re-frame.

White balance

Auto white balance is fine if you are taking RAW images and are happy to adjust later on the computer. Using Auto may result in the loss of some of the golden colours you want to portray. Experiment with different settings but using 'Daylight', 'Shade' or 'Cloudy' will result in warmer tones.

Up at the crack of dawn as the day breaks on a spring morning in the Cotswolds. Be up early for the golden light. Nikon D4, 500mm, ISO 800, 1/500 sec at f/11

Below: morning light highlights the brown hare against dark shadows. Nikon D4, 500mm, ISO 2500, 1/1250 sec at f/9

Night Photography

'Luck is preparedness in the face of opportunity.' – Anon

Night photography offers the opportunity to capture those secretive creatures of the night. This is an exciting time to be out in the wild and alongside the expected badgers, bats and owls, many other species are abroad at this time including deer, foxes and otters.

Flash

With the lack of light comes the opportunity or necessity for flash photography. There are ethical questions raised here: firing a flash in the face of a nocturnal animal like an owl is likely to alarm the creature and at least temporarily affect its night vision. Some animals such as the badgers pictured here have become accustomed to flash and these are a good subject for night photography. Using remote triggered flash is becoming an increasingly common method of capturing an image at night. For those who regard the experience of being there at the moment as an essential part of the process a dedicated flash gun or even a built in camera flash can be sufficient to obtain a quality image.

Focusing

In pitch black it is pretty impossible to focus the camera and autofocus is certainly out of the question. Either set up external lighting at a feed point to allow you to get a fix on the subject or carry a small torch to highlight the subject so you can focus. Alternatively with birds coming to a perch or animals to a feed point focus manually in advance using daylight or with a torch on the point you know the subject will visit.

Badger climbing on a tree trunk. Nikon D800E, 70-200mm at 116mm, ISO 2000, 1/250 sec at f/2.8 , Nikon inbuilt flash

Badger sniffing the air. Nikon D4, 70-200mm at 195mm, ISO 2000, 1/250 sec at f/2.8, Nikon Speedlight Flash

Processing

Using normal light bulbs to spot the subject usually lends a yellow tinge to the colour. This can be corrected if you shoot in RAW files by adjusting the white balance in processing. Most processing software has an application to adjust the white balance. This can be used to pinpoint an area on the animal that is known to be white, the software uses this as a reference and re-adjusts. Note that badgers are not necessarily black and white.

Red eye or green eye from the flash is a common problem and again this can be adjusted in processing. Occasionally the red eye healing tool works well but if not use a spot healing brush.

Hedgehog emerging from the flower border. Nikon D4, 70-200mm at 185mm, ISO 4000, 1/250 sec at f/2.8 , Nikon Speedlight flash

About the Author

Andrew Marshall ©Anna Riddle

Andrew had the good fortune to be brought up in the English Lake District surrounded by nature: woodlands full of roe deer, great spotted woodpeckers and red squirrels, and lakes full of pike and perch. At that time many of the iconic species were rare and elusive; otters had been hunted to the edge of extinction, and birds of prey shot and poisoned by chemicals such as DDT. Happily, thanks to conservation efforts, we now see otters and ospreys returning to the lakes once more.

Andrew's first camera was a Kodak Instamatic with which he took photographs of animals in zoos and parks trying to emulate the images he saw in National Geographic and wildlife magazines. He studied Biological Sciences in Manchester with the Lake District and its wildlife never too far away.

Andrew has travelled widely since, including South Africa, Australia, North America, Tanzania, Venezuela and Nepal, combining exploration of wild places with his love of photography. In anticipation of another visit to the Kruger Park in South Africa in 2011 he bought his first professional quality camera and lens. This marked a turning point in his photographic career.

Back home Andrew realised this passion could be continued and he began to research the best places in the UK to photograph wildlife. An influx of short-eared owls in the winter of 2011 at his local RSPB reserve encouraged him further. An inspirational visit and close encounter with wild otters on the Isle of Mull cemented his passion for UK wildlife photography.

Now living in the Cotswolds, Andrew balances work as a wildlife garden designer and landscaper with wildlife photography. He is a contracted contributor to the RSPB photography library.

Over the last three years he has visited wildlife locations all across the UK, many several times, researching and photographing for this guidebook.

Andrew is available for one-to-one or group tuition in wildlife photography and is offering guided visits to all the locations in this guidebook.

Email Andrew at: **Gowild@freeuk.com**

To find out more about Andrew and his photography visit:
www.gowildlandscapesphoto.com
www.facebook.com/Gowildphotos

Andrew's current camera kit comprises of:
Nikon D800E and Nikon D4 bodies and the following lenses: 17-35mm f/2.8, 70-200mm f/2.8, 300mm f/2.8, 500mm f/4 along with 1.4 x and 2 x converters. Manfrotto tripod and head.

Opposite right: Courting gannets on Bass Rock. Nikon D800E, 500mm, ISO 1000, 1/1250 sec at f/11

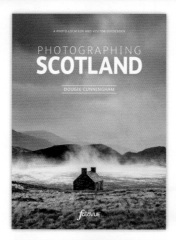

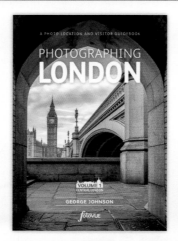

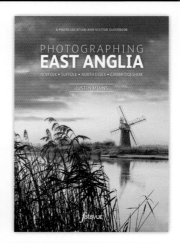

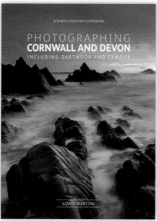

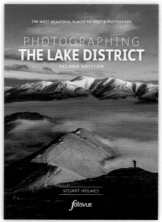

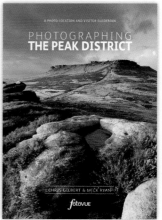

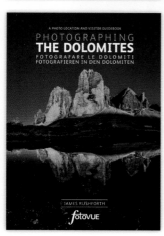

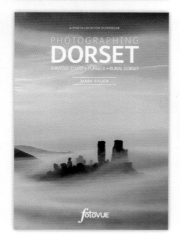

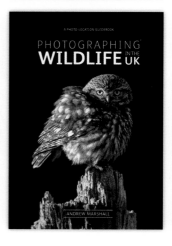

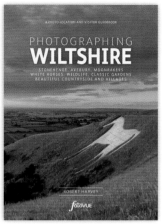

A PHOTO LOCATION AND VISITOR GUIDEBOOK

PHOTOGRAPHING
WILTSHIRE

STONEHENGE, AVEBURY, MOONRAKERS
WHITE HORSES, WILDLIFE, CLASSIC GARDENS
BEAUTIFUL COUNTRYSIDE AND VILLAGES

ROBERT HARVEY

fotovue

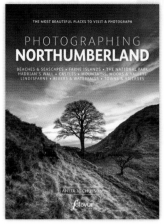

THE MOST BEAUTIFUL PLACES TO VISIT & PHOTOGRAPH

PHOTOGRAPHING
NORTHUMBERLAND

BEACHES & SEASCAPES • FARNE ISLANDS • THE NATIONAL PARK
HADRIAN'S WALL • CASTLES • MOUNTAINS, MOORS & VALLEYS
LINDISFARNE • RIVERS & WATERFALLS • TOWNS & VILLAGES

ANITA NICHOLSON

fotovue

THE *fotovue*
ICELAND
adventure
& travel
MAP

A TOPOGRAPHIC MAP OF ICELAND
150 beautiful locations to visit,
enjoy & photograph

also includes:
• REYKJAVÍK CITY MAP
• THE BLUE LAGOON
• THE GOLDEN CIRCLE ROUTE MAP
• THE SUN, DAY & NIGHT LENGTH • CLIMATE & WEATHER
• THE TOP TEN PLACES TO VISIT IN ICELAND
• HOW TO PHOTOGRAPH THE NORTHERN LIGHTS

travel advice • best places to see wildlife • facilities • accommodation • natural & cultural features

///WHAT3WORDS & SCANNABLE QR-CODE DIRECTIONS FOR ALL LOCATIONS
∞ PRINTED ON WATERPROOF & TEAR RESISTANT PAPER ∞
www.fotovue.com

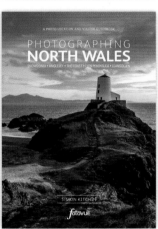

A PHOTO LOCATION AND VISITOR GUIDEBOOK

PHOTOGRAPHING
NORTH WALES

SNOWDONIA • ANGLESEY • THE COAST • LLŶN PENINSULA • LLANGOLLEN

SIMON KITCHIN

fotovue

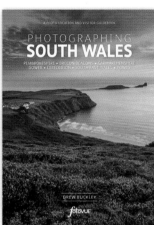

A PHOTO LOCATION AND VISITOR GUIDEBOOK

PHOTOGRAPHING
SOUTH WALES

PEMBROKESHIRE • BRECON BEACONS • CARMARTHENSHIRE
GOWER • CEREDIGION • SOUTH-EAST WALES • TOWNS

DREW BUCKLEY

fotovue

Forthcoming title

Photographing The Night Sky

By Alyn Wallace

Check **fotovue.com** for the latest on release dates and a list of all our forthcoming titles.
Contact:
mick@fotovue.com

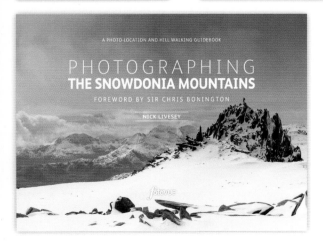

A PHOTO LOCATION AND HILL WALKING GUIDEBOOK

PHOTOGRAPHING
THE SNOWDONIA MOUNTAINS

FOREWORD BY SIR CHRIS BONINGTON

NICK LIVESEY

fotovue

Order at:
www.fotovue.com
and use code: **FVFV**
at checkout to get:
15% off all books

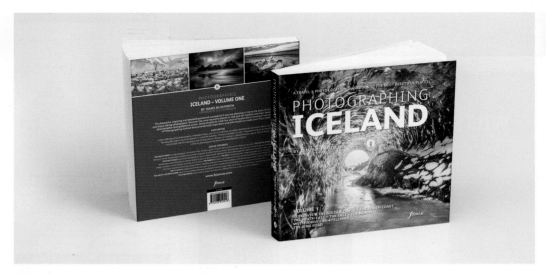

What people say about fotoVUE photo-location and visitor guidebooks

"The best photographer guidebooks by a mile."
"The quality of product is surpassed only by the attention to highly relevant detail."
"This could be the best location-oriented photoguide I have yet to come across."
"A fantastic book and an amazing travel guide."
"The template for all photography location guides."

Please subscribe to our newsletter at **fotovue.com**
for our latest news and newsletter only deals.